Growth, Trade, and Systemic Leadership

Growth, Trade, & Systemic Leadership

Rafael Reuveny and William R. Thompson

UNIVERSITY OF MICHIGAN PRESS

Ann Arbor

Copyright © by the University of Michigan 2004
All rights reserved
Published in the United States of America by
The University of Michigan Press
Manufactured in the United States of America
⊚ Printed on acid-free paper

2007 2006 2005 2004   4 3 2 1

A CIP catalog record for this book is available from the British Library.

Library of Congress Cataloging-in-Publication Data

Reuveny, Rafael.
Growth, trade, and systemic leadership / Rafael Reuveny and
William R. Thompson.
p.   cm.
Includes bibliographical references and index.
ISBN 0-472-09850-0 (Cloth : alk. paper) —
ISBN 0-472-06850-4 (Paper : alk. paper)
1. International trade.   2. Tariff.   3. Protectionism.
4. Economic development.   5. Leadership.
6. United States—Commercial
policy.   7. Free trade—United States.
I. Thompson, William R.   II. Title.

HF1379 .R48   2003
382—dc21   2003014224

ISBN13 978-0-472-09850-7 (cloth)
ISBN13 978-0-472-06850-0 (paper)
ISBN13 978-0-472-02423-0 (electronic)

For my dear wife Ronit
and my amazing children
Adi and Noam.
—*R.R.*

This one is for George Modelski
who is to blame
for initiating this research program.
—*W.R.T.*

Contents

Figures

Tables

Acknowledgments

At various points, several individuals have been quite helpful in this enterprise. Our thanks to Joshua Goldstein, Bart Kerremans, Brian Pollins, David Rapkin, James Lee Ray, Bruce Russett, Jeremy Shine, Robert Switky, Peter Taylor, Jarrod Weiner, and a plague of anonymous reviewers over the years. Parts of this book have appeared in various forms at earlier points, and we are grateful for permission to republish them within what we hope is a more coherent whole. Chapter 2 is based on "Leading Sectors, Lead Economies, and Their Impact on Economic Growth," *Review of International Political Economy* 8 (November 2001): 689–719. Chapter 3 first saw the light of day as "War, System Leadership and Economic Innovation: The United States Case," *Journal of Conflict Resolution* 43 (October 1999): 570–95. An earlier version of chapter 4 appeared as "Explaining Protectionism: Seventeen Perspectives and One Long-Term Common Denominator," *Global Society* (summer 2001): 229–49. Chapter 5 was first published as "The Timing of Protectionism," *Review of International Political Economy* 4 (spring 1997): 179–213. Chapter 6 is based on "Tariffs and Trade Fluctuations: Does Protectionism Matter as Much as We Think?" *International Organization* 52 (spring 1998): 421–40. "Systemic Leadership and Economic Openness" in *International Interactions* 29 (June 2003): 83–110, was the basis for chapter 7. Finally, chapter 8 was first published as "Trade Regionalization and Tariffs: The Correlates of Openness in the American Long Run," in Robert Switky and Bart Kerremans, eds., *The Political Consequences of Regional Trading Blocs* (London: Ashgate, 2000).

1. An Introduction to Growth, Trade, and Systemic Leadership

As we enter the twenty-first century, international political economy (IPE) concerns encompass a wide range of topics. New technology promises to make obsolete many of the conventional ways of making and doing things. If the nature of economic activity changes radically, so, too, will the nature of political economy—both domestically and internationally. Not coincidentally, signs of globalization seem literally everywhere, just as resistance to increasing economic interdependence is equally widespread. Global inequalities appear to be increasing and accelerated by the latest round of technological innovation, as embodied by the ongoing revolution in information technology. Some parts of the world are becoming increasingly wealthy and wired. Other parts of the world may be destined to being left further behind than they were earlier. Global institutions are evident but are clearly struggling to carry out their missions. Peacekeeping in Africa appears especially problematic, especially given the twin reluctance of local actors to cooperate and the most powerful states to become involved. Financial institutions such as the World Bank and trade institutions such as the World Trade Organization (WTO) are confronted with riots outside their meetings and limited agreement on what to do within their meetings. Doubts are raised about whether the World Bank and International Monetary Fund (IMF) facilitate or hinder economic growth in the Southern Hemisphere. While considerable success has been realized in reducing tariffs and expanding trade, other types of barriers to trade have been expanded. Regional trading arrangements are proliferating, presumably to reduce further local barriers to trade but always retaining some potential for reverting to older-fashioned regional trading blocs.

In short, the problems of international political economy may seem novel, but it is doubtful that they really are. They can be reduced to the customary by-products and stresses associated with long-term economic growth and change. The degree of interdependence may be increasing quickly but the types of problems being experienced are not completely new. These changes occur within a global political economy in which there are winners and losers as a consequence of growth and change. The winners do not necessarily rule the world economy, but they do get more than their proportional share (from a population perspective) of the benefits. They also get to devise the world economy's governance rules. Yet governance at the level of the world economy and global political economy is an awkward concept. We are socialized by international relations theory to think of international politics and political economy as anarchic. That does not quite mean that international relations is a ruleless, junglelike, survival of the fittest. But it does highlight the absence of a central authority that we usually assume to be necessary to some semblance of government and governance.

In this respect, we suggest that the conventional emphasis on anarchy is at best misleading. Governance, for better or worse, does take place in the world economy and global political economy. It operates, and has operated for several centuries, without much in the way of the formal institutions of a central government. It is (and has been) supplied primarily by the system's preeminent winner in the ongoing contest over capturing the benefits of long-term economic growth. Not surprisingly, the level and type of governance supplied depends on who is preeminent and whether anyone is preeminent at any given time.

Winners bias the rules in their own favor. The United Nations, World Bank, IMF, and WTO's predecessor, the General Agreement on Tariffs and Trade (GATT), were all created by the U.S.-led coalition that won World War II. Global combat is certainly a primitive way of determining who wins, but, so far, it has emerged as a trial-by-fire exercise for determining who governs in the global political economy—imagine what sort of institutions for governing international political economy transactions would have emerged if the opposing coalition (Germany, Italy, and Japan) had won World War II. Still, while we are aware that various battles could have turned out differently, the winning side prevailed thanks to superior resources and technology and a superior strategy for coalition building (including enlisting the Soviet Union and its important contribution to the war effort) and war making. That is what the global combat was about: not simply winning battles on land and at sea, but demonstrating superior resources, technology, and strategy or, in other words, fitness for leader-

2

ship. The side that demonstrates superiority then gets to devise the rules governing growth, trade, and finance on an increasingly worldwide scale.

There are some obvious problems with this type of approach to governance. The intermittent, trial-by-fire combat is an archaic and inefficient way to "elect" new leadership. The best chances for rule and institution making follow shortly after the end of the global war when one state is relatively all-powerful and the rest of the world is exhausted. As other states begin to catch up with the system leader, the likelihood of resistance to system leadership governance increases. To some extent, then, the likelihood of successful governance depends on whether the system leader can maintain or renew the preeminence enjoyed immediately after the last global war. If its capability lead erodes, so, too, will global governance. That is one quick way of explaining many of the IPE problems being encountered at the beginning of the twenty-first century.

Nevertheless, this book is not about explaining or even addressing all of the current IPE problems that we are experiencing. We wish to focus more on some of the implications of the centrality of systemic leadership to IPE governance. Our view on the salience of systemic leadership is not without its controversies. These controversies persist in part because it has not yet been demonstrated conclusively enough that the asserted salience is indisputable.[1] The primary mission of this study is to contribute to the demonstration that systemic leadership matters and that it matters quite significantly in IPE processes. Since we cannot take on all IPE processes at one time, some selectivity is in order. We have chosen to focus on economic growth, protectionism, and trade this time around. Subsequent studies will take on a host of other topics including North-South conflict, Southern debt problems, global inequality, and the prospects for economic convergence on a worldwide scale.

The Growth-Trade-Leadership Nexus

The title of the present study, *Growth, Trade, and Systemic Leadership,* implies that we think these three topics are related in some way. We most certainly do think they are not only related but also highly interdependent. It is of course common to link economic growth and trade. As economies grow and become more complex and affluent, trade is likely to expand. Conversely, trade is thought to promote economic growth. New tastes are acquired, which can lead to increased demand. New demands from abroad can expand domestic efforts to supply those demands. This reciprocal rela-

3

tionship is therefore not particularly controversial. More controversial, however, is the third component of our featured trio. We argue that economic growth and trade fluctuations take place within a politicoeconomic context constructed by systemic leadership. Unless we appreciate the nature of the context, we are unlikely to develop accurate growth and trade interpretations. Hence, an appreciation for systemic leadership is absolutely necessary for an understanding of growth and trade.

Our argument is doubly controversial because we do not simply assert that growth and trade processes work differently in the presence or absence of systemic leadership. That is only part of the argument. Rather, we think that systemic leadership processes actually generate the long-term sources of economic growth and trade. Politicoeconomic leadership at the systemic level is predicated on radical technological innovation, which brings about long-term economic growth, influences the incentives for trade (and barriers to trade), and also pays for the politicomilitary expenses associated with systemic preeminence. These processes are hardly constant. Systemic leadership is not forever. Economic growth is not continuous. Trade is also capable of contraction. The awkward and destabilizing transitions from one cluster of technological innovation to the next depress economic growth. They encourage national political intervention into the international exchange of goods and services. These same transitions also represent opportunities for new system leaders to emerge and old system leaders to be supplanted. Thus, as systemic leadership waxes and wanes, so do the prospects for economic growth and trade. This bring us to the main or meta-proposition of this examination.

> H1: World economic growth, trade, and systemic leadership covary
> causally and significantly.

Supportive evidence for this assertion is suggested by the data arrayed in table 1.1. Figure 1.1 summarizes the nearly three hundred years worth of trade and industrial growth data listed in the table. The table's observations are not evenly dispersed, which renders the figure a bit more subjective than might otherwise be the case. To aid in the visualization, we filled in missing data between any two given points using linear interpolation. But the observations, for the most part, are for the same time-intervals, which aids comparison immensely. The two series clearly appear to be related. Industrial production began to accelerate in the second half of the eighteenth century until it peaked toward the middle of the next century. A brief inter-

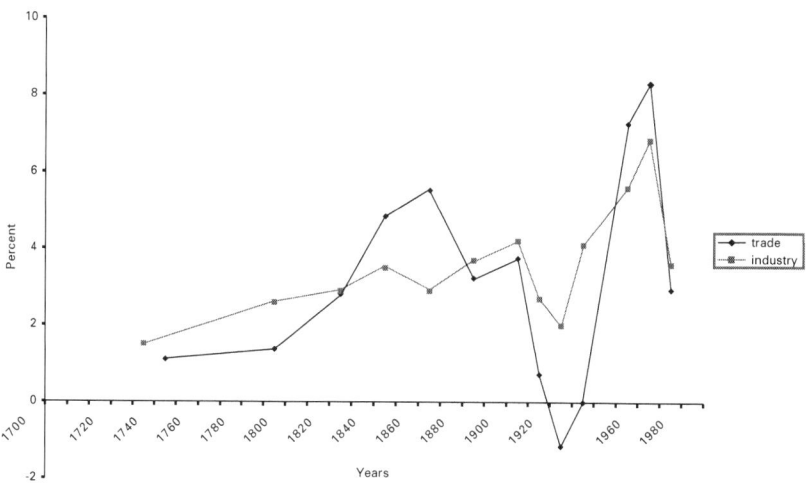

Fig. 1.1.   World trade and industry growth rates

TABLE 1.1.   Growth Rates in the Volume of World
Trade and Industry

Time Period	Annual Average Growth (%)	
	World Trade	World Industry
1705–85		1.50
1720–80	1.10	
1780	1.37	2.60
1820–40	2.81	2.90
1840–60	4.84	3.50
1860–70	5.53	2.90
1870–1900	3.24	3.70
1900–1913	3.75	4.20
1913–29	0.72	2.70
1929–38	−1.15	2.00
1938–48	0.00	4.10
1948–71	7.27	5.60
1971–74	8.31	6.84
1974–80	4.15	3.60
1980–86	2.94	2.65

Source: Holtfrerich (1989: 2). Holtfrerich's own sources were Rostow (1978)
and various GATT references.

ruption in industrial expansion is noted around the 1870s, with a second peak taking place just before World War I. Slow industrial growth characterized the interwar years, with a very strong surge following World War II. That surge had peaked by the early 1970s. A period of slow growth marked the 1970s and 1980s until the most recent upturn of the 1990s.

The first trade expansion peak occurred only after the mid–nineteenth century. It also is followed by a second pre–World War I peak, although in the case of trade the average rate of expansion was much less impressive than the rates attained in the first peak. Little expansion of trade occurred until after World War II. The next expansionary peak parallels the industrial expansion profile, although the heights attained are something less than double those reached in the mid–nineteenth century. After the early 1970s, the rate of expansion slowed, much as in the case of industrial production, before also returning to an upward trajectory.

Two points need to be made about the past three hundred years of industrial and trade growth. First, as already noted, the two different processes have expanded at roughly similar rates, suggesting that they are closely related. A second point that is rather easily discernible is that neither process expanded at a constant rate. Both processes experienced intervals of acceleration and slowing down. Both also had similar periodicities, with peaks in the mid–nineteenth and twentieth centuries and immediately prior to World War I. Both experienced a major depression in the interwar years of the twentieth century and minor depressions in the mid- to late nineteenth and late twentieth centuries.

How are we to explain the timing of these phenomena? A thorough if conventional answer, labeled the "determinants of international trade," is offered by the economic historian Carl-Ludwig Holtfrerich (1989: 10–23). Holtfrerich advances five causal factors: (1) technological and organizational progress in primary production, industry, and trade; (2) fiscal innovations and the lowering of trade barriers; (3) technological and economic revolutions in transportation and communication; (4) innovations in international financial and monetary relations; and (5) innovations in international law. Of the five, the prime mover since the eighteenth century is pinpointed as the "continuously innovative process of industrialization and modern economic growth" that led to breakthroughs in increasingly capital-intensive agriculture and industry (10–11). The increases in productivity expanded the supply of commodities for exchange. To fuel their production, the new commodities also required new supplies of energy that had to be transported from their source origins.

Introduction

High tariff rates in the nineteenth century were a legacy of older ideas about the desirability of mercantilistic strategies to reduce international dependence. They also were a convenient way to pay for war debt servicing. As the world economy moved into the mid–nineteenth century, these older motivations faded in significance. Tariff rates slowly declined, albeit with occasional relapses into protectionist frenzies, but still gradually reducing some of the barriers to trade expansion. Britain had led the tariff reduction process in the nineteenth century while the United States assumed the leadership of this process in the mid- to late-twentieth-century GATT negotiations.

The movement of commodities, people, and information, plus their transaction costs, were affected greatly by a series of innovations in transportation and communication mechanisms. Canals, railroads, steamships, automobiles, trucks, and airplanes reduced the time it took to move goods from one place to another. Costs declined after these innovations became increasingly routine. Telegraphs, telephones, radios, satellites, and most recently, the internet greatly facilitated the exchange of information.

Monetary interactions were made more convenient by the gradual movement toward the late-nineteenth-century gold standard that created a system in which "participating countries were *de facto* linked by a common currency, managed by the Bank of England as the international lender of last resort at the centre of international trade and finance in London" (Holtfrerich 1989: 18). This system broke down after World War I and was only slowly replaced by a Bretton Woods U.S. dollar–based system after World War II that functioned formally through 1971 and less formally thereafter. Similar gains came from reducing some of the uncertainties in international exchange as European commercial law diffused throughout the world (Holtfrerich's fifth causal factor).

We have no great quarrel with standard economic history's outline of nineteenth- and twentieth-century industrial and trade expansion. All of these factors, undoubtedly, were important and, for that matter, continue to be important. But one factor is definitely underplayed. It is most explicit in the treatment of tariff reductions and monetary exchange. It needs to be more explicit in the accounts of innovations in industry, transportation, and communications. It easily deserves to be a sixth general factor underlying the modern expansion of industry and trade. That factor is systemic leadership.

Industrial innovation was not widely dispersed throughout the nineteenth and twentieth centuries. At first, such innovations were highly concentrated in Britain in the late eighteenth and the first half of the nineteenth centuries. Germany and the United States competed to supplant Britain as industrial leader in the second half of the nineteenth and first half of the twentieth centuries. Transportation and communication innovations were no less concentrated in conception. Railroads, automobiles, and jet engines were developed most successfully by British and U.S. firms. Telegraphs, telephones, radios, satellites, and the internet were all British and U.S.-led innovations. As already noted, Britain led the nineteenth-century effort to lower barriers to trade, not only in terms of tariffs, but also in opening up Spain's Latin American colonies in the early part of the century. The United States championed free trade after the 1930s and pressed for European decolonization after World War II. The world economy's monetary relations increasingly revolved around the British pound as the system's central currency in the nineteenth century until it was supplanted by the U.S. dollar after World War II.

Therefore, we suggest that systemic leadership deserves a central place in explanations of the expansion of industry and trade. There is some irony in that the economics discipline has a strong fixation on micromotivations and yet is reluctant to extend agency to the most consistently central actors in the world economy. Economic historians have even less excuse since their stories of technological innovation and postwar settlements are focused clearly on systemic leadership behavior by default. Whether they admit it or not, these accounts must revolve around British and U.S. activities in the nineteenth and twentieth centuries because they were the lead actors in innovation and reorganization of the world economy. Scholars of international political economy are prepared to recognize that economies require some underlying infrastructure of governance, yet they too are reluctant to accept the ubiquity of systemic leadership in IPE activities. A few IPE students have worried about "hegemonic decline," but most IPE analysts are content to subscribe to the economics discipline's reluctance to acknowledge that technological innovations, tariff reductions, central currencies, and lenders of last resort do not simply happen courtesy of some Smithian invisible hand or the vagaries of economic history. Rather, they come from behavior that is spatially and temporally concentrated and predominantly generated by the world economy's lead economy.

Returning to figure 1.1, the upsurge in industrial production of the late eighteenth and early to mid–nineteenth centuries was predicated on the British Industrial Revolution and its impact on textiles, iron, and steam. So, too, was the nineteenth century's midcentury trade expansion as the techniques and economic implications associated with the British Industrial Revolution diffused to parts of Western Europe and North America. The pre–World War I upswing in the pace of industrial and trade growth was led by the United States. The post–World War II golden age reflected a diffusion of American techniques and products experienced before in the mid–nineteenth century. The 1990s upswing also appears to be essentially U.S.-led.

Or so we claim. Since systemic leadership is not embedded in our explanations of industrial and trade expansion as solidly as are technological innovations or transaction cost reductions, we cannot assume that readers will take our word for the accuracy of this generalization. The case for systemic leadership needs to be made—not assumed. Our slant on systemic leadership privileges two related concepts—leading sectors and the lead economy. Neither concept is well-established. Both require and deserve elaboration.

The Leading Sector and Lead Economy Concepts

The basic idea underlying the leading sector concept is that any economy is characterized by varying sectors of production activity. Some sectors not only grow rapidly but also have major implications for accelerating the growth of the macroeconomy. A leading sector, therefore, represents the introduction of novel technology; it is expanding faster than most other sectors. The novel technology may come from a new industry, but could also include new trade routes or financial innovations of sorts. The impact of the novel technology is highly significant in reshaping the rest of the economy. The presumption is that long-term economic growth comes in concentrated temporal and spatial spurts and is carried by these radical innovations in specific sectors.

New technology comes in clusters in some sectors, diffuses throughout the lead economy—the economy most responsible for introducing and adapting the new technology (and the one that profits most from its introduction)—and then diffuses to receptive areas in the rest of the world.[2] In this respect, the lead economy plays a role in the world economy that is similar to the role of leading sectors in its own economy. The leading sector and the lead economy are important drivers of economic growth. No one claims that they are the exclusive drivers of economic growth, but their impact is viewed as fundamental.[3]

Leading sectors are also fundamental to politicomilitary leadership at the global level. The profits from pioneering economic innovation fund the development of military instruments and networks of global reach. Systemic leaders of the past five centuries have constructed large blue-water fleets and support bases around the world to police the main trade routes and to contain emerging challengers to the world order created in the aftermath of global wars. Those same fleets also made important contributions to winning global wars in the first place, thereby deciding whose version of world order would prevail. But the profits of pioneering economic innovation have also helped finance other aspects of systemic political leadership, which include the financial aid necessary to keep wartime (and peacetime) coalitions together and to assist postwar reconstruction efforts. They also encompass the related leadership functions of shaping and maintaining international politicoeconomic order, and provide the lion's share of the world economy's capital and loan flows, just as new commercial and industrial activities stimulate the expansion of trade.

In many respects, this type of argument resembles hegemonic stability theses. One might argue that the simplest way to summarize such theses is to suggest that the world works much differently in the presence of a hegemon than in its absence. At the global level (as opposed to the regional level) *hegemon* is simply another term for system leaders. Whether they are viewed as benevolent (altruistic) or malevolent (self-interested), their leadership is essential to the stable functioning of the international political economy in a variety of ways (Lake 1993).[4] However, one difference between hegemonic stability theses and other interpretations of systemic leadership is that the former do not focus on the question of why hegemons come and go. Our emphasis on the life cycles of specific leading sector complexes is one answer for the question of why "hegemony" or systemic leadership tends to be transitory. The rise and relative decline of hegemons is predicated on pioneering national economic innovation in one era that is not sustained or reproduced in a subsequent era. The politicoeconomic leadership mantle spatially follows the movement of radical innovation.

A second difference between the lead economy and hegemonic stability interpretations is that the latter stresses political functions that occur exclusively after the advent of hegemony. Hegemons are responsible for keeping world economies functioning. One might call this a damage-control perspective on leadership. It is not surprising, then, that hegemonic stability theories were initially stimulated by Kindleberger's (1973) study of world economic depression between two distinct eras of leadership.

The emphasis on lead economies and sectors does not discount the various order-maintenance roles played by system leaders. It emphasizes instead the growth-generating role of the leader that is largely absent from hegemonic stability arguments. One of the fundamental ironies of the global political economy is that system leaders are least able to exercise damage control when the world economy is experiencing its most serious growth problems. The political failure to exercise damage control may well aggravate the economic problems, but the more fundamental problem is the need for new growth stimulants. In turn, the stimulants need to come from the same source as the damage control. In this interpretation then, the primary explanation for the failure of global political leadership is emphatically structural in origin.

The Mainstream Economic Growth Literature

It must be acknowledged that the concepts of leading sector and lead economy are not prominent in the mainstream economic growth literature. This literature is extensive, and we do not intend to fully review it here.[5] Instead, we list a few examples for each line of work. In general, there are two main approaches: the neoclassical and endogenous growth models, neither of which focuses on specific lead economies or leading sectors. The specific historical and spatial context of economic growth and the political implications are ignored for the most part. The focus is on the behavior of a representative macroeconomy comprised of similar economic agents.

The neoclassical growth model assumes the existence of a utility-maximizing, representative, consumer/producer agent that operates in a competitive market for an aggregated output. Utility is assumed to grow with consumption, output is produced from labor and capital (machines), production technology exhibits constant returns to scale, and technological progress is assumed to be exogenous. The agent decides how to allocate output among consumption and saving (Shell 1966). Saved output is used to produce capital. In the absence of technological progress, the economy converges on constant output and consumption per capita. The economy can increase consumption per capita over time only through technological progress. If technology and other model parameters are similar across countries, their economic growth rates will converge.

Starting in the mid-1980s, endogenous growth models focused on the determinants of technological progress, a subject not treated by the neoclassical approach. While the variables used vary across these models, they typically include aggregates of physical capital, human capital, knowledge, consumption, population, and output.[6] There are six types of endogenous growth models, the last two of which begin to overlap the political economic concerns of our technologically based, leading sector economic leadership models.

The first type of model posits a certain aggregate production function for the macroeconomy. It is assumed that the marginal product of capital declines with capital, but it never declines below some asymptotic threshold that is higher than the going interest rate.[7] Operating in perfect competition, investment in capital is therefore always profitable. Agents will continue to accumulate capital, and this accumulation enables output growth.

In a second type of model, the advance of knowledge is the key determinant of economic growth. Basically, it is assumed that when a firm invests in some generic research and development, some of the benefits from the innovation are not captured by the innovating firm; these lost benefits are said to be external to the firm (e.g., Romer 1986). Firms cannot capture all the benefits associated with their innovations. Private innovation creates a positive spillover into the economy, positively affecting firms that did not participate in the original innovation and thus generating aggregate growth.[8]

In a third type of model, economic growth is driven by profit-seeking, innovating entrepreneurs. This idea goes back to Schumpeter (1939). Firms engage in technological innovation because they believe they can capture monopoly profits if they succeed. The important point is that growth is determined by the ability of firms to capture temporary monopolies through innovation. Such monopolies in turn require well-developed systems of property rights and patent law enforcement.[9]

In a somewhat less mainstream argument, a fourth type of model argues that population growth drives innovation and economic growth. Simon (1981) argues that increased population raises the demand for innovation (by necessity) and the supply of innovation (by labor specialization and higher probability of innovators). Boserup (1981) argues that high population density drives innovations not only due to the potential gains from progress, but also because it raises the efficiency of transportation and communication and stimulates urbanization and labor specialization.

In a fifth type of model, Brezis, Krugman, and Tsiddon (1993) argue in the spirit of Olson (1982) that the economic success of a leading country actually prevents it from leading (possessing the highest labor productivity) in the future.[10] The model includes two trading nations and two goods, either technically stagnant or progressive. Initially, one country is more productive in the progressive good and exports it to the other country (the other sector's productivity is the same). When a new technology is introduced in the progressive sector, the leading nation does not adopt it since its experience with older technology makes the new one inferior. The lagging nation adopts the new technology, it becomes more productive in the progressive sector, trade patterns change, and leadership "leapfrogs."[11]

The sixth type of model focuses on "general purpose technologies" (GPTs). Helpman and Trajtenberg write, "in any given era there typically exists a handful of technologies that plays a far reaching role in widely fostering technical change and thereby bringing about sustained and pervasive productivity gains" (1998). The same authors go on to offer the steam engine, electricity, and microelectronics as specific examples of GPT engines of growth. While these GPTs sound very much like leading sectors, GPT analysts seem unaware of the older leading sector arguments, especially ones involving political economy, and so far have been content to confine themselves to formal theory exercises pertaining to economic growth.

Leading Sectors and the Mainstream Growth Literature

The preceding discussion illustrates that leading sectors are generally not emphasized by most economists. We are also well aware that the concept of "leading sectors" is contested among political economists. A good part of the problem is that economists have chosen to focus on macroeconomic models that seemingly demand aggregated data on economic activity. But as Metcalfe and Gibbons (1991: 485) note, macroeconomic models also tend to assume equilibrium growth with fixed sets of commodities. That does not correspond very well to long-term growth patterns in which new ways of doing things periodically displace, albeit unevenly, old ways of doing things. In fact many scholars have noticed that technological change in the most advanced economies is more likely to resemble a spasmodic movement from one set of discontinuities to another, rather than a smooth and continuous process. Shifting emphases on new industries that eventually become old industries and that may be supplanted in Schumpeterian fits of "creative destruction" seem to offer a better fit with long-term realities.

Another part of the problem with the leading sector concept is that it is actually employed in one form or another under a number of different names. These kindred conceptualizations do not refer to identical interpretations, but they do overlap considerably. For instance, Rostow (1978) defines leading sectors as new industries, reflecting the introduction of major new technology, characterized by above average growth, absorbing more than their share of investment monies, and often accelerating urban growth. Rostow argues that new technology is not introduced into some constructed aggregate such as gross national product, but rather into specific industries and by specific firms, and the process is not continuous, but rather is manifested in temporal and spatial clusters.

This conceptualization conforms well to Schumpeter's (1939) wider emphasis on new products, processes, markets, and sources of supply. The leading sector notion also matches well with Landes's (1969, 1998), Gilpin's (1975, 1981, 1987), and Kurth's (1979a, 1979b) emphases on the introduction of major new technologies. Other analysts seem to employ much the same conceptualization under different rubrics: Lewis (1978)—new ways of doing old things and making new commodities; Mensch (1979)—basic innovations; Mandel (1980)—technological revolutions; Bousquet (1980)—radical innovations; Hall and Preston (1988)—key technologies; Chase-Dunn (1989)—leading-edge industries; Jovanovic and Rob (1990)—fundamental innovations; Tylecote (1991)—technological styles; Kitschelt (1991)—newly emerging technologies; Murphy (1994)—lead industries; Arrighi (1994)—new capital goods; Adams (1996)—sociotechnical systems; Wallerstein (1996)—leading industries; and Murakami (1996)—major technological innovations.

What might be called the Sussex school emphasizes technological paradigms (Dosi 1982, 1983; Freeman and Perez 1988; Freeman and Soete 1997; Dicken 1998), sometimes using terms like *leading sectors* and *main carriers of the new technological paradigm.* Other analysts, such as Nelson and Winter (1982), adopt similar ideas when they introduce technological regimes as part of a firm's environment. As noted, more recently some economists have also begun to focus on the economic growth impacts of *general purpose technologies*—another close cousin of leading sectors and new technological paradigms (Bresnahan and Trajtenberg 1995; Aghion and Howitt 1998a; Helpman and Trajtenberg 1998; Lipsey, Bekar, and Carlaw 1998).

We do not suggest that all of these analysts are studying precisely the same phenomenon—only that what they are examining is closely related: the intermittent introduction of radically new technology into the economy and its consequences. These studies are not forms of economic reductionism or technological determinism. They simply begin with certain

14

premises about the discontinuous nature of technological change and then proceed in a host of different ways to map some of the implications. However, while the terminology is more prolific than most people might think, the actual measurement of leading sectors is far less common, an issue to which we return later.

On a more general level, the basic idea that technological innovation generates economic growth is compatible with the concepts of leading sectors and lead economies. The difference is that mainstream economic growth arguments prefer to treat new technology in the most abstract sense, while leading sector arguments prefer to be more specific about which new technologies are most responsible for economic growth. This difference is also reflected in the questions being asked. Mainstream growth analysts model growth processes in general. Leading sector analysts argue that specific technologies in specific nations have led to periodic bursts of economic growth at specific times, which in this literature are termed long waves. Given this assumption, the questions tend to revolve more around inquiries into the implications, or consequences, of long waves of technologically induced growth, and less around the influences on, or sources of, intermittent innovation. The leading sector school's emphasis on the close relationships between lead economies, politicomilitary leadership, and war is one such focus. Another question is whether growth in one economy systematically leads growth in the rest of the world. It is not that these implications could not be treated by mainstream growth models; rather, so far they have not received much attention.

We think there are two main reasons for the analytical neglect of the concepts of leading sectors and lead economies in the mainstream economic growth literature. One is that most of these models either leave technological change as a residual category, as in the neoclassical model, or do not deal with technological change in specific sectors or nations, as in endogenous growth models. To the extent that certain sectors are differentiated, the distinctions are apt to be more generic, as in the case of labor, land, and capital. In the context of such an approach, the idea that specific technologies play significant roles in specific times and places (and are less significant at other times and places) may appear to be anecdotal and countertheoretical.

A second reason for the low profile may be that of the few economists who have taken long wave hypotheses seriously enough to examine the evidence, most conclude there is insufficient evidence that clusters of technological innovation have had a discernible and systematic input on aggregate growth.[12] These analysts do not dispute the fact that long-term economic growth is discontinuous and characterized by alternating phases of rapid and slow growth. However, they view the shifts from phases of rapid to slow and back to rapid growth as governed by accidental, random, and ad hoc disturbances.

Unfortunately, the evidence examined in those studies is often only indirectly related to the leading sector thesis. Instead of examining the impact of leading sectors (e.g., cotton, textiles, railroads, steel, automobiles) on economic growth per se, there has been a tendency to remain tied to aggregated activities such as production, productivity, investment, and inflation. When the focus is applied to specific sectors, the target almost invariably has been the nineteenth-century railroad case.[13] Other sectors are sometimes examined, but the analysis is usually conducted for a single year.[14] In any case, we believe that all of the possible avenues of critical examination of the leading sector idea have not yet been exhausted.

A Leadership-Long Cycle Perspective on Economic Growth

The particular politicoeconomic environment in which system leaders emerge and prosper is critical to an understanding of the outcomes associated with leadership. We contend that systemic leadership is made possible by the development and confluence of concentration in certain key politicoeconomic resource processes. Furthermore, it is the underlying resource concentration, as much as the systemic leadership, that helps account for such outcomes as global economic stability and world trade openness.

Put differently, we study whether actors respond to the spatial concentration of economic and political resources in the system leader's country. But even that may simplify our problem too much. For example, perhaps it is an interactive, nonlinear dynamic. Are system leaders more successful when they control the most resources than when they no longer do so? While we do not focus on the domestic politics of the hegemon, slow domestic elite realignments and sticky political institutions may complicate the problem even further. It is conceivable that system leaders may not act like system leaders until their principal policy-making centers are captured by elites who wish to assume systemic leadership roles. These realignments do not happen overnight. Similarly, once a political system has grown accustomed to behaving like a system leader, its political elites may continue the attempt to lead even if the appropriate resource foundation is no longer there. Therefore, is it necessary to possess a preponderant resource foundation, proactive leadership strategies, elites committed to the idea of leadership, and the appropriate supporting domestic and international institutions for there to be a discernible link between systemic leadership and politicoeconomic outcomes?

While we may not yet be fully up to the challenge of interrelating the leader's resources, strategies, elites, and institutions with precision, one place to start the investigation is with an overview of a theory that focuses on the resource platforms for systemic leadership, namely, the leadership–long cycle theory (for a detailed exposition see Modelski 1982, 1987; Thompson 1988, 1990, 1992, 2000; Rasler and Thompson 1994, 2000; and Modelski and Thompson 1996, 2000). The discussion here summarizes this theory for the sake of linking it theoretically and empirically to the notion of economic growth.

The leadership–long cycle theory with which we will be working is predicated on four assumptions.

A1: Long-term economic growth is discontinuous and dependent on spurts in the development of radical innovations (leading sectors) that produce new products, technologies, and ways of doing things. The more difficult the transition from one growth spurt or wave to the next, the greater is the extent and duration of economic depression and instability between them.

A2: National economies are organized hierarchically along a global technological gradient. Radical innovation is monopolized primarily at or near the top of the gradient, with subsistence activities characterizing the bottom. Yet some movement up (via technological innovation, imitation, and diffusion) and down the gradient is possible.

A3: The principal source of radical technological innovation is concentrated in a single lead economy. Radical innovation generates temporary leads in monopoly profits, efficiency, and productivity, which enable systemic leadership. As the new technologies become routine and dispersed, pioneer economies will experience diminishing returns.

A4: Lead economies benefit from two waves of innovation. The first (ascent) wave is especially destabilizing and encourages intensive conflict among states that are located high on the technological gradient. The benefits associated with leading in the first wave make the pioneer innovator's victory in the conflict more probable by funding global reach capabilities and war coalitions. The lead in the first wave and the intensive global war mobilization enable a second (catch-up) growth wave. It is in this second wave that competitors are able to close the gap between the lead economy and its rivals.

These assumptions are not merely abstract generalizations. Assumption A1 is quite compatible with the way in which many historians of technological progress describe macroeconomic change. Assumption A2—that there is a state hierarchy and that some movement up and down is conceivable— is rather difficult to challenge. Assumptions A3 and A4 are more controversial, but they are also based on a substantial body of literature. While we take these assumptions as given in this chapter, some supportive elaboration may be helpful at this point.

The leadership-long cycle theory asserts that radical technological innovation and global reach capabilities are the principal foundations for systemic leadership. This generalization is compatible with the arguments of more than one school of thought in the literature on international political economy (e.g., Gilpin 1975, 1981, 1987; Kennedy 1987; Wallerstein 1983, 1996). The technological innovations create the system's lead economy that, in turn, funds and necessitates the development of predominance in global reach capability. It should hardly be controversial to point out that cotton textiles, iron production, steam engines, and railroads were prominent foundations of British economic leadership in the nineteenth century. Steel, electricity, automobiles, semiconductors, and aerospace have been equally prominent industries in the emergence of U.S. economic leadership in the twentieth century. However, it is not necessary that we capture every facet of these leading sectors. This would be a rather ambitious task. For our purpose, it should suffice if we are able to generally capture the relationships between the rise and decline of leading sectors in the lead economy and economic growth.

H2: Leading sector growth in the lead economy drives the lead economy's aggregate economic growth.

H3: Leading sector growth and aggregate economic growth in the lead economy drive world economic growth.

H4: After some lag, world economic growth and leading sector growth in the lead economy are negatively related.

Introduction

Testing hypotheses involving leading sectors requires empirical measures or indices of these sectors. One possible index of the rise and decline of the system leader's leading sectors is their rate of growth. A related index is the share of global leading sector production controlled by the system leader. As the leader's share rises, so does the economic platform for systemic leadership. One would expect the system leader's leading sector growth rates and leading sector production share to wax and wane in a corresponding fashion. However, global war and military mobilization have become necessary to defend the fruits of the first growth surge and to facilitate the emergence of a second growth surge. This twin-peaked, economic base of the leader enables its political preponderance. The leader's share of naval capability, a major index of the ability to project military force on a global scale, should rise and decline in roughly synchronized fashion, albeit subject to some sort of lagged relationship to the economic foundations that both motivate and finance the expansion of naval power. We suggest that the trinity of leading sector growth rate, leading sector production share, and naval power share should capture the politicoeconomic and military foundation for systemic hegemonic leadership. But we need to keep in mind that they do not necessarily measure the success or the exercise of systemic leadership. What they measure is the capability platform from which leadership can be exercised.

H5: Leading sector growth in the lead economy supports the attainment of economic superiority in leading sector production.

H6: Leading sector growth and economic superiority in leading sector production encourage the development of superiority in global reach capabilities.

H7: The development of superiority in global reach capabilities reinforces an ascending system leader's mobilization for warfare.

H8: Leading sector growth and economic superiority in leading sector production make the system leader's military mobilization for warfare more probable, which, in turn, encourages further leading sector growth and economic superiority.

Understanding the functioning of this platform for systemic leadership is only a beginning. We also need to understand how this platform relates to other politicoeconomic phenomena. We have already suggested strong linkages to long-term growth prospects. Now we suggest strong linkages to trade and the openness of the system to international commerce.

Growth, Trade, and Systemic Leadership

A Leadership–Long Cycle-Based Theory of Trade Openness

So far, we have presented the concepts of leading sector and the lead economy. We have also advanced our interpretation of long-term economic growth, which is predicated on the notion of long waves of economic and political systemic leadership. We now use these same ideas to construct a leadership–long cycle-based theory of technological change and world trade openness.

New technology and products are introduced in the first (ascent) growth wave. At this stage, the technological gap between innovational pioneers and other economies is great, and the returns from new technology are high. Innovational pioneers thus will move toward unilaterally reducing trade barriers in order to reduce import costs, subject to the overcoming of domestic resistance, because their new products have little in the way of genuine competition. Similarly, pioneers will also move to open access for their products in other countries' markets. The intensity of the leader's motivation for political action on global trade policy, however, will also hinge on the extent to which the particular system leader's economy is dependent on trade. Greater trade dependence is conducive to a more intense motivation to move toward free trade.

The domestic political impact of the new technology in the first growth wave, in any event, is not likely to be abruptly pervasive. Old ways of doing things and entrenched interests that need protection can be supplanted only gradually. As a consequence, the movement toward freer trade is slow in all economies, including the lead economy. Some, but certainly not all, countries will respond to the lead economy's lowered trade barriers with comparable reductions in trade barriers in order to better obtain the new products innovated by the leader. There are also strong incentives to learn and imitate the tricks of the new leading sectors, the desire to exploit new abilities to compete, and the associated benefits from the expanded trade associated with growth surges. The actors most resistant to lowering their trade barriers will be states with considerable potential for moving up the technological gradient but whose decision makers perceive the need for protection in order to do so.

In the second growth wave, other countries master the new technology. The systemwide impetus to free trade will be greater in the second wave than in the first wave because competitiveness and trade benefits are then less concentrated. But, eventually, the returns from new technologies diminish. Multiple producers will then find themselves capable of producing more than markets can absorb, foreign exports will appear more threatening, and collective action to obtain protection will be more likely to be sought and to be successful. Diminishing returns are most probable in the downswings of, and the transitions between, the long-term growth waves. Diminishing returns are especially evident in the lead economy as it fails to renew its technological edge (after leading two growth waves). Consequently, its relative decline is due to a combination of various types of political and social rigidities, the successful catching-up of its economic rivals (thanks in part to freer trade), and the relative absence of new innovation due to such factors as complacency. Free trade policies, then, are beneficial for the lead economy in the short term but less so when viewed from a longer-term perspective.

The story includes lags on both the ascent and descent phases of leadership due to domestic political alignments in the leading nation. On the ascent phase, system leaders come to prefer free trade, but they may not do so immediately. That will depend on how much domestic political baggage (older elites, institutions, and ideas) must first be shed. Ultimately, though, the primary producer of new technologies and products will embrace free trade if there is little to fear from foreign competition. As promoters of free trade, system leaders will push others to follow their lead. In some cases, this push may be coercive, but we would expect such to be the case only for weaker actors who thwart major power export strategies. Usually, system leaders will be content to avoid conflict with strong actors and are thus more likely to negotiate for reductions in trade barriers, either bilaterally or multilaterally.

On the descent phase of leadership, after leading the struggle for freer trade and becoming heavily socialized in the free trade doctrine, political elites in a relatively declining, lead economy will be among the last to succumb to the attractions of downswing protectionism. These pro–free trade elites are no more easy to supplant than the ones they replaced. The situation is made even more ambiguous if the incumbent lead economy demonstrates some potential for reestablishing its lead for an additional set of two economic growth waves.

Exceptions to these generalizations may be expected. Significant parts of the world economy may be beyond the leader's influence, especially if there is concerted resistance by states reluctant to participate fully in the world economy, or to participate on terms established by the leader and its regime. Moreover, in pursuit of strategic aims, a leader may look the other way if allies use protectionist measures to rebuild their economies. In general, though, we expect world trade openness to respond, subject to variable lags, to the concentration of politicoeconomic capabilities in the system leader's economy. This interpretation suggests several more testable hypotheses.

> H9: Systemic leadership and long waves of economic growth and trade impose fundamental constraints on protectionist behavior.
>
> H10: In the short term, protectionist behavior influences the volume of trade; in the long term, declining growth and trade influence the probability of protectionism.
>
> H11: The long-term influence (trade $\rightarrow$ protectionism) is stronger than the short-term influence (protectionism $\rightarrow$ trade).

Hypotheses H9 through H11 follow from the idea that long-term economic growth and trade are closely related. Growth leads to expanded trade, which, in turn, leads to more growth. The converse holds as well. We depart from the norm in many international political economy studies by assuming that protectionist behavior in the long term is more a function of fluctuations in growth and trade than the other way around. We do not need to argue that protectionist behavior has no impact. Rather, we suggest that protectionism tends to reinforce propensities toward diminished growth and contracting trade—as opposed to being the prime mover. Similarly, systemic leadership is closely linked to growth and trade prospects and therefore also linked to trade openness. However, the effect of the system leader on protectionism is not primarily coercive. Openness is not imposed. Instead, the system leader creates new incentives and opportunities for expanded trade. And that, in conjunction with the leader's example in unilaterally lowering tariffs and its ongoing negotiating pressures, encourages greater openness as long as the economic environment is suitably conducive.

> H12: After some lag, world trade openness will be positively influenced by systemic leadership, as reflected in the leader's leading sector production superiority and global reach capability.

Still, if the system leader itself only moves slowly toward freer trade due to domestic resistance, the initial growth spurt in leading sectors may not be accompanied by an immediate lowering of trade barriers—either on the system leader's part or anyone else's. If the long-term growth impulses are double-gaited (i.e., there is an ascent wave followed by a catch-up wave that is particularly conducive to expanded trade), the upswing in the second growth wave may follow significant reductions in trade barriers on the part of the system leader. Other states will perceive different cues depending on which wave is prevailing. The catch-up wave, as opposed to the ascent wave, should be a more favorable context for others to lower their trade barriers. This variety of mixed effects suggests our next hypothesis.

H13: The influence of leading sector growth in the lead economy on world trade openness is likely to be weak.

The theory suggests, moreover, that trade ultimately is a leveling process—at least at the upper end of the technological gradient. Competitors learn the new skills of the leading sectors, produce more of them, and eventually outproduce and outsell the leader. Some states may also surpass the leader in innovational productivity. Therefore, we should expect the leader's leading sector growth and production shares to generally decline, as world trade openness rises. As the leader's relative economic position erodes, its incentives for possessing global reach capabilities and its relative advantage in funding them decays. Consequently, its naval power erodes, again subject to some lag.

H14: After some lag, systemic leadership and the leader's leading sector growth, leading sector production superiority, and shares of global reach capability will be negatively influenced by world trade openness.

The relationships formulated in hypotheses H12 through H14 imply an overarching causal chain: economic and global reach leadership → a rise in world trade openness → a decline in economic and global reach leadership. These relationships clearly do not exhaust all of the implications of the theory presented earlier.[15] For instance, they do not touch upon the advent of diminishing returns, differential responses to trade strategies, depressions and their linkage to growth wave transitions, or structurally encouraged domestic political realignments in the leader and follower nations. We do not regard these topics as inconsequential, but due to their inherent complexity, they seem better dealt with in separate contexts.

Finally, we turn to the latest twist in the development of regimes influencing trading patterns—free trade agreements (FTAs) that are regionally based. Ostensibly, these efforts to reduce trade barriers on a selective geographical basis are being undertaken currently because more global efforts have either gone as far as they can and/or have encountered resistance that is more likely to be overcome by more local efforts. To the extent that they are successful in reducing trade barriers in regional arenas, they contribute to a more open system. But if they open the region at the expense of the region's contacts with the outside world, FTAs could become conduits to a more closed world economy, not unlike the beggar-thy-neighbor trading blocs encouraged by the 1930s world depression.

Thus, for some observers, these arrangements portend a return to the exclusivist blocs of the 1930s and, therefore, represent movement toward world trade closure. For others, the arrangements are more benign and reflect a variety of short-term politicoeconomic motivations, as well as natural proclivities toward trade regionalization. To the extent that regional free trade arrangements break down highly resistant barriers to trade, they can even further the cause of world trade openness.

Since the United States, the current system leader, is heavily involved in a North American regional trade arrangement and is working toward a pan-American extension, it is appropriate that we take a closer look at these trade regionalization activities. If the reigning system leader is constructing a regional enclave, the omens for world trading openness are less than good. However, given some of the short-term political considerations at work, our best guess is that a system leader's trade regionalization activities do not necessarily portend world trade closure or even the abandonment of free trade doctrines by the United States. This brings us to our last hypothesis.

> H15: Trade regionalization activities on the part of the system leader and the closure of world trade are not necessarily synonymous.

Outline of the Book

Chapters 2 and 3 develop what we refer to as the *leadership platform*. This platform provides a literal and figurative foundation for subsequent arguments about how systemic leadership is related to other important processes. In chapter 2, we examine the assertion that leading sectors within the lead economy are causally related to the lead economy's aggregate economic growth. Leading sectors such as steel, automobiles, and computers represent radical technological innovations that we contend are critical to long-term growth. We also evaluate the claim that the world economy's economic growth is dependent upon the lead economy's leading sector production as well as its aggregate economic growth. All of these assertions are amply supported by the empirical evidence pertaining to the role of the United States as a spark plug of economic growth and, ultimately, the system leader in the second half of the twentieth century. Both U.S. leading sector and aggregate growth drive world growth in its leadership era. But we also find that the causal arrows do not all point in one direction from the United States to the rest of the world.

After establishing the significance of leading sectors in chapter 2, chapter 3 explores in greater depth the linkages among the constituent parts of the leadership platform. We focus on three variables: (1) leading sector growth, (2) superiority in leading sector production, and (3) global reach capability primacy. We argue that leading sector growth leads to leading sector dominance and global reach capability primacy and that leading sector dominance also leads to primacy in global reach capabilities. These assertions are amply substantiated in the U.S. experience. We also add a fourth variable to the platform ensemble, war mobilization, which we suggest is also a function, in part, of leading sector dominance. Why this should be the case requires some amplification (chap. 3). Briefly, though, wealth and economic predominance lead to military protection costs and warfare over whose version of order will prevail in the global political economy. This argument is also amply supported in the U.S. case. Moreover, while we find that the economic processes tend to drive the politico-military processes, there is also feedback from the political processes to the economic processes. These findings add up to a tight coevolutionary pattern between economic and politicomilitary predominance in the world system.

In the second part of this study, we shift analytical gears from an emphasis on growth per se to an emphasis on growth and trade. Having made a strong case for the existence and role of systemic leadership in chapters 2 and 3, how does systemic leadership generate a context for the functioning of other politicoeconomic processes? There are a number of processes that we might have focused upon (and hope to do so in future studies), but we chose to concentrate here on protectionism and the trading openness of the world economy. There are two main reasons for choosing this particular topic. One is that the role of systemic leadership in creating and maintaining trading openness is contested. Some authors see systemic leadership or hegemony as critical to openness, while others regard the linkage as largely irrelevant. Not surprisingly, we side with the former camp. Yet we also think that the topic has not received appropriate theoretical and empirical attention to date. Thus, the contestation is predicated in part on insufficient analysis—a problem we can address directly.

A second reason for focusing on protectionism and trade openness is that these processes have been approached from a bewildering number of perspectives. In chapter 4, for instance, we outline seventeen different perspectives on protectionism and make no claim that we have exhausted the diversity that exists in the literature. Most of these perspectives focus on domestic considerations. That is, protectionism is seen primarily as a subsystemic process in which local actors pursue local self-interests, sometimes with systemic consequences. We do not argue that these domestic emphases are wrong—only that they are incomplete. What actors do locally is executed within a larger systemic context that is strongly flavored by the ups and downs of systemic leadership. Chapter 4's mission, as a consequence, is to survey the protectionism literature and briefly outline the various interpretations. Given the diversity in points of view, chapter 4 then attempts to show how the seventeen perspectives can be linked to the waxing and waning of systemic leadership. The argument is that what we see as domestic processes do not take place in a vacuum. While protectionism represents domestic attempts to insulate local processes from external forces, there is a limit to how much these attempts are insulated from the influences of structural or systemic constraints and opportunities.

Chapter 5 takes our ecumenical approach one step further, focusing on a number of interpretations of the history of the last two centuries of protectionist efforts. These interpretations lend themselves to sometimes overlapping, sometimes conflicting categorizations of sequences of increasing and decreasing protectionism. To assess the relative validity of these claims, we develop serial indices of tariff protectionism for several important economic actors and for the world economy as a whole. The question then is, Whose interpretative story comes closest to the empirical tariff information mark? We find that perspectives that emphasize systemic shocks, long waves of economic growth, and systemic leadership do best in this debate. Such a finding does not mean that only these variables should be credited with fluctuations in tariffs. Rather, it generates additional support for developing perspectives that integrate these emphases into their explanatory webs.

While chapters 4 and 5 focused on two related bodies of literature, chapters 6 and 7 take the empirical testing begun in chapter 5 much farther. If protectionism is essentially a domestic process with international implications, we should expect various attempts at opening or closing markets to influence the volume of trade. Chapter 6 asks a simple question: To what extent do protectionist efforts drive trade volumes? If, on the other hand, our emphasis on systemic leadership contexts is correct, we should expect protectionism to be more reactive to external growth considerations that are not wholly controllable. In this sense, we should anticipate that fluctuations in trade lead to protectionist efforts. For instance, as the world economy contracts, local agents should attempt to insulate themselves from the external threat of economic deterioration. But which impulse is stronger? Does protectionism drive changes in trade volume, or do changes in trade volume drive protectionism? Or, do both processes occur more or less simultaneously? We find that, in the longer term, trade drives protectionism much more so than the other way around. This finding should be seen as reinforcing our argument that the greater context within which protectionist efforts take place is critical to an understanding of why, when, and where protectionist attempts are made.

Chapter 7 returns explicitly to the systemic leadership platform. If we are right in contending that the openness or closure of the world economy to trade is tied closely to systemic leadership processes, we should be able to demonstrate an empirical linkage between the systemic leadership platform and world economic openness. We anticipate and find strong support for a positive causal connection between both economic primacy and global reach predominance and world trade openness. We also find support for an equally anticipated negative causal connection between world trade openness and systemic leadership. Ironically, an open system benefits a system leader's advantages and interests in the short run. Over the longer run, a price is paid by the leader to the extent that trading openness facilitates the catching up of challengers and new leaders.

Chapter 8 examines one of the latest wrinkles in the history of protectionism—the turn to FTAs or regional, free trade agreements. We examine this phenomenon very selectively. We cannot predict whether FTAs will become more protectionist in the future. What we can do is to examine the history of U.S. trade regionalism tendencies. In particular, we focus on the United States because of its status as the current system leader and because our current emphasis is on systemic leadership. If we find that the current system leader is hedging its bets by developing a North American enclave to which it can retreat should the world economy become "too" competitive, we would need to seriously rethink some of our arguments about the relationship between systemic leadership and trade openness.

Chapter 8 asks whether U.S. trade regionalism has been highly correlated with other possible forms of trade closure such as tariffs and the relative size of trade. All three have been advanced as alternative indicators of protectionist tendencies. However, we find that they are not very well correlated in the U.S. experience at least. U.S. trade regionalization tendencies and the closure of the U.S. market have not gone hand in hand. A closer look at NAFTA (the North American Free Trade Agreement) suggests some of the reasons for regarding FTAs as hitherto benign elements in world trade. While they possess some potential to facilitate world trade closure, to the extent that NAFTA is a sign of things to come, they are not currently detracting from world trade openness.

What do all of these chapters add up to? Figure 1.2 provides a cursory answer. We are attempting to develop an empirical map of the relationships in international political economy—or at least some of the more important ones. On our "empirical map," we mean to show what is related to what. Our chosen point of departure is the systemic leadership platform, which, in turn, is predicated on spatially and temporally clustered technological innovations that bestow preeminence on one actor at a time. The coming and going of systemic leadership, we think, is fundamental to the tempo of international political economy processes. The presence or absence of systemic leadership and the strong capability concentration that it implies do not dictate what happens. Rather, they establish a macrostructural context within which other processes function. Some things are simply more likely when systemic leadership is strong, while others are less likely when leadership is weak.

This is not the place to go into detail about the interconnections suggested in figure 1.2. That is, after all, the work of the next eight chapters. We will return to this figure and some of its implications in chapter 9. In the interim, and subject to some qualifications to be discussed later, we can say that protectionism is one of those processes that is most prevalent when leadership (and the systemic leadership platform) is weak. Systemic openness to trade, in addition to economic growth and trade, is one of those processes that is more prevalent when leadership (and the systemic leader-

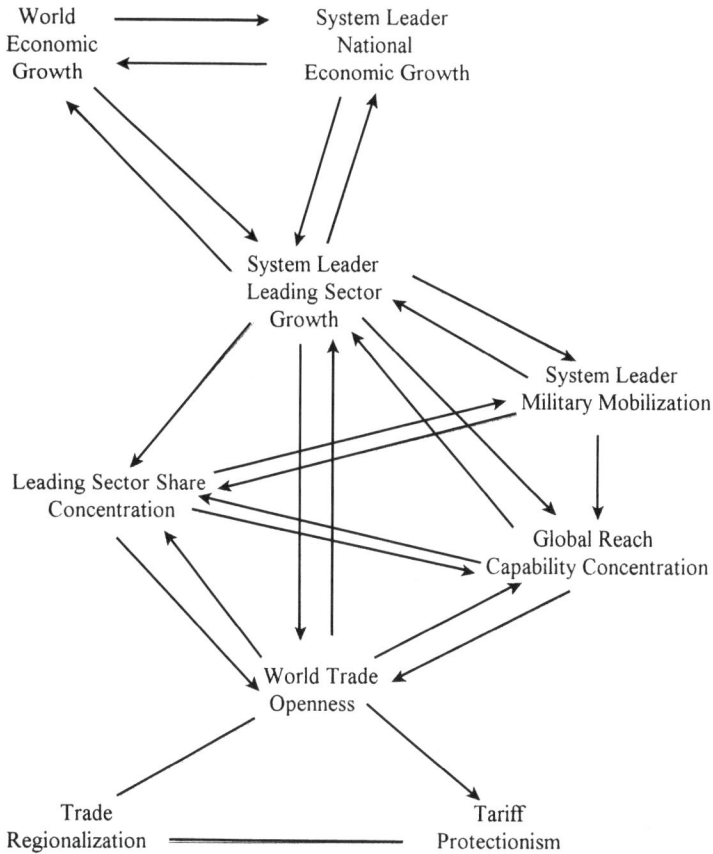

Fig. 1.2.   The overall model

ship platform) is strong. However, it is equally important that protectionism and openness are embedded in a network of variables and processes, as suggested by figure 1.2. Leading sector growth, leading sector dominance, global reach capability predominance, military mobilization for war, lead economy growth, world economy growth, and trade openness are all interrelated, coevolve, and, in varying degrees of predictability, feed back on one another. This is not the end of our story. What we are attempting to do is to unravel what might be called the IPE structural genome. This book represents a major start—but it is only that, a start and not its final conclusion. We, and hopefully others, need to build on this start and to continue the unraveling process for it is clear that there are a host of other connections to be made.

The next chapter initiates the unraveling process by focusing on the linkages from the system leader's leading sectors to its aggregate growth and, ultimately, the aggregate growth of the world economy. As the world's lead economy, the system leader generates radical economic innovations in commercial and industrial sectors that serve as the core of the platform for global politicomilitary leadership. The economic pioneering is extraordinarily profitable for the lead economy's own growth. The innovations diffuse throughout the lead economy and then to the rest of the world that is in a position to adopt the innovations. Thus, leading sectors are viewed as important drivers of the aggregate growth of the lead and world economies, and, indirectly, they generate the economic infrastructure for the global political system.

While others have demonstrated that lead economies monopolize the production of economic innovation, we provide the first test for the empirical relationships among one lead economy's leading sectors, its aggregate growth, and the growth of the world economy as a whole. Focusing on the 1870–1990 experience of the United States, we find that U.S. leading sector activity and aggregate growth both drive world economic growth. However, these relationships do not appear to be continuous. Rather, they wax and wane according to the life cycles of leading sector innovations and the intermittency of systemic leadership. In general, though, the more basic point is that economic development is and has been a global process and one strongly influenced by first the concentration and then the diffusion of major innovations via the agency of politicoeconomic leadership in the world economy.

Part I. The Systemic Leadership Platform

2. Leading Sectors, Lead Economies, and Economic Growth

Conventional economic growth models tend to be restricted by national boundaries. External inputs are certainly conceivable (trade, foreign aid, technology transfers, remittances, and so forth), but otherwise the primary ingredients for growth are found domestically and are typically conceived in such generic terms as population growth, capital accumulation, labor, education, human capital, technological progress, infrastructure, investments, and savings. In contrast, some nonmainstream models assume that the prospects for national economic growth trajectories are affected by the larger international system in which national economies are embedded. In these models, the internal ingredients for growth are not dismissed, but they are unlikely to be sufficient for growth in the absence of a favorable systemic context. Moreover, the favorable systemic context hinges to some extent on the system's political hierarchy. Innovative systemic leadership (in both economics and politics) is required to ensure sustained growth. In the absence of systemic leadership, the systemic context is likely to be less favorable to economic growth.

However, global political leadership is unlikely unless it can draw on an economic resource foundation established by radical innovations in commerce and leading sectors. This fundamental interdependency makes it extremely difficult to separate "economics" from "politics" at the global level. It makes more sense, therefore, to view systemic leadership from a political economy perspective. The preconditions for leadership are simply too intertwined to treat the processes as distinct.

Nevertheless, models that make use of concepts such as leading sectors and economic leadership are anything but monolithic. Analysts disagree about the significance and meaning of capitalism, how long a world system has been operating, whether long waves of growth and/or prices exist and what drives them, and the relative importance of core-periphery divisions of labor. They also disagree about epistemology and the necessity or even the possibility of theory construction. Yet there are four arguments on which analysts working in this area increasingly converge: (1) economic leadership in new commercial activities and new industries is a precondition for politicomilitary leadership; (2) these same innovations drive the aggregate growth of the most advanced economies; (3) these leading sectors are monopolized initially by the lead economy in which they are pioneered before being diffused to other receptive economies; and, most importantly, (4) the growth of the lead economy is a major propellant of the growth of the world economy and, less directly, a mainstay of the global political system.[1] Reciprocal effects of the lead economy's growth on leading sector growth and the world economy's growth on the lead economy are also possible but are typically not emphasized.

One problem with these generalizations, though, is that the arguments are usually assumed instead of being put to the empirical test. We challenge that tendency by testing the two generalizations that have so far received the least empirical attention. Strong empirical linkages between leading sector growth and economic preeminence in holding the largest world shares of these sectors, and between these two to naval concentration, military mobilization, and global war for the nineteenth-century British era and the American twentieth century have already been established (Rasler and Thompson 1994; Modelski and Thompson 1996; and see chap. 3). The argument that innovations first appear in a single lead economy and then are diffused to other receptive economies may well be the least controversial of the four generalizations. This proposition, in any event, has already been corroborated.[2] It is quite another matter to insist that the new innovations drive national aggregate economic growth in the other technologically advanced economies, and that the growth of the lead economy in the development of these innovations drives world economic growth. To our knowledge, these propositions have yet to be tested.

We test these propositions over the last 120 years in the context of U.S. leading sector growth and gross domestic product (GDP) growth and world GDP growth. We first inspect plots of our time-series, then examine cross-correlations between all the variable pairs that can be formed among them. Next, we perform causality tests, always keeping in mind that causality is a contested term. We follow Granger (1969) and assume that the statement "x causes y" minimally means that changes in x temporally precede changes in y. It is also possible that x and y will be coterminous in time, which implies that the causality is reciprocal. As argued by many analysts, Granger causality tests are useful in establishing which variable, if any, came first. That may not be enough to establish causality in the full sense of the concept, but it is a start.

Summarizing our results, world economic growth is found to be positively correlated with, and Granger caused by, the growth of the lead economy and its leading sectors. The lead economy's growth is found to be positively correlated with the growth of its leading sectors. The causality link between the growth of the leading sectors and the growth of the lead economy is reciprocal. Thus, world economic growth is a function of the economic success of the system leader. Its economic innovations propel its own and the world's aggregate growth in periods of strong leadership. Hence, standard economic growth explanations are overlooking an important part of the growth puzzle. The implications of these findings for attaining global political leadership also need to be considered.

In the rest of this chapter, we first briefly recapitulate the theoretical argument that was put forward in the preceding chapter, then discuss our research design, describe our data and empirical measures, and present the results.

The Causality between Leading Sectors
and Economic Growth

One of our arguments is that long-term economic growth is fueled by the periodic emergence of new commerce and industries that alter fundamentally the way commodities are produced or marketed. We call these new commercial and industrial activities *leading sectors.* Leading sectors are not the exclusive source of long-term growth. They act more like intermittent spark plugs that keep economies expanding by developing ways to do novel things or to do less-than-novel things more efficiently and/or faster, even if that only means moving old commodities more effectively than before. These developments do not occur randomly or constantly. Rather, they appear to emerge every forty to sixty years and have been doing so for the last millennium. In addition, they emerge initially in one place. One economy, referred to as the *lead economy,* pioneers in introducing the innovations and reaps monopoly profits for doing so. These leads are temporary. Eventually, competitors learn how to copy and to improve upon the innovations. As the innovations diffuse selectively throughout the system, they also gradually become more routine and less profitable, thereby setting up circumstances for the emergence of new leading sectors.

If this interpretation has validity, we should expect to find that both the aggregate growth of the lead economy and that of the rest of the world economy are stimulated significantly by the lead economy's leading sector rates of growth. The lead economy's aggregate economic growth should also be a source of stimulation for the world economy in that the system's leading economy becomes not only the primary source of innovation but, thanks to its economic expansion and affluence, also a preeminent source of demand for the world's goods. Yet we should also anticipate a negative feedback loop at some point. Eventually, growth in the world economy should be linked negatively to further leading sector growth in the lead economy, as these industries become successively more diffused, more routine, and less profitable. Thus, referring back to chapter 1, we have our main hypotheses for this chapter.

H2: Leading sector growth in the lead economy drives the lead economy's aggregate economic growth.

H3: Leading sector economic growth and aggregate growth in the lead economy drive world economic growth.

H4: After some lag, world economic growth and leading sector growth in the lead economy are negatively related.

One of the problems in assessing the impact of leading sectors is how to select indicators that simplify the incredibly complex changes under way while not attempting to measure all possible facets of the new technological regimes. This emphasis on indicators cannot be overemphasized. For instance, if leading sectors in the mid–nineteenth century are measured in terms of the rate of expansion of railroad lines, it does not mean that railroad infrastructure was the only economic activity that mattered in driving long-term economic growth. Rather, the expansion of the railroad infrastructure is simply one index of the movement toward steam propulsion in the mid–nineteenth century. But, if we focus on, say, automobile production, how do we best aggregate luxury and entry-level units? At what cost do we ignore the related petroleum, steel, tire, glass, upholstery, used vehicle, repair, and part-supply industries?

Assuming we have overcome these challenges to index construction, we need to determine whether leading sectors have actually made a measurable difference to aggregate growth, in their respective time periods. We attempt to model linearly a rather discontinuous growth process. It is quite probable that new industries have their greatest growth impacts when they are small and expanding, rather than when they are at their most mature size. But it would be naive to assume that these sectors do not interact with other growth stimuli manifested at the aggregate levels. In fact, rather complex feedback processes may also characterize the interplay between leading sectors and other sources of economic growth.

In terms of causality, if new industries appear in temporal and spatial spurts—as opposed to emerging randomly—and if they do indeed stimulate the growth of the economy in which they emerge and the growth of the world's economy, we may expect that the growth of leading sectors will precede aggregate economic growth more than aggregate economic growth will precede the growth of the leading sector, or at least the causality should be reciprocal. Yet, the direction of the causality between these variables may also change depending on the time period used in the empirical analysis. Suppose that leading sector growth spurts occur at times t_1 and t_3, and the economy in which this growth occurred grows vigorously at time $t_1 < t_2 < t_3$. A sample that includes t_1 and t_2 but not t_3 will most likely show Granger causality from leading sector growth to aggregate economic growth, or changes in the leading sector preceding changes in aggregate economic growth. On the other hand, a sample that includes t_2 and t_3 but not t_1 may show Granger causality from economic growth to leading sector.

That said, the strongest evidence for leading sector stimulation should be associated with the life cycle of the new industries. As the new industries emerge as major forces, their stimulus to overall growth should be greatest. As they diffuse to other economies or as they become routinized, their stimulus to overall growth should diminish. Hence, periods that include greater leading sector growth are most likely to be characterized by a causal link from the growth of leading sectors to aggregate growth.

As the lead economy develops new industries that stimulate its own growth, its impact on the world economy should be greatest. At the same time, some lag in the transmission of this effect from the lead economy to the world is likely because the impact of the leading sector is related to the relatively slow diffusion of the knowledge associated with the new sectors. Thus, while the impact on growth in the lead economy is beginning to wane, it may still wax in other countries, to the extent that the sectors in question retain novelty in other, follower economies. In terms of causality, we expect to find that the growth of the lead economy will precede the growth of the world's economy, just as leading sector growth may precede the growth of the lead economy.

There could also be some payoff from the diffusion of the new technology, in the short term at least, to the lead economy as some sections of the world import more from the lead economy. This effect may translate into a reciprocal effect of the world economy on the lead economy. That is, while the lead economy's growth is expected to stimulate the world economy more than the other way around, and more or less in step with the timing of the introduction of new leading sectors, we do not rule out some evidence of reciprocal relationships. But we expect the lead economy's influence (in terms of Granger causality) to be discernibly greater on the rest of the world than the other way around. Prior to the full emergence of a new lead economy, or as the incumbent lead economy loses its lead, we should expect the old lead economy to be responsible for a much weaker stimulation of world system growth. We may even find the causal arrow reversed in these circumstances, with the growth influence of the rest of the world being stronger than the "lead" economy's influence on the world.

Finally, we cannot ignore the possibility that leading sector growth in the lead economy directly affects the world's economy. In an age in which globalization seems to be an all-engulfing phenomenon, this interpretation seems all the more attractive to explore. The lead economy innovates new ways of doing things. Some parts of the world economy are in positions to adopt, and adapt to, these ways. Therefore, we expect that growth in the lead economy's leading sector will also have a direct effect on the world economy and that the effect will be most discernible after 1945. It is conceivable that the two processes (lead economy growth and leading sector growth driving world growth) work together in transmitting the innovative effect of the lead economy to the world.[3]

Research Design Considerations

Focusing on the most recent example of a lead economy (the United States), we pose three questions, each in two variants: (1) Has U.S. leading sector growth preceded or anteceded, or is it correlated with, U.S. GDP growth? (2) Has U.S. GDP growth preceded or anteceded, or is it correlated with, world GDP growth? (3) Has U.S. leading sector growth preceded or anteceded, or is it correlated with, world GDP growth? These questions are likely to be interrelated to some extent, both conceptually and empirically. However, in order to simplify, we investigate them separately from one another.

Our emphasis on the U.S. case is neither random, arbitrary, nor chauvinistic. We begin with the strongest case possible in the double sense that most analysts will concede U.S. credentials as a twentieth-century system leader, and there are fewer data problems associated with this most recent case, in comparison to its predecessors. There also is a tendency in the international political economy literature to argue over whether Britain was a system leader in the late nineteenth and early twentieth centuries. From our perspective, this tendency has the liability of focusing on a time period that is undeniably a period of relative economic decline for Britain. One should expect at best relatively weak systemic leadership on the part of Britain in the years leading up to World War I.

If we were then to focus on data from the late nineteenth century onward (because of the availability of data) from Britain, we would be in effect biasing the examination toward years in which Britain was least likely to act as an engine of growth for the world economy. We prefer, instead, to examine the U.S. case in the period leading up to and including its peak years of influence. Consequently, our empirical focus is solely on the United States as it slowly emerged in the years prior to 1945 as the system leader and the years after 1945 when it clearly performed as the system leader. We choose to accentuate the ascendancy of systemic leadership in this analysis, and not the relative decay of its influence.

Our general approach to empirical testing assumes that statistical tests are complements to one another rather than emphasizing one test as a substitute for any others. Along these lines, we plan to apply a battery of tests and integrate their results. The tests will be applied in ascending order by complexity and amount of empirical information they may supply. Along these general lines, our investigation consists of visually inspecting time-series, cross-correlation tests, and Granger causality tests.

Similar to Berry's (1991) analysis of American long waves, we plan to inspect visually the dynamics of our series. Yet time-series of growth rates are quite noisy. To gain further insights, we sum the growth rates over periods of ten years to create a depiction of per-decade growth. The smoother time-series so generated will be investigated both visually and with cross-correlation analysis. As we demonstrate later, our series exhibit leads and lags relative to one another. Therefore, in addition to contemporaneous cross-correlations, we will also compute the cross-correlations between series that lag or lead each other. Put formally, we will compute the cross-correlation between x_t and y_{t-n}, where x and y are time-series, n is the number of lags or leads of y ($n < 0$ denotes leads), and t denotes time.

Two methods are used to find whether the cross-correlation results are statistically significantly different from zero (Spiegel 1988). In one method we compute a t-statistic to check if the null hypothesis, $\rho = 0$, should be rejected in favor of the alternative $\rho > 0$ (or $\rho < 0$ if the observed correlation is negative). In the second method we compute Fischer's test statistics to find if ρ is as small as 0.00001 (or –0.00001). We will analyze results only if they are significant at a certain level in both tests. Two significance levels are used, 5 and 10 percent.

The cross-correlation results, while illuminating, cannot pinpoint which series causes the other. We therefore include in our research design a causality test developed by Granger (1969). We perform three tests from the raw yearly data. The first test inspects the causality between U.S. leading sectors growth and U.S. GDP growth, the second inspects the causality between U.S. GDP growth and world GDP growth, and the third inspects the causality between U.S. leading sector growth and world GDP growth.

Given limitations on the availability of standardized aggregate growth series, our data start in 1870. The period before World War I is a decline phase of Britain as a system leader while U.S. leadership was still emerging. The period between the world wars was one in which U.S. leadership was forming. The period after World War II, at least until the mid-1970s, is one in which the United States clearly was the lead economy and politicomilitary system leader. When these periods are combined into one sample, competing effects may distort the empirical outcome. Hence, we need to consider the temporal structure of our causality tests.

We have two reasons for examining periods shorter than the full 1870–1990 period. First, no single state led consistently in the 1870–1990 period. As noted, a declining Britain led prior to World War I, and the United States led after World War II. A second reason for using shorter time periods is the question of robustness. Ideally, robust findings should be consistent across time. Yet we suspect that this may not be the result in our case. The long wave argument is that the peak influence of the United States should occur in the post–World War II period, but possibly before as well, since the first U.S. leading sector wave in our period peaks just before World War I. But, while there may be some question as to when the causality should be manifested, there is no uncertainty about when the evidence should be strongest. The most clear-cut support for the argument for the United States should be manifested in the post-1945 period, as this is the most obvious period of its leadership.

We do not have any ideal solutions for the methodological problems concerning handling discontinuities in history appropriately with linear and continuous techniques. One imperfect approach involves conducting tests within four periods: 1870–1990, 1870–1913, 1870–1945, and 1946–90, with the periods being, respectively, a full sample, Britain leadership in decline, Britain leading in part with U.S. leadership emerging, and finally the U.S. as the lead economy.[4] We realize that the examination of periods that may be too short for long-term relationships to be fully manifested could introduce as much distortion as looking only at a longer period without being concerned about heterogeneity across time. Our compromise is to look at the longer and shorter periods simultaneously in hopes of expanding our ability to correctly read the statistical outcomes.

Next we turn to rather technical Granger causality test design issues. The stationarity of the time-series, the adequacy of the test's specification, and the choice of a distributed lag length may be important in Granger tests. The significance of these issues, for the most part, continues to be debated.[5] Yet, acknowledging them alerts us to the possible limitations of Granger's approach.

We discuss one such technical issue here, however. In an investigation of economic growth, we believe that the most important control variable to include is the timing of recessions. Recessions represent a faster, shorter-term dynamic than long waves and are caused by different forces. By controlling for recessions, then, we attempt to distinguish them from long wave processes. These recession periods are marked by setting a dummy variable to a value of one in years in which they occur. As we cannot include all variables of possible interest, we follow Hoole and Huang's (1989: 147) advice that it is reasonable to assume that excluded variables will not affect the causality when the residuals are white noise.

The limitations notwithstanding, as pointed out by Freeman (1983) and Hamilton (1994), Granger causality testing retains considerable utility in assessing patterns of antecedence. The causality test is based on F-tests from the coefficients of series x and y in equations (1) and (2), where y_t and x_t are growth rates at time t, y_{t-k} and x_{t-k} are growth rates k years ago, x_0 and y_0 are intercept terms, R_N and R_w are dummy variables denoting

41

national and world recessions respectively, L_x, L_y, L'_x, and L'_y are the number of lags, u_t and u'_t are white noise error terms, and Greek symbols denote coefficients.[6]

$$x_t = x_0 + \sum_{k=1}^{L_y} \alpha_k x_{t-k} + \sum_{k=1}^{L_y} \beta_k y_{t-k} + \gamma R_{Nt} + \delta R_{Wt} + u_t \tag{1}$$

$$y_t = y_0 + \sum_{k=1}^{L_y'} \alpha_k' x_{t-k} + \sum_{k=1}^{L_y'} \beta_k' y_{t-k} + \gamma' R_{Nt} + \delta' R_{Wt} + u_t' \tag{2}$$

If the coefficients β_k in (1) are significantly different from zero, the inclusion of past values of y will yield better forecasts of future x than the use of x alone. Hence, one would conclude that y Granger causes x. The roles of x and y are then reversed in (2) to test if x Granger causes y. This is done by determining whether the coefficients α_k' are significantly different from zero. If both β_k and α_k' are significantly different from zero, both variables Granger cause each other.

Another issue concerns the significance threshold to use in evaluating causality results. In some studies causality results are reported with 5 and 10 percent significance levels. However, there is a debate in the literature about the utility of conventional levels in this case because Granger models are considered exploratory, and since (by construction) they exhibit collinearity that, while not biasing the results, increases their variance.[7] At least one author, for example, reports results with 20 percent significance levels (Moore 1995). Taking a middle-ground position in this debate, we report results with 5, 10, and 15 percent significance levels.

Finally, it is important to note that Granger causality tests are unlikely to generate the last word on our research questions. The statistical outcomes from a Granger test should be viewed as preliminary to the development of a more fully specified model. Our current goal is not to model fully the economic growth relationships that pertain to the lead economy, its leading sectors, and the world's economic growth, but rather to probe them, with the intent of formulating more ambitious models in the future.

Data and Indicators

Our empirical analysis requires data on aggregated economic growth, leading sectors, and recessions. Long series for world economic growth inevitably require some construction and, no doubt, some bias toward data that are readily available in comparable format. Annual real gross domestic product (GDP) data for seventeen major industrialized countries from 1870 to 1990 are taken from Angus Maddison's (1992) database. These countries include Australia, Austria, Belgium, Britain, Canada, Denmark, Finland, France, Germany, Italy, Japan, the Netherlands, New Zealand, Norway, Sweden, and Switzerland. Data are available from 1870, except for Japan, which enters the summation in 1885, and Switzerland, which enters the summation in 1899. The GDP data of the sixteen countries without the United States are aggregated to represent the rest of the world. The contributions of each country are expressed in constant dollars, using 1990 as the base year. Growth rates are then computed from both U.S. and world data.

While discussed in many studies, the actual measurement of leading sectors is far less common. Other than Rostow's (1978, 1998) efforts, the primary exception to this observation is the leadership-long cycle research program, which has consistently attempted to quantify the timing of leading sector spurts. The early conceptual work appeared in Modelski (1981, 1982), with the first measurement efforts appearing in Thompson (1988) and later refined and extended historically in Modelski and Thompson (1996). Utilization and discussion of these data in earlier empirical analyses are found in Thompson (1990, 1992, 2000); Rasler and Thompson (1991, 1994, 2000); and Thompson and Vescera (1992).

To best measure leading sectors or technological trajectories one must select indicators that simplify the complex changes under way while not attempting to measure all possible facets of the new technological regimes. At the same time, it is essential that we select sectors that indeed made a difference in their respective time periods. Table 2.1 lists the leading sectors to be used here. High growth dates identify the periods during which the particular sectors became leading. Start-up dates indicate the periods during which the particular sectors were in a phase of preliminary development. The leading sectors in table 2.1 have been consistently highlighted as applicable to the nineteenth and twentieth centuries by leadership-long cycle analyses (Thompson 1988; Modelski and Thompson 1996) and others.

Once the leading sectors are identified for each time period, the next problem is one of aggregating multiple indicators where applicable and developing a schedule of the entry and exit of leading sectors. For the periods immediately prior to 1973, we use the schedules of leading sector entries and exits generated by Rostow (1978) and Modelski and Thompson (1996). For all indicators, we calculate growth rates and shares by indicator and then aggregate them across the overlapping years. Shares are computed by calculating the U.S. share of the aggregated production of the principal global economic powers (Britain, France, Germany, United States, and Japan—although not all of these states existed or were globally competitive throughout the nineteenth century) per indicator. Both sums are then divided by the number of indicators aggregated per year to create one composite growth index and one composite share index.

Leading sector series are aggregated longitudinally in a conservative way. Yet the schedule in table 2.1 does not tell us how to develop continuous series. Data are not usually available for leading sector production in the earlier start-up periods. The primary operational question, therefore, is not so much when to begin counting a leading sector but, rather, whether to abruptly discontinue a former leading sector after its high growth period is concluded.

Since the early leading sectors are predicated on the British leadership phase, we maintain the nineteenth-century indicators of innovation for the United States through the following high growth periods. This practice assumes some lag in the transmission of British innovations to the American economy. Beginning with electricity consumption, however, we continue to employ a leading sector indicator through only the following start-up phase. This procedure yields the following indicator schedule: cotton

TABLE 2.1.   Lead Industries, Indicators, and Timing

Industry	Indicator	Start-Up	High Growth
Cotton	Cotton consumption	1740–63	1763–92
Iron	Iron production		
Railroads	Railroad track open	1792–1815	1815–50
	Railroad track density		
Steel	Steel production	1850–73	1873–1914
Chemicals	Sulfuric acid production		
Electrics	Electricity consumption		
Motor vehicles	Motor vehicle production	1914–45	1945–73
Electronics	Semiconductor industry sales		
Information	Industry production (ISIC group 3825, 3832, and division 385)	1973–2000	2000–2030

Note: For the periods prior to 1973, entries are based on Modelski and Thompson (1996: 69, 75). The idea for the ISIC code indicators is taken from Hall and Preston (1988: 190).

consumption (1800–1850), iron/steel production (1800–1945), railroad expansion in terms of absolute line laid and line laid/total area (1830–1914, with both indices given equal weight), acid production (1868–1945), electricity consumption (1903–45), motor vehicle production (1914–92), and semiconductor production (1954–92). For the post-1973 period, we follow Hall and Preston (1988: 190) in aggregating data on three United Nations International Standard Industrial Classification (ISIC) categories: 3825 (office, computing, and accounting machinery), 3832 (radio, television, and communications equipment), and 385 (scientific, controlling, measuring, and photographic/optical equipment). With this last indicator cluster, we are attempting to capture the ongoing development of the information age's leading sectors without the full benefit of much hindsight.

The system leader's leading sectors growth rates, thus generated, are used in the empirical analysis of this chapter. The shares of leading sectors held by the system leaders are used in chapters 3 and 7. We make no exaggerated claims that these indicators are capable of overcoming all of the challenges associated with measuring leading sectors. It is also apparent that our analysis eliminates all leading sector data available prior to 1870. We claim only that our indicators zero in on some of the most important economic sectors of the past two hundred years. To attempt to do more over a two-century time span assumes heroic dimensions.

Finally, we need to specify periods of U.S. and world recessions in an attempt to isolate short-term economic influences on growth. Data on the timing of recessions are not readily available in our period for all countries. To capture world recessions, we emulate Maddison's (1991) procedures by using a dummy variable set to one when the aggregated GDP of the United States, Germany, Britain, France, and Japan declines. These countries are a good proxy for the bulk of the world economy. A similar method is used to mark U.S. recessions.[8]

Empirical Results

The empirical analysis consists of visual inspections of the time-series data, cross-correlation analyses among our variables, and Granger causality statistical tests.

Visual Inspections

Our raw growth rate time-series fluctuate around zero and do not exhibit a time trend. Given this behavior, the variables used here are most likely stationary without a random trend (unit root) or a deterministic time trend.

This is attributed to the fact that we are employing growth rates. It is also established elsewhere that the variables in our test most likely do not include a unit root.[9] Accordingly, no further differentiation of the variables is needed.

For visual purposes, the raw time-series are filtered or smoothed by summing them over decades. The smoothed series so generated are presented in figure 2.1 for U.S. GDP growth and world GDP growth, in figure 2.2 for U.S. GDP growth and U.S. leading sector growth, and in figure 2.3 for U.S. leading sector growth and world GDP growth. Forty- to fifty-year long waves are visually discernible in all figures. Their length, however, is not precisely the same. Further, the waves in each variable do not follow exactly the same time periods—that is, our series give the impression of exhibiting lags or leads, of one series relative to the other. We chose to present these data in pairs as our statistical analysis is also performed for each of these pairs.

In figure 2.1, the time-series of world GDP growth rate peaks in the 1880s, the 1920s, and the 1960s. The most prominent peaks in the time-series of U.S. GDP growth rate seem to precede the world peaks with some regularity. Visually, then, we have some reason to suspect that U.S. economic growth has anteceded the economic growth of the rest of the world.[10]

Figure 2.2 also appears "long waveish." Three leading sector peaks are shown: one in the 1870s, a second one around World War I, and a third one that crests in the 1950s. The 1870s peak may be something of an artifact of the end of the American Civil War and the near-simultaneous beginning of the sulphuric acid industry (one of our production indicators). The second two peaks, more or less interrupted by World Wars I and II and the intervening interwar years, are commonly stressed in most long wave studies of the American economy. Modelski and Thompson (1996), for example, refer to this twin-peaks phenomenon as a standard characteristic of lead economy long waves throughout the last millennium.

Comparing the plots of leading sector growth and GDP growth for the U.S. economy, GDP growth appears to have more bumps than peaks. The two most noticeable ones after the 1870s occurred roughly at the turn of the century and at the end of World War II. Even more gentle bumps can be discerned in the 1920s and 1960s. The leading sector series, on the other hand, seems to have a more peaklike behavior. The visual impression is thus one of GDP growth rate bumps bracketing leading sector peaks.

The presentation of the data in figures 2.1 and 2.2 implies that till now

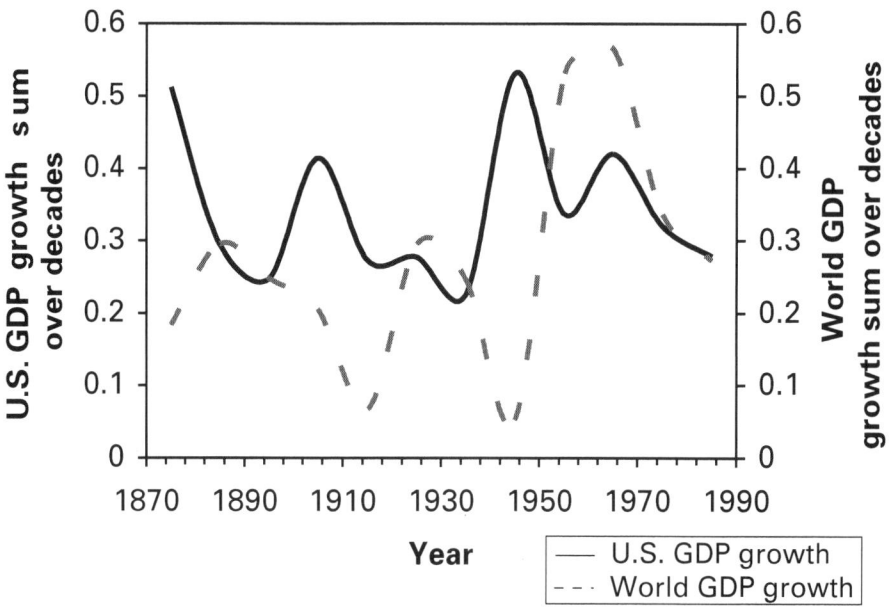

Fig. 2.1.   U.S. and world GDP growth

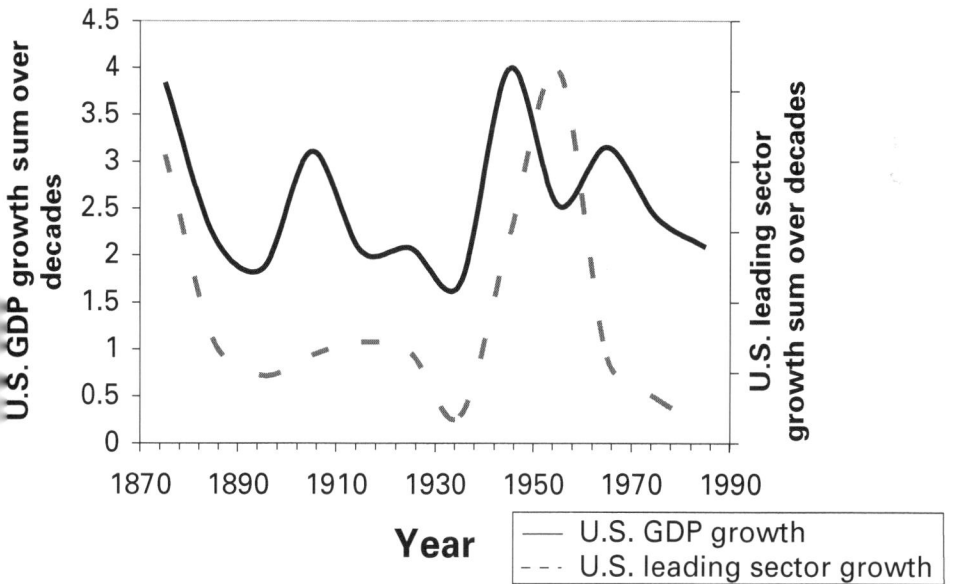

Fig. 2.2.   U.S. GDP and leading sector growth

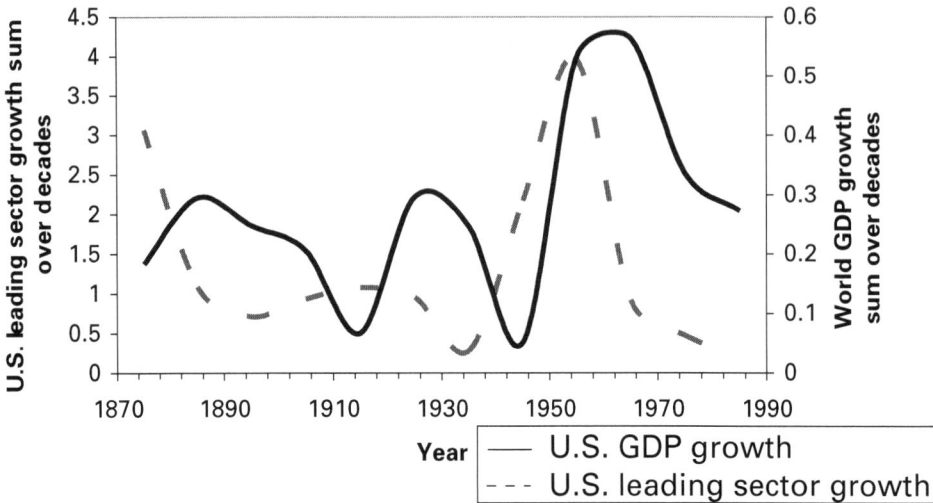

Fig. 2.3.   U.S. leading sector and world GDP growth

we have been implicitly thinking in a linear manner. That is, we have suspected that U.S. leading sector growth causes U.S. aggregate economic growth, which then causes world economic growth (hypothesis H2). Yet, as we have discussed earlier, we also wish to investigate the possibility of a direct relationship between U.S. leading sector growth and the world economy's growth (hypothesis H3). To that effect, figure 2.3 presents the leading sector growth rate for the U.S. economy together with world GDP growth.

In figure 2.3, peaks in U.S. leading sector growth seem to come before peaks in world GDP growth. The leading sector growth peak of the 1870s is followed by the 1890s peak of world economic growth, the leading sector expansion of the early 1920s is followed by the 1920s world expansion, and the leading sector growth peak of the 1950s is almost immediately followed by a visually similar peak of world economic growth. That the correspondence between the dynamics of U.S. leading sector growth and world growth seems clearer after 1945 may indicate two interrelated points. First, in a more global economy (one that is relatively open for trade, capital movement, and, most importantly, the flow of technology and knowledge) the links between the lead economy and the world should be stronger. Second, the U.S. leadership peaked in the decades immediately after 1945, before declining, which supports hypothesis H4. We do not view openness and leadership as coincidental phenomena. It is therefore likely that the effects of the U.S. leading sectors on the world's economy would be most pronounced after 1945.

Cross-Correlation Analysis

Cross-correlation coefficients from the series in figures 2.1 to 2.3 are presented in table 2.2. As is common, we denote leads as negative numbers. Leads or lags refer to the series written on the right of the slash in the title of columns. Since these series are given in a ten-year frequency, each lag or lead in the cross-correlation tests implies a ten-year interval. Using ρ to denote the correlation coefficient, the result $\rho = 0.430$, for example (located in the intersection of row -1 and column US GDP / WR GDP) is the cross-correlation between U.S. GDP growth at time t and world GDP growth at time $t + 1$. That is, in this example, U.S. GDP growth is positively and significantly associated with the first lead (ten years into the future) of world GDP growth. Such an outcome provides support for hypothesis H4.

Focusing on statistically significant cross-correlation coefficients, we start with the correlation between U.S. GDP growth and U.S. leading sector growth. From $\rho = 0.544$, we reject the null hypothesis of no correlation at the 5 percent significance level. Hence, U.S. GDP growth is significantly associated with U.S. leading sector growth, as we anticipated in hypothesis H2. From $\rho = -0.412$ we reject the null of zero correlation at the 10 percent significance level. This result implies a negative association of current U.S. GDP growth and the second lead of U.S. leading sector

TABLE 2.2.   Cross-Correlations from 1870–1990 Sample

Lead/Lag	GU/LU	LU/GW	GU/GW
−3	−0.332	−0.188	−0.170
−2	−0.412*	0.163	0.351
−1	0.361	0.692**	0.430*
0	0.544*	0.139	−0.142
1	0.035	−0.478*	0.125
2	−0.092	−0.114	0.019
3	−0.070	−0.053	−0.292

Note: For "lead/lag," negative (positive) values denote leads (lags). Lead/lag refer to series to the right of the slash in each title. LU denotes U.S. leading sector growth. GU denotes U.S. GDP growth rate. GW denotes world GDP growth rate.

*Significance at the 10% level; **significance at the 5% level.

growth. As each lead and lag in this test represent ten-year intervals, these results imply that current U.S. GDP growth decline is associated with an increase in leading sector activity roughly twenty years or so into the future. This correlation may reflect the emergence of new leading sectors in response to economic decline, in conformance with our long wave–based interpretation.

Moving to the results for U.S. leading sector growth rate and world GDP growth, we observe a robust correlation of 0.692 (significant at the 5 percent level) between the growth rate of U.S. leading sectors and the first lead of the growth rate of world GDP. U.S. leading sector growth does appear to be a driver of the world economy, just as we have predicted in hypothesis H3. From $\rho = -0.478$ we reject the null of zero correlation at the 10 percent significance level. The result implies a significant negative association of current U.S. leading sector growth and the first lag of world economic growth. As before, and still in harmony with a long wave inter-pretation, it seems to capture the initiation of the rise of the next leading sector that follows economic decline. The negative correlation also sup-ports hypothesis H4 on the reciprocally negative effect of world economic growth on the lead economy's leading sector growth.

For the cross-correlation results for U.S. and world GDP growth, we reject the null of no correlation given that $\rho = 0.430$, at a 10 percent significance level. Hence, current U.S. GDP growth is significantly associ-ated with the first lead of world GDP growth. This points to a direct influence of U.S. economic growth on world economic growth (not only through the effect of its leading sector growth), as anticipated in hypothe-sis H3. While not tested explicitly here, this influence could well reflect an increased tendency of the United States to trade with, and invest in, other countries when it grows faster. It is also plausible that as the lead economy becomes more open to trade at periods of higher growth, the increase in world exports to the lead economy stimulates the growth of the world's economy.

Granger Causality Tests

When used with leads and lags, the correlation results supply some limited amount of information on temporal relationships between variables. Corre-lations have their limitations, however, including not telling us enough about the precedence and antecedence of variables. To that effect, Granger causality examinations provide more information than correlations and also provide some clues about which variables cause other variables. These examinations are computed from the raw data. Hence, lags and leads in these tests refer to one-year intervals.

Tables 2.3 to 2.5 present the best significance level from the causality tests, for each sample used. The best causality test (or F-test) outcome is defined as the lowest significance level, among all the lag structures tried for that sample, provided that the error term in the Granger regression is white noise. A significance value lower than 0.1, for example, represents rejecting the null hypothesis of no causality at a 10 percent level. The tables also delineate the direction of causality in each time period.[11]

Table 2.3 investigates the causality between U.S. GDP growth and leading sector growth. For the period 1870 through 1990, GDP growth causes leading sector growth at the level of 5 percent, while leading sector growth causes GDP growth at the 15 percent level. For the period 1870–1945, the causality is reciprocal at the 15 percent level. For the period 1870–1913, GDP growth causes leading sector growth at the level of 5 percent, but leading sector growth does not cause GDP growth. For the period 1946 through 1990, the causality is reciprocal at the 5 percent level.

From these results, the relationship between U.S. GDP growth and leading sector growth is mostly reciprocal. Periods that exhibit large positive (such as in the 1950s) or negative (the 1930s and 1970s) spurts of leading sector growth tend to Granger cause (positive or negative) economic growth, as anticipated by hypothesis H2. In particular, as expected, in the 1946–90 period the Granger impact of U.S. leading sector growth on U.S.

TABLE 2.3. Causality from U.S. GDP Growth and Leading Sector Growth

Period	Significance from F-test		Causality Direction	
	LU → GU	GU → LU	LU → GU	GU → LU
1870–1990	0.125 (1)	0.021 (13)	LU → GU*	GU → LU***
1870–1913	0.182 (10)	0.029 (2)		GU → LU***
1870–1945	0.132 (12)	0.128 (2)	LU → GU*	GU → LU*
1946–90	0.014 (15)	0.009 (14)	LU → GU***	GU → LU***

Note: An arrow (→) denotes the direction of the Granger causality. Empty entries denote no causality. LU denotes U.S. leading sector growth. GU denotes U.S. GDP growth rate.

*Significance at the 15% level; **significance at the 10% level; ***significance at the 5% level. Entries are the best F significance levels from F-tests. Numbers in parentheses denote lag structure for which the best F is obtained.

economic growth is found to be most pronounced.[12] Similarly, the 1870–1913 period is the one period in which the growth of the U.S. leading sector does not significantly Granger cause U.S. economic growth. Yet we also find that U.S. GDP Granger causes leading sector growth.

Table 2.4 investigates the relationship between the growth of U.S. GDP and world GDP. In the period 1870 through 1990, the causality is unidirectional at the 5 percent level, running from U.S. GDP growth to world GDP growth. In the period 1946–90, the causality is reciprocal at the level of 5 percent. In the period 1870–1913, U.S. GDP growth did not cause world GDP growth. In periods including relatively more years in the nineteenth century (1870–1913 and 1870–1945), the world economy's GDP growth was Granger causing U.S. GDP growth at the 15 percent level, yet the effect gets weaker when the sample includes more years in the twentieth century (significance level of 0.119 for 1870–1913 and 0.137 for 1870–1945).

The causality between the growth of U.S. leading sectors and the growth of world GDP is investigated in table 2.5. As in table 2.4, the weakest causal relations are revealed in the 1870 to 1913 period. In this period, U.S. leading sector growth and world economic growth do not cause each other. U.S. leading sector growth Granger caused world growth from the 1870 to 1945 period at a 5 percent level, and world GDP growth caused U.S. leading sector growth at the 15 percent level. The causality turns reciprocal when the periods 1870–1990 and 1946–1990 are used.

Integrating results from tables 2.4 and 2.5, we find that the U.S. economy exerted a strong effect on the world economy in all the time periods tested, except the period 1870–1913. Our results support the claim,

TABLE 2.4.   Causality from U.S. GDP Growth and World GDP Growth

	Significance from F-test		Causality Direction	
Period	GU → GW	GW → GU	GU → GW	GW → GU
1870–1990	0.000 (12)	0.282 (12)	GU → GW***	
1870–1913	0.197 (12)	0.119 (4)		GW → GU*
1870–1945	0.001 (7)	0.137 (11)	GU → GW***	GW → GU*
1946–90	0.023 (11)	0.000 (4)	GU → GW***	GW → GU***

Note: An arrow (→) denotes the direction of the Granger causality. Empty entries denote no causality. GU denotes U.S. GDP growth rate. GW denotes world GDP growth rate.

*Significance at the 15% level; **significance at the 10% level; ***significance at the 5% level. Entries are the best *F* significance levels from *F*-tests. Numbers in parentheses denote lag structure for which the best *F* is obtained.

expressed in hypothesis H3, that the U.S. economy transmits growth to the world economy in two ways. U.S. macroeconomic growth induces world growth. This process presumably works through the conventional conduits of trade and foreign investment. In a second way, the growth of its leading sectors induces world growth, presumably through technological diffusion, knowledge spillover, and imitation. Investigating and ranking the importance of these effects, while interesting, is a matter deferred to future research.

The effect, albeit weak, of the world's economy on the U.S. economy in the 1870–1913 and 1870–1945 periods is explained by noting that in these periods the British economy, while still influential, was in relative decline. Other economies were still relatively small. In addition, the U.S. economy in this period remained relatively closed in terms of trade, and one would expect trade barriers might diminish the effects of other countries on the U.S. economy.[13] The 1946 to 1990 reciprocal causality, with opposite signs depending on the direction (negative from world to U.S. as we observed and as suggested by hypothesis H4) is corroborated by the phenomenal (U.S.-induced) growth of Japan and Germany during the 1950s and 1960s, as well as by the relative decline of the U.S. position in the world economy in the 1970s and 1980s. As the economic position of the United States eroded, and other economies grew, its economy became more sensitive to external economic growth development. The shortness of the 1946–90 period is an analytical handicap, but it is possible that the statistical outcome is "averaging" a strong → U.S. world influence in the early part of the period, followed by a stronger world → U.S. influence in the latter part.

TABLE 2.5. Causality from U.S. Leading Sector Growth and World GDP Growth

Period	Significance from F-test		Causality Direction	
	LU → GW	GW → LU	LU → GW	GW → LU
1870–1990	0.028 (13)	0.055 (15)	LU → GW***	GW → LU**
1870–1913	0.364 (10)	0.232 (2)		
1870–1945	0.014 (14)	0.140 (9)	LU → GW***	GW → LU*
1946–90	0.036 (13)	0.01 (12)	LU → GW***	GW → GU***

Note: An arrow (→) denotes the direction of the Granger causality. Empty entries denote no causality. LU denotes U.S. leading sector growth. GW denotes world GDP growth rate.

*Significance at the 15% level; **significance at the 10% level; ***significance at the 5% level. Entries are the best F significance levels from F-tests. Numbers in parentheses denote lag structure for which the best F is obtained.

Conclusion

We began by questioning two important general assumptions about long-term growth and political economy patterns. In chapter 1, we demonstrated that some analysts proceed with the understanding that leading sector growth in new technologies drives the lead economy's growth. As the argument goes, that same leading sector growth tends to be monopolized initially by the originating lead economy before the new ways of doing things are diffused selectively to the rest of the world. It follows then that the growth of the lead economy, and its leading sectors, are significant drivers of the growth of the world economy.

These are hardly weak assumptions. Nor are they trivial. It is also difficult to view the processes involved as strictly "economic." They represent fundamental politicoeconomic processes because the interaction between the economic foundations for leadership and the exercise of politicomilitary leadership are highly interdependent. If leading sectors propel economic growth, they do so within an interrelated political order. That same political order is underwritten by leading sector growth—or so the arguments go. Yet critical aspects of these arguments have gone untested, and not without reason. Most of the generalizations are not particularly easy to test. Nonstandard data have to be assembled to create leading sector and world growth series to encompass respectable lengths of history. Even then, the extent to which the indicators are capable of capturing the desired phenomena well remains highly imperfect. Even more unsettling, we are trying to isolate discontinuous growth impulses within a complex field of continuous economic activities without, at the same time, being able to control for all possible influences on economic growth.

Despite these hurdles, supportive empirical evidence for the leading sectors/lead economy assumptions emerged in the 1870–1990 data that we have inspected. The first generalization—that leading sector growth drives the aggregate economic growth of the lead economy (hypothesis H2) and the world economy (hypothesis H3)—was corroborated by the data, but not without qualification. The strongest impact occurred, as anticipated, in the post–World War II era. Still, the evidence also points to a reciprocal relationship that was anticipated. Leading sectors and the U.S. national economy have mutually stimulated each other, with the leading sector impact fluctuating in terms of its strength. We also find a reciprocal relationship between U.S. leading sector growth and world economic growth. Leading sector growth positively stimulates world economic growth, while continuing world economic growth comes at the expense of continued leading sector growth, as anticipated by hypothesis H4. These results lend some credence to a more global view of long waves, operating in what amounts to a world politicoeconomic system, with initially positive effects and, later, negative feedback loops.

The second major generalization—that the overall economic growth of the lead economy is a driver of world economic growth (hypothesis H3)— was also corroborated by the data. Over the whole 1870–1990 period, the causality between lead economy growth and world economy growth is uni-directional, flowing from the lead economy to the world. It may be that other parts of the world economy are, or have been, important drivers of the world economy as well. We have not tested these other possibilities mostly because we are unaware of compelling arguments to do so. The major exception to this statement would be the influence of British economic growth as the nineteenth century's lead economy. But to do more with the nineteenth century we would need a different economic growth database. We would rather defer that challenge to a separate analytical effort.

It may seem unremarkable to find that U.S. economic growth has been an important stimulant of world growth. We are unaware of contrary posi-tions—that is, that U.S. economic growth has not been an important stim-ulant of world economic growth. However, whether the United States has or has not stimulated world economic growth is not really our question. Rather, the more general argument is that there has been at any point in time (within the last millennium) a lead economy (for which the United States is but the most recent example) that generates and monopolizes major innovations. With the passage of time, these innovations diffuse on a selective basis to more receptive parts of the world. These are more con-troversial ideas than the more descriptive question of whether U.S. eco-nomic growth is or has been critical for the rest of the world's growth in the twentieth century (and perhaps beyond). They are also closely related to the question of just how much emphasis should be given to the role of concentrated political-economic-military power in our explanations of world politics and world economics.

What we have attempted to do in this chapter is interpret in what way U.S. economic growth has been critical over the past century or so. It is not simply because the U.S. economy grew large and rich that its impact has been so great. The question is more focused on why the U.S. economy grew large and rich and how these developments are then transmitted to the world. Other analysts have demonstrated that major economic innovations

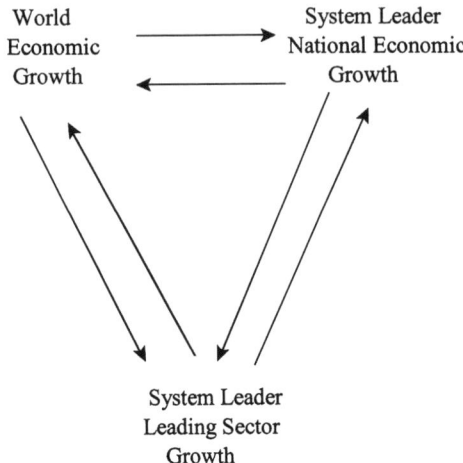

Fig. 2.4. System leader and world economic growth

cluster temporally and spatially. We empirically link U.S. technological innovation not only to U.S. aggregate growth but also to the growth of the rest of the world as part of a systematic process of long-term growth that is depicted in figure 2.4. Therefore, some of the more important elements of long-term economic growth, we argue, are innovations, lead economies, and technological diffusion.

Yet it needs to be repeated that lead economies and leading sectors are not strictly speaking economic processes. These concepts cannot be separated easily from coevolving processes that pertain to the concentration of political influence and military capabilities for global reach. Technological innovation leads to economic, political, and military primacy. Two corollary processes associated with this politicoeconomic complex of central processes are linkages to the national economic growth of the lead economy and, moreover, to the aggregate growth of the world economy.

Approaches that include these processes as an integral part have not been part of the international political economy mainstream. Our evidence suggests that these assumptions deserve more attention by all analyses of economic growth and political economy. Economic growth, it would appear, is not a process that can be modeled exclusively on a national basis. Nor can it be divorced easily from the historical context of successive technological regimes. For that matter, economic growth is not an exclusively economic process. It is contingent on the emergence and eventual erosion of politicoeconomic structures of concentrated innovation, wealth, and power, that are in turn partially contingent on bouts of intensive conflict. Yet growth is hardly determined by these patterns of concentration and conflict. Nor are the patterns of concentration (in the form of the lead economy and system leader's economic growth) immune to exogenous influences from the rest of the world. We have only begun to tap into the interdependencies between leadership and followership in the world's political economy.[14]

We turn next to the interdependencies of innovation, wealth, power, and conflict as they are manifested within the political economy of the system leader. Economic growth is usually analyzed in isolation from the structure and flux of world politics. Fortunately, the converse is less true. In chapter 3 we present an initial, and potentially expandable, four-variable model (leading sector innovation, leading sector concentration, naval capability concentration, and military preparation for warfare) with a vector autoregression analysis of U.S. data for the 1801–1992 period that demonstrates a substantial degree of interrelationship consonant with our approach. The two leading sector variables Granger cause the two military-political variables (naval capability concentration and military preparation for warfare). Eight of nine other anticipated relationships linking specific variables in our theory also obtain, as are two unanticipated relationships linking naval concentration negatively to the leading sector variables.

In particular, the next chapter will show that leading sector growth positively affects leading sector share, the two leading sector variables positively affect naval capability concentration, leading sector share positively affects war preparations, and war preparations positively affect the two leading sector variables and naval capability concentration. In sum, and in marked contrast to arguments to the contrary, a very tight, coevolutionary pattern is found to characterize the economic growth-systemic leadership-military mobilization experience of the United States, thereby underlining the constraints of structural change. Everything is not related to everything else. But a clear causal nexus of interrelationships emerges to specify how the systemic leadership platform coheres.

3. Economic Innovation, Systemic Leadership, and Military Preparations for War

If the system leader's leading sector growth is linked to its own national economic growth and to world economic growth (as shown in the previous chapter), what other linkages are plausible? While a host of possible connections come readily to mind, the most salient linkages should be ones that work toward fleshing out the foundation for systemic leadership. Leading sector growth is an important part of this foundation, but it does not constitute the whole foundation. Rasler and Thompson (1994) have argued that two other components in the foundation are leading sector share concentration and global reach capability concentration. *Leading share concentration* refers to the relative proportion of a leading sector that is produced or controlled by the system leader, whereas *global reach capability concentration* refers to the relative proportion of naval coercion controlled by the system leader for the purposes of protecting its homeland and foreign market access. In this chapter, we reexamine the linkages among leading sector growth, leading sector share concentration, and global reach capability concentration. To this ensemble, we also add a concomitant of the first three variables—the system leader's military mobilization for warfare.

The Systemic Leadership Foundation and Preparation for Conflict

Why and how states engage in interstate conflict is a classically "political" question. One simple answer to this question is that states engage in interstate conflict in order to advance national interests, which may range from the expansion of one's own territorial sovereignty to thwarting the expansion of one's enemies. For instance, in 1812 the United States is said to have fought the British over violations of American rights at sea and perhaps as well over the prospect of acquiring some Canadian territory. In 1846 the Mexican-American War began in order to defend Texas and to fulfill U.S. manifest destiny in reaching the Pacific. In 1898 the war with Spain involved liberating Cuba, reducing European influence in the American Mediterranean, and perhaps, somewhat inadvertently, acquiring a new colony in maritime southeast Asia. Of course, this particular list could be extended to encompass the Germans, the Japanese, the North Koreans, the Chinese, the North Vietnamese, the Iraqis, the Serbs, and the Taliban.

Yet however neutrally one describes these affairs, it is also clear that they are embedded in broad-gauged, politicoeconomic dynamics. Warfare, and preparations for warfare, have had implications for state expansion and economic growth, whatever the intentions of decision makers. It should not seem far-fetched to expect reciprocal impacts—the effects of state expansion and economic growth on warfare and preparations for warfare. In this context, classically political and economic questions are quickly transformed into classical international and domestic political economy questions involving the reciprocal relationships between external conflict and internal economic growth.

Relationships and long-term dynamics there may well be, but should we expect them to be loosely or tightly structured? A loosely structured set of relationships would suggest variable and weak politicoeconomic interactions over time. War might sometimes impact economic growth and do so positively or negatively. The converse could hold as well. A tightly structured set of relationships would suggest less variance and stronger linkages. Warfare and economic growth would be systematically and reciprocally interdependent processes.

But why should it matter if the relationships are loose or tight? One obvious answer is that we seek to understand how these processes work. Whether the relationships are strong or weak, intermittent or continuous, we want to know how and to what extent economic growth and conflict are linked. Yet wanting to know how variables are interrelated is one thing. Do we *need* to know? If economic growth and international conflict were relatively independent processes, we could continue to explain economic (political) processes, and develop policies for promoting and regulating them, as if international politics (economics) hardly mattered. If, on the other hand, economic growth and international conflict are interdependent, we need to reconsider some of our myths about the respective autonomies of economics and international politics. Along the way, we may also need to reconsider the perceived insularity of domestic processes from the vicissitudes of the outside world.

Moreover, the 1990s has been a decade marked by considerable politicoeconomic and military change. One partial consequence of post–Cold War triumphalism (or merely surviving it) is an enthusiastic embrace of new analytical foci. Rational choice perspectives are clearly in the ascendancy. Regime type is everyone's favorite variable. Seemingly less salient, in contrast to the 1970s and 1980s, is the idea of structural context. Yet whatever latitude one ascribes to the decision maker's degrees of freedom, and however significant regime type proves to be, structural context, we maintain, still matters. In particular, it matters very much to the dynamics of politicoeconomic change and its behavioral implications.

Structural analyses emphasize the role of hegemony or systemic leadership. But it is not enough to demonstrate, as is customary, the presence or absence of hegemony. We need to move beyond this minimal step and attempt to model simultaneously the roots and outcomes of structural change. In this chapter, we address these "tight versus loose" questions of political economic interdependency and structural constraints, roots, and outcomes by focusing on the empirical linkages among innovation in leading economic sectors, systemic economic leadership (shares in leading sectors), global reach capability (in the form of naval forces), and military mobilization encompassing nearly two hundred years of U.S. history. As the leading economic and politicomilitary power of the twentieth century (and perhaps beyond), the U.S. case is hardly a trivial one. Moreover, it is an unusual major power case in the sense that it affords us the opportunity to begin more or less at the beginning, or perhaps a little in advance, of the U.S. ascendancy to politicoeconomic preeminence. At the same time, it is a case characterized by a mythology of exceptional and highly endogenous economic growth due primarily to its natural resource endowment and technological creativity.

For the most part, U.S. warfare has not been close to home or particularly destructive—at least in comparison to the experience of the other major powers. And yet there has also been a pervasive sense that the politicomilitary costs of American preeminence after 1945 have been undermining the economic foundation for that preeminence (see, for instance, Gilpin 1981, 1987, 1996; Kennedy 1987, 1993). Surviving the Cold War and winning the Gulf War handily may have dulled at least temporarily the appeal of "declinist" arguments, but the underlying empirical questions have yet to be fully addressed. For all of these reasons, the U.S. record provides an especially attractive case for study of the relationship between war preparation and economic performance.

Extending earlier arguments and empirical analyses (Rasler and Thompson 1991, 1994), we find predictable and strong interrelationships in the U.S. empirical record that support the notion that economic innovation and preparations for war are closely and systematically intertwined. Economic innovation and economic leadership lead to an expansion of global reach capabilities and military mobilization for warfare, and vice versa. Some support for the notion that military preeminence has economic costs is found, but it is not as strong as is argued by some authors. Before elaborating further on these findings, we need to first describe and discuss the substantive model on which the analyses are predicated, the appropriate data to be examined, and the multivariate vector autoregression (VAR) statistical model that will be used in the empirical examination. After these preliminary tasks are accomplished, we turn to reporting and interpreting our findings.

The Substantive Model

In our perspective, the main contribution to the defining hallmark of systemic leadership is pioneering innovation in leading economic sectors and the development of a lead economy that acts as a principal source of long-term economic growth for the world economy.[1] Economic innovation is linked to economic and naval concentration as two concomitants of pioneering commerce and production. Economic concentration occurs within the leading sectors of the lead economy following radical innovations. The lead economy enjoys at least temporarily an economic monopoly position, due to the great economic importance and spillover effects of the leading sectors. This position eventually gives way to diffusion of knowledge and catch-up by other economies. Nevertheless, the advancement and protection of long-distance commerce and leading-edge production leads to the development of a global reach capability position that is superior to those possessed by the main competitors. In the past, global reach capabilities have been equated with naval capabilities (Modelski and Thompson 1988). Recently, they have begun to encompass aerospace and space capabilities—although still often with a strong naval flavor.

Global politics, from this perspective, is not synonymous with all international politics. Rather, global politics, it is argued, is predominantly about the management of policy problems that stem from participation in the global economy. The global economy, in turn, is viewed as focused on transregional transactions that are linked (depending on the century) to the world economy's most sophisticated commercial and production techniques.

For the past five hundred years, a specific pattern of economic growth and warfare has characterized global system activities. Long-term growth in the global economy is stimulated by intermittent growth spurts led by the lead economy in a twin-peaked fashion (Modelski and Thompson 1996). The first growth spurt gives the pioneer economy an edge but it is also destabilizing for the rest of the system. The first growth spurt thus tends to lead to a period of particularly intensive conflict (global war) among the main challengers for succession to systemic leadership. The old incumbent system leader is in decline. Although the dynamics of coalition building for the succession struggle have been fused with attempts at European hegemony, what tends to happen is that the new leader emerges during the global war as an ally of the old leader and the combination, with the assistance of other powers, defeats the primary challenger and its coalition.

Global warfare thus has a number of effects (Modelski and Thompson 1988). It is a succession struggle that leads to and anoints a new leadership era in the global political economy. The new leader's capability platform for global reach has been enhanced by responding to the emergency nature of the global war crisis (Thompson 1988). The naval capabilities of its main competitors, on the other hand, are likely to have been reduced. Moreover, participation in and winning the global war increase the probability of a second growth spurt that builds on the first growth spurt, before succumbing to the processes of relative decline and setting up the conditions that encourage the macroprocesses of structural change to cycle through another iteration (Modelski and Thompson 1996).

But we argue that it is not just global wars that are of interest even if they have constituted the most intensive warfare in the system. They are not the only wars that influence the politicoeconomic processes of ascent and decline. Our basic assumption is that all U.S. military mobilization has been linked in varying degrees to the ascent (and relative decline) of the U.S. as the global economy's system leader. Hence, if we wish to assess the ultimate relationship between systemic leadership and war, we should not exclude smaller wars or between-war activities. Thus, our approach differentiates between greater and lesser intensities in war preparation, as indicated by resource mobilization and allocation to war and defense-related activities.

Military Preparations for War

Both the great and less intense variations of warfare are very much part of the story of the United States' ascent to, and maintenance of, systemic leadership. In the nineteenth century, the U.S. participated in a segment (1812–15) of the Napoleonic phase of the 1792–1815 global war and then expanded its territorial platform in a war with Mexico (1846–48) and its global reach network in a war with Spain (1898). The American Civil War (1861–65) established the hegemony of New England and Midwestern industry and commerce over the Southern plantation political economy—a prerequisite to the United States' subsequent ascent to leadership in industrial production. World Wars I and II, without doubt, were critical stepping-stones in the rise to preeminence. In the second half of the twentieth century, the Korean, Vietnam, and Gulf Wars were linked closely to leadership maintenance burdens.

With this in mind, we do not focus solely on the most intense manifestations of U.S. warfare (World Wars I and II), nor do we treat all wars as if they were alike in terms of their relationship to the economic innovation and leadership processes we model. Our measurement strategy thus is one of attempting to capture varying degrees of military mobilization partially as a proxy for the intensity of wars of different scale, but also to capture the costs of war preparations between wars.

Our primary interests for the empirical work to be presented later are linked to several specific hypotheses. First, if we are correctly identifying the principal source of systemic change, economic innovation in leading sectors should be positively related to economic concentration in leading sectors (economic leadership) and global reach or naval capability concentration. Second, economic concentration should contribute positively to naval capability concentration, which is developed to protect and extend systemic leadership. Third, the anticipated relationships involving military mobilization, in part, are contingent on the identity and timing of the actors being modeled. For an ascending actor, as the United States is for most of the period to be examined empirically (1801–1992), rising economic innovation and concentration, both the economic and naval varieties, should increase the probability of warfare and preparations for war. Systemic leadership is not acquired passively. Aspiring leaders must fight their way up the hierarchical system, not unlike professional boxers. They must first demonstrate some level of autonomy and security in their home region before they can take strong positions in the global arena. Once in the global arena, they can anticipate intensified rivalries with some of the system's most capable major powers. Eventually, systemic leadership must be gained, at least so far, in global combat (Thompson 1988). Once attained, a position of preeminence must be protected against challengers. There will also be constant demands on the system's strongest actor for intervention in regional and local disputes. Contrarily, we would expect the concentration relationships to be characterized by negative signs for descending system leaders (deconcentration → warfare and preparations for warfare), as in the case of Britain were it to be modeled over the same time period.

The approach outlined here cannot be described as uncontroversial. A number of very different types of authors (Keynes 1919; Trotsky 1923; Angell 1933; Hansen 1964; Organski and Kugler 1980; Olson 1982; Brenner 1985; Goldstein 1988, 1991; Liska 1990; Williams 1993; Williams, McGinnis, and Thomas 1994; Pollins 1996; Pollins and Murrin 1997; Kindleberger 1996, 1999) have argued for much weaker and not necessarily consistent connections between long-term economic and politicomilitary fluctuations. The argument is not that the dynamics of these long-term processes are completely unrelated (although see Schumpeter 1939 and Connybeare 1990) but that there are strong and weak versions of the connections.

Some researchers (for instance, Goldstein 1988, 1991; Pollins 1996) advocate a weak relationship in which changes in the "political" and the "economic" realms proceed at different paces subject to different rhythms and only intermittently overlapping. Goldstein (1991), in particular, argues that economic expansion can encourage intensive warfare by creating surplus resources that are available to be devoted to warfare if decision makers are so inclined. When intensive war breaks out, its impact on prosperity is negative. On the other hand, the impact of economic expansion and warfare on capability distributions is variable. Sometimes the impact is destabilizing, while at other times it is less so. Thus, we have economic expansion facilitating the possibility of warfare, the occurrence of warfare influencing the probability of economic contraction, and economic change and warfare occasionally upsetting the capability distribution status quo.[2]

Other researchers (Boswell and Sweat 1991; Rasler and Thompson 1994; Modelski and Thompson 1996) argue for a stronger relationship in which economic changes drive politicomilitary changes that, in turn, drive further economic changes. The most intensive wars are fought because a new round of economic expansion has destabilized the field of competitors, because there is an opportunity for a new leader to emerge, and because there are competitors prepared to pursue coercive strategies for improving their relative and absolute positions. From this perspective, the outcome of the most intensive warfare increases the probability not of economic contraction but of another long-term growth spurt.

Clearly, there are rather basic disagreements about how these long-term dynamics work. While preliminary empirical evidence tends to support the notion that there are interrelated, politicoeconomic long-term dynamics at play, just how, and how closely, these processes are interrelated remains contested. We admit that the debate may not be on the order of realist versus liberal exchanges, or even the putative significance of relative versus absolute gains, but we do lack consensus on what leads to what. Accordingly, there is considerable room for continued exploration of these questions. Precisely how we propose to explore these questions further is delineated in the next two sections discussing our measurement strategy, research design, and statistical model.

Data and Measurement

Four hypotheses from chapter 1 are explored in this chapter.

H5: Leading sector growth in the lead economy supports the attainment of economic superiority in leading sector production.

H6: Leading sector growth and economic superiority in leading sector production encourage the development of superiority in global reach capabilities.

H7: The development of superiority in global reach capabilities reinforces an ascending system leader's military mobilization for warfare.

H8: Leading sector growth and economic superiority in leading sector production make the system leader's military mobilization for warfare more probable, which, in turn, encourages further leading sector growth and economic superiority.

These hypotheses require us to operationalize four variables: leading sector growth, economic superiority in leading sector production (economic leadership), superiority in global reach capabilities, and military mobilization. Leading sector growth in the lead economy is measured from growth rates of our leading sector index (chap. 2).[3] The superiority or concentration variables are measured as the U.S. share of system aggregates within the context of a group of relevant countries. In terms of the fourth variable, military mobilization, our strategy is to use the ratio of military personnel to total population. For all variables we include the years from 1801 to 1992.

As discussed previously, the basic idea underlying the leading sector concept is that any economy is characterized by varying sectors of activity—some relatively stagnant, others growing incrementally, and a few that not only grow rapidly but also have major implications for accelerating the growth of the macroeconomy. This last type of sector is linked directly to the idea that long-term growth comes in spurts and is carried by specific and radical breakthroughs in commerce and production in certain sectors. The underlying assumption is that new technology comes in clusters in some sectors, diffuses throughout the pioneering economy, and then diffuses to receptive areas in the rest of the world. The U.S. leading sector data used here are similar to those used in chapter 2. In this chapter we also use the data on the shares of leading sectors held by the system leader, the generation of which was described in chapter 2.

Our global reach capabilities measure is based on an index developed by Modelski and Thompson (1988). This index captures world shares of naval weapons systems and frontline battleships. From 1801 through 1945, the average share of naval expenditures and battleships (1800–1860, warships with 60 guns or more; 1861–1909, first-class battleships; 1910–45, Dreadnought-class battleships) is used in order to ameliorate the impact of experimentation in battleship design during the second half of the nineteenth century. From 1946 through 1959 the index is based on the number of heavy aircraft carriers. From 1960 through 1993, the average share of aircraft carriers, nuclear attack submarines, and nuclear ballistic missiles at sea attributes (countermilitary potential and equivalent megatonnage) is used.

The country pool for calculating global reach capabilities varies over the nineteenth and twentieth centuries due to minimal share threshold requirements. The naval data are from Britain and France (1801–1945), Spain (1801–8), the Netherlands (1801–10), Germany (1871–1945), Japan (1875–1945), Russia/the Soviet Union (1801–1992), and the United States (1816–1992). The index values for the United States are zero until 1816 when the United States first satisfied the minimal threshold requirements, as discussed in Modelski and Thompson (1988).

Other researchers have measured warfare preparation by the ratio of military expenditures to gross national product (GNP). The basic premise is that this ratio rises in conjunction with the level of war or war preparation. Yet while a GNP divisor may assist in controlling for the effects of inflation, it may also introduce the effect of business cycles into the analysis. Moreover, it is debatable whether one would want economic information in a warfare preparation indicator, especially in the context of a model in which two of the three other variables are also economic in nature and presumably related to aggregated product.

In this analysis, we use U.S. military personnel as a proportion of total population as a continuous measure of preparations for warfare. The basic rationale behind this measure is that higher levels of mobilization should be associated with higher levels of conflict (which are not readily measurable in the type of model we are using).[4] This series records the mobilization associated with all U.S. wars in the time period of our study: World Wars I and II, the American Civil War, and the relatively high levels of manpower mobilized during the Soviet-American Cold War (and encompassing the Korean and Vietnam Wars), and the smaller War of 1812, the Mexican-American War, and the Spanish-American War. With the exception of the Civil War mobilization, we would argue that the series accurately reflects participation in, and preparation for, interstate warfare. Such an interpretation takes us one step away from the global system leader emphasis with which we began without forcing us to relinquish it altogether. But, at the same time, it also allows us greater latitude in examining the impact of increased military mobilization on U.S. economic innovation and leadership (leading sector growth rates and production shares) and vice versa.

Statistical Model

We wish to investigate the preceding relationships with a statistical model that includes all of our four variables. To that effect, we reevaluate and significantly extend two earlier analyses. Rasler and Thompson (1991, 1994) investigated the Granger causalities between separate pairs of variables (that is, which variable comes first) chosen from the set of leading sector growth rates, economic concentration in leading sectors, naval capabilities concentration, and military expenditures as a proportion of gross national product. The analysis included British (1780–1870) and U.S. (1870–1980) phases of systemic leadership. For the United States, the Granger causalities between economic innovation and leadership and military expenditures were found to be reciprocal. Economic leadership and military expenditures were found to Granger cause naval capability leadership.[5] Other causalities were found to be statistically nonsignificant.

In this chapter, we focus exclusively on the U.S. case. We extend the earlier analysis in three major ways. First and most important, we move beyond the earlier bivariate Granger analysis by developing a multivariate vector autoregression model in which all the included variables are considered endogenous. In general, Granger results need to be viewed as a first step aimed toward specifying a more elaborated, multivariate, empirical model. One of the clear liabilities of the previous findings is their bivariate nature. Indirect relationships cannot be addressed. Furthermore, such results are not well suited to investigate signs of effects in relationships or their strengths. We, however, wish to identify causalities as well as the signs and the strengths of both direct and indirect effects. To that effect we will employ a certain type of multivariate statistical analysis. Second, we introduce a different measure of military mobilization. As we already explained, we believe that the new measure is better at capturing war preparation. Third, the earlier work focused on separate phases of systemic leadership. We seek to expand this analysis to earlier as well as more modern U.S. data, for there is no obvious reason why we cannot employ systemic arguments to examine specific cases—as long as we have arguments that suggest that some cases may be more distinctive than others. We also need to keep in mind that system leaders emerge and decline slowly. If possible, we should strive to capture the full evolution of these processes—as opposed to artificially singling out distinctive segments or phases. To that effect, we expand the time period analyzed to 1801 through 1992.

Our theoretical perspective defines four endogenous variables that interact with each other. Two approaches may be used in such cases, the VAR model and the simultaneous equations model (SEM). When theories contain sufficient information to permit specification with substantial confidence, a SEM would be preferred over a VAR model. In many cases (including our own), however, theories do not specify the information needed to formulate a full SEM. The estimation of SEMs requires imposing identifying restrictions. When theory can not identify restrictions with great certainty, the results from a SEM may be biased. In such cases, a VAR model would be preferred over a SEM model. The two approaches to multivariate modeling of endogenous interactions are not unrelated, however. Several researchers (e.g., Zellner and Palm 1974) have noted that a VAR model may be viewed as an unrestricted reduced form of a SEM in which the independent variables are all lagged endogenous variables.

VAR models are not without critics, however. Some researchers argue that VAR models are basically atheoretic (unrestricted lags of all variables are included). They also point out that the individual coefficients of long distributed lag structures cannot be estimated precisely. Other researchers note the basic sensitivity of VAR results from variance decompositions and impulse responses to the chosen order of the variables in the model (see next section).[6]

In principle, the atheoretical nature of VARs can also be viewed as an asset. VAR models can be useful precisely because they are flexible and do not impose many restrictions on the relationships between variables. But even less than fully specified theories are likely to suggest certain interactions among variables. Such theories may also help in choosing the order of the variables in the model. Limitations not withstanding, the VAR methodology has been used in several studies in political science.[7] In particular, Goldstein (1991), Williams (1993), and Williams, McGinnis, and Thomas (1994) used VAR models to investigate the relationships between war and economic variables for the world system. While our substantive questions overlap with these studies, we employ different variables from the ones they used.

Our VAR model includes four variables: the U.S. leading sector growth rates (L), the U.S. share of leading sector production or economic concentration (S), the U.S. share of global reach or naval capabilities (G), and the U.S. record of military mobilization or war preparations (W). Each variable in the model is regressed on a constant term, its own lags, and the lags of the other variables in the system.

Leading sector growth rates equation:

$$L_t = L_0 + \sum_{i=1}^{N} \alpha_l L_{t-i} + \sum_{i=1}^{N} \alpha_s S_{t-i} + \sum_{i=1}^{N} \alpha_g G_{t-i} + \sum_{i=1}^{N} \alpha_w W_{t-i} + \varepsilon_t \qquad (3)$$

Leading sector share equation:

$$S_t = S_0 + \sum_{i=1}^{N} \beta_l L_{t-i} + \sum_{i=1}^{N} \beta_s S_{t-i} + \sum_{i=1}^{N} \beta_g G_{t-i} + \sum_{i=1}^{N} \beta_w W_{t-i} + v_t \qquad (4)$$

Global reach equation:

$$G_t = G_0 + \sum_{i=1}^{N} \gamma_l L_{t-i} + \sum_{i=1}^{N} \gamma_s S_{t-i} + \sum_{i=1}^{L_T} \gamma_g G_{t-i} + \sum_{i=1}^{N} \gamma_w W_{t-i} + u_t \qquad (5)$$

Military mobilization equation:

$$W_t = W_0 + \sum_{i=1}^{N} \delta_l L_{t-i} + \sum_{i=1}^{N} \delta_s S_{t-i} + \sum_{i=1}^{N} \delta_g G_{t-i} + \sum_{i=1}^{N} \delta_w W_{t-i} + v_t \qquad (6)$$

In (3) through (6), the subscripts t and i denote time, the subscript 0 denotes a constant term, N denotes the number of lags, α, β, γ, and δ denote coefficients to be estimated, and ε_t, v_t, u_t, and v_t are the error terms, or innovations, assumed to be white noise. This model is a typical VAR: the same lag length is used for all variables, the same variables appear in each equation, constant terms are used in all equations, and the model does not include a time trend term, contemporary independent variables, and error correction terms.

Empirical Analysis

Our empirical analysis includes seven steps. Technical details are provided in appendix B. A 10 percent significance level is used throughout the analysis. In the first step, we test if our variables are stationary. Based on the results from these tests, we conclude that our four series are stationary. Hence, we decided to use the series in their original form.[8]

In the second step, we choose the lag length for the VAR. This is done from the method suggested by Sims (1980) and recommended in Doan (1992). If the lag length is not appropriate, it will most likely be reflected by serial correlation in the error term. To that effect we estimate the VAR from that lag length and inspect the error terms of all equations for the presence of serial correlation. Based on these tests, we decided to use six lags in the analyses that follow.

In the third step, the VAR is estimated from linear least squares for the whole time period. We use the whole time period for several reasons. First, in our perspective, the basic politicoeconomic forces that drive structural change did not change much in our time period. Second, as in many studies, we wish to measure the average behavior of the model over time, and not to best fit the model in separate periods. Third, as we show, our F-test results are significant. Since our error terms do not contain serial correlation, the F-test results mean that our model captures the systematic behavior of our variables. This supports our view on the nature of the forces that drive our system. Fourth, assume for a moment that the model's coefficients changed at some point in time. Since we estimate the model from the whole time period, this would only make it harder for us to find statistically significant coefficients. Finally, from a philosophical point of view, finding the best fit of the model for each period precludes using the model for prediction since one can never be sure that a structural change will not occur in the near future. However, we believe the past has some ability to predict the future. This, of course, is the basic rationale for studying the past in all social science econometric exercises.

In the fourth step, statistical tests on the joint significance of the lag coefficients (Granger causalities) are conducted from F-tests for each equation. The results in table 3.1 show that the lags of all variables, with two exceptions, are all jointly statistically significant. Hence, the Granger causalities conveyed in this analysis are strongly reciprocal. This generalization supports the use of a multivariate model and is fundamentally different from the bivariate analysis of Rasler and Thompson (1991, 1994). The majority of the causalities reported here are reciprocal, a result also not obtained by Rasler and Thompson. The exceptions to the generalization on the reciprocal relationships are the two nonsignificant effects of leading sector share and global reach capabilities on the leading sector growth rates. These outcomes, however, are not inexplicable. A high leading sector growth rate is expected to affect leading sector share (and wealth) and therefore the nation's ability to acquire global reach capabilities. We have no reason to assume a reverse causality—namely, that wealth and naval power will lead to innovation. As anticipated, the causal effects of leading sector growth rates on global reach capabilities and leading sector share are strongly significant in table 3.1.

Results from F-tests are reported by many VAR modelers. While important, they may tell a partial story since they are computed separately from each equation. This could be a limitation since in a VAR the lags of one variable may affect a dependent variable through their effect on the lags of another variable. We therefore augment the F-test analysis with investigations involving more equations.

In the fifth step, we perform block exogeneity tests. The test consists of comparing two VARs, a restricted model and a nonrestricted model, by partitioning or dividing the variables into two blocks and testing if one block of variables affects (as a group) the other block of variables. These results, however, need to be interpreted with caution. We will therefore check their consistency with our F-tests and cross-check them in light of our substantive argument. Limitations notwithstanding, similar to the Granger causality test, the test can assist in choosing the order of the variables in the full VAR model.

Although many partitions of variables into blocks are conceivable, the one to be investigated here is related to our substantive argument. By dividing the variables into a political block (global reach capabilities and military mobilization) and economic block (leading sector growth rates and share) we first test whether the economic block of variables enters the equations of the political variables.[9] The test is repeated by ascertaining whether the political block of variables enters the equations of the economic variables. The results in table 3.2 suggest that the political block does not affect the economic block, while the economic block does affect the political block. These results are consistent with the F-test results since the lags of global reach capabilities do not exert a significant effect on leading sector growth rates. The results could also be interpreted as supporting the claim that the economic block of variables needs to be written first in the model.

In the sixth step, we conduct variance decompositions from the full VAR model. The order of variables may matter in a VAR variance decomposition and impulse response analysis (conducted in the seventh step).

TABLE 3.1.   Significance Levels from F-Tests in Individual Equations

Dependent Variable	Independent Variable	Significance Level
Leading sector growth rates	Leading sector growth rates	0.005
	Leading sector share	0.545
	Military mobilization	0.036
	Global reach capabilities	0.214
Leading sector share	Leading sector growth rates	0.001
	Leading sector share	0.000
	Military mobilization	0.031
	Global reach capabilities	0.011
Military mobilization	Leading sector growth rates	0.071
	Leading sector share	0.019
	Military mobilization	0.000
	Global reach capabilities	0.001
Global reach capabilities	Leading sector growth rates	0.010
	Leading sector share	0.001
	Military mobilization	0.000
	Global reach capabilities	0.000

Note: Significance levels are from F-tests. Small values indicate that the null hypothesis that a variable's group of lags is jointly not significant can be rejected.

This, however, need not be viewed necessarily as a limitation. We believe that the order of variables is part of a theory, in the same way that the identity of variables is part of a theory. In this spirit, our approach in choosing the order of variables is based on a semistructural interpretation combined with the results from F-tests and block exogeneity tests. If the empirical evidence is consistent with our hypothesized relationship we will interpret it as supporting our chosen order of variables. For this order, the VAR is orthogonalized, and a one-step forecast error variance decomposition is computed for each variable. Variance decompositions are further used to verify the chosen ordering, as suggested by Doan (1992: 8–14).

In the spirit of our previous results, and in line with our theoretical interpretation, we assume that the economic block precedes the political block in the model. Within the economic block, it makes sense to assume that growth (L) should antecede shares (S). Within the political block, it makes sense to assume that military mobilization (W) antecedes global reach capabilities (G), as previous analysis (Thompson, 1988) has demonstrated that naval capabilities tend to peak at the conclusion of the most intensive wars. In sum, we order the variables in the model as L, S, W, G. As discussed in Freeman, Williams, and Lin (1989), this implies that innovations, or shocks, in L will have lagged and immediate effects on all the model's variables, including L. Innovations in S will have lagged effects on all the variables in the model but immediate effects only on itself and the variables that come after it in the ordering (W and G), and so on.

Next, we compute the variance decompositions. Results from decomposing a one-step, twenty-year horizon, forecast variance of each variable into individual contributions are presented in table 3.3. We report results for every fifth year of analysis. As shown, considerable portions of the one-step forecast error variance in leading sector growth rates and shares are

TABLE 3.2. Significance Levels from Block Exogeneity Tests

Variables in the Restricted Model	Variables in the Nonrestricted Model	Significance Level	Decision
Political	Political + Economic	0.057	Reject restricted
Economic	Economic + Political	0.515	Accept restricted

Note: Significance levels are from Sims's (1980) test statistics. A small value indicates that the hypothesis that a block of variables does not enter the equations of another block of variables should be rejected. The political variables include share of global reach capabilities and military mobilization, and the economic variables include share of leading sector and leading sector growth rates. The restricted variable includes a subset of variables as regressors. The nonrestricted model includes all the variables as regressors.

explained by the effect of their own past values. Using peak values, leading sector shares contribute less than 2 percent to the variance in growth rates, while military mobilization and global reach capabilities contribute 8.7 percent and 6.7 percent, respectively. The contribution of leading sector growth rates to leading sector shares is larger than the other way around and peaks at 5 percent. The contribution of military mobilization peaks after eight years at 8 percent, and that of global reach capabilities peaks at 4.7 percent. The contribution of leading sector growth rates to military mobilization is 13.6 percent, that of shares peaks at 11.4 percent, and that of global capabilities peaks around 15.5 percent. The contribution of military mobilization's previous values to military mobilization decreases over

TABLE 3.3.   Variance Decompositions of Forecast Error

Step	Std. Error	L	S	W	G
Leading Sector Growth Rates					
1	0.17	100.0	0.00	0.00	0.00
5	0.19	87.28	1.09	5.90	5.73
10	0.20	83.79	1.38	8.23	6.60
15	0.20	83.06	1.54	8.73	6.68
20	0.20	82.80	1.76	8.76	6.68
Leading Sector Share					
1	0.02	1.41	98.59	0.00	0.00
5	0.05	3.89	91.21	4.09	0.80
10	0.08	3.55	88.60	7.29	0.57
15	0.09	2.66	89.56	5.95	1.83
20	0.10	2.07	88.45	4.70	4.77
Military Mobilization					
1	5.13	13.62	7.09	79.28	0.00
5	10.38	6.20	8.65	69.84	4.24
10	10.51	6.30	9.51	68.72	15.47
15	10.66	6.32	10.69	67.71	15.28
20	10.73	6.28	11.43	67.09	15.20
Global Reach Capabilities					
1	0.04	1.57	3.71	12.15	82.57
5	0.08	6.45	14.05	25.34	54.16
10	0.14	10.32	21.33	27.00	41.35
15	0.17	9.02	26.05	28.33	36.60
20	0.19	8.19	30.23	28.69	32.89

Note: Values are the percentage of one-step forecast error variance due to another variable. Std. Error is the standard error of forecast error, Step is the point in time, *L* is leading sector growth rates, *S* is leading sector shares, *G* is global reach capabilities, and *W* is military mobilization.

time to 67 percent. More than 30 percent of the variance of global reach capabilities is explained by leading sector shares, while the contribution of growth rates peaks around 10.3 percent. The contribution of military mobilization to this variance peaks around 28 percent, while the contribution of the lags of global reach capabilities to global reach capabilities' forecast variance declines rapidly to 32 percent.

The forecast error variance decomposition results suggest that the effect of growth rates on shares is stronger than the effect of shares on growth rates.[10] The political variables are affected by the economic variables more than the other way around, which seems to agree with our basic argument. In particular, global reach capabilities are strongly affected by leading sector shares. Overall, the results support a variable ordering in which the economic variables come before the political variables in the model.

The forecast error variance decomposition analysis, however, does not indicate the signs of the effects of variables in the model, and its interpretation is to some extent subjective as the literature does not provide a significance test for variance decompositions. Further, in this exercise we are not explaining the data but rather work in a point forecast mode of analysis. That is, the estimated coefficients are treated as deterministic while in effect they are random numbers.

The results, so far, support our hypotheses in the sense that we have shown that our variables are significantly interrelated. But the statistical outcomes do not indicate the signs of the effects, which are specified in our hypotheses. In the seventh and last step, we perform impulse response simulations to inform the signs of the variables' effects. These simulations compute the reaction of the system's variables to a positive impulse (shock) in each variable, applied one at a time. Reacting to the shock, each variable will follow a certain dynamic path to be presented graphically, where the signs of those reactions may change over time. Impulse responses depend, however, on the model's estimated coefficients. As these coefficients are random numbers, the impulse responses might have changed had we done the analysis from repeated samples. Yet, as in all such exercises in the social sciences, we only have one realization of our variables with which to work. Alternatively, a 10 percent confidence interval is chosen to investigate the sensitivity of responses in repeated runs, so-called Monte Carlo simulations.

Many VAR software packages have a built-in Monte Carlo simulation feature. We have used this feature from version 4.2 of the RATS package.[11] Figure 3.1 presents impulse responses and their confidence intervals over a

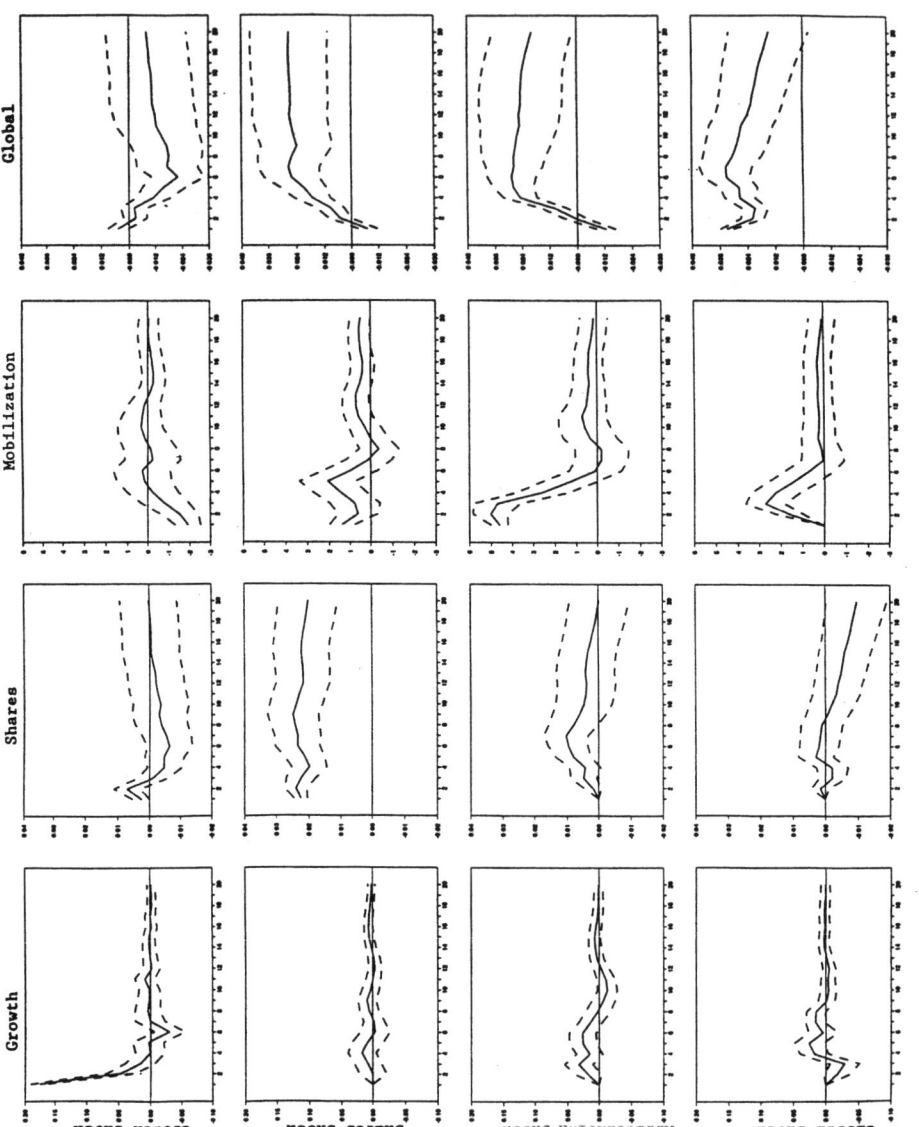

Fig. 3.1.   U.S. impulse responses

twenty-year interval. A column corresponds to *the response of a variable,* and a row corresponds to *the shock in a variable.* For instance, the leftmost plot in the first row is the response of leading sector growth rates to a shock in leading sector growth rates. Similarly, the second picture from the left in row three is the response of leading sector shares to a shock in global reach capabilities. Confidence intervals are computed and plotted using dashed lines around each response. If a portion of confidence interval includes the zero line, the particular portion of this response is not statistically significantly different from zero. The size of all shocks is one standard deviation, and they are all positive. Only statistically significant impulse responses are discussed later.[12]

The effects of shocks in a variable on the same variable, presented along the diagonal, are all significant and positive. The statistically significant cross-effects of variables are investigated next. A shock in leading sector growth rates raises leading sector shares (or economic superiority as anticipated in hypothesis H5), reduces military mobilization at first but increases military mobilization in the longer run (as expected in hypothesis H8, military mobilization becomes less negative), increases global reach capabilities in the short run (in conformance with hypothesis H6), but reduces global reach capabilities in the long run. A shock in shares slightly raises growth in the long run (hypothesis H8), considerably raises global reach capabilities (hypothesis H6), raises military mobilization in the short run (hypothesis H8), but reduces it in the longer run (military mobilization becomes less positive). The second half of hypothesis H8 is supported by the shock in military mobilization increasing growth, economic shares, and global reach capabilities. A shock in global reach capabilities reduces growth in the short run—but the effect is marginal, increases growth in the longer run (hypothesis H7), raises military mobilization in the short run but reduces it in the medium run, and reduces leading sector shares marginally.

The results establish that the United States has exhibited positive economic and political inertia as historical values exert significant effects on their own contemporary values. Domestic economic innovation in leading sectors is a prerequisite to attaining world economic and political leadership. Importantly, military mobilization increases leading sector growth rates and shares (hypothesis H8)—a finding that supports the Modelski and Thompson (1996) twin-peak idea and one that speaks against the generic war → postwar economic contraction assertion that some analysts have posited over the years (Hansen 1932; Davis 1941; Bernstein 1941; Dickenson 1941; Rose 1941; Imbert 1959; Mensch 1979). World economic leadership is a prerequisite to attaining political leadership in the form of global reach capabilities (hypothesis H6). Building global reach capabilities constrains economic innovation in the short run but only marginally.

Table 3.4 clarifies the extent to which we found corroboration for our anticipated relationships. Of the twelve possible directional relationships (not including the effects of lagged variables on their own contemporaneous value), we expected positive relationships in nine. Eight of these expectations were borne out empirically. The one exception is the innovation → military mobilization relationship. Since economic innovation is destabilizing, we had thought that the relationship would be a positive one. Instead, it is found to be negative yet with tendencies to diminish over time (an effect that supports our initial assertion). In addition, since the positive innovation → economic concentration and economic concentration → military mobilization relationships are supported, we conclude that while economic innovation has some inhibitory effect on military mobilization, it also indirectly leads to more military mobilization.

Other qualifications of the anticipated relationships were also detected. The positive relationship between innovation and naval concentration is evident in the short term. The relationship between innovation and naval concentration changes signs (from positive to negative) over the longer term. Why the shift in signs takes place is not obvious and may be due to factors that are idiosyncratic to the U.S. experience. For instance, the United States experienced major bursts of economic innovation immedi-

TABLE 3.4. Anticipated and Obtained Relationships in Impulse Responses

Relationship	Expected	Obtained
Innovation → economic concentration	+	+
Innovation → naval concentration	+	+ short term / –long term
Innovation → military mobilization	+	– and diminishing
Economic concentration → innovation	N/A	not significant
Economic concentration → naval concentration	+	+
Economic concentration → military mobilization	+	+
Naval concentration → innovation	N/A	– and marginal
Naval concentration → economic concentration	N/A	– and marginal
Naval concentration → military mobilization	+	+
Military mobilization → innovation	+	+
Military mobilization → naval concentration	+	+
Military mobilization → economic concentration	+	+

Note: N/A denotes 'not anticipated' by the model.

78

ately prior to World War I and shortly after World War II. Naval concentration would have been increasing or extremely high in these instances, followed by declines in naval concentration (after World War I and the 1960s).

The model has no specific predictions for three of the twelve relationships: economic concentration → innovation, naval concentration → economic concentration, and naval concentration → innovation. We found no significant relationship between economic concentration/leadership and innovation. We did find, however, some negative impacts of naval concentration on innovation and economic concentration that offer marginal support for naval concentration—a proxy for politicomilitary leadership—suppressing economic growth. Another advantage, then, of a comprehensive VAR modeling is the discovery of empirical evidence that had hitherto been overlooked.

Conclusions

In the prominent case of the United States, we have found strong evidence for systematic and reciprocal relationships between economic innovation/leadership and military mobilization for war. Economic and military concentrations of power are intimately related to the economic growth-conflict linkage as well. Therefore, the coevolution among long-term economic and politicomilitary processes is fairly tight in at least this important national case. Moreover, U.S. economic growth, military mobilization, and systemic leadership are intricately intertwined. It probably makes little sense to examine U.S. economic performance in isolation from world politics. The converse would appear to hold as well.

Recapping our results, eight of the nine anticipated relationships among economic innovation, economic concentration, naval concentration, and military mobilization were substantiated by our empirical results. Figure 3.2 attempts to quickly outline these relationships. Leading sector growth positively affects leading sector share, the two leading sector variables positively affect naval capability concentration, leading sector share positively affects war preparations, and war preparations positively affect the two leading sector variables and naval capability concentration. The one relationship from innovation to military mobilization that was not fully supported by the results, and the two marginally negative impacts of naval concentration on innovation and economic concentration, do not threaten the fundamental utility or integrity of our four-variable VAR

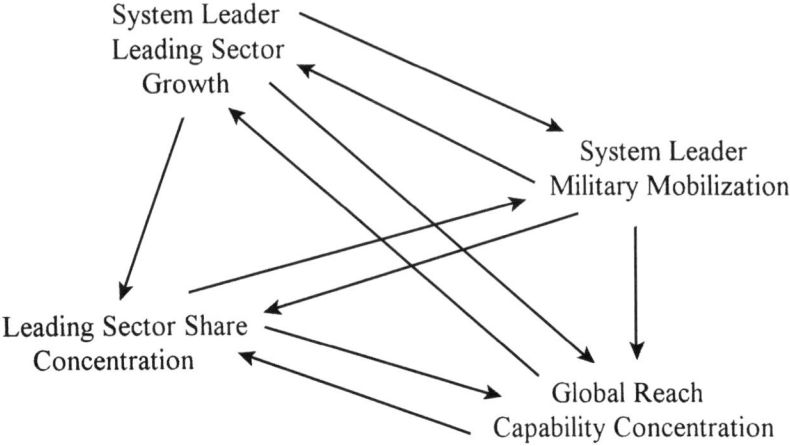

**Fig. 3.2. The foundation for systemic leadership
and military mobilization**

model. For the United States, economic innovation, economic concentration, naval concentration, and military mobilization are found to be related significantly and systematically.

Of course, we have only investigated one case. Whether these same relationships identified here for the United States characterize other cases as well remains to be seen. It could also be profitable to examine less prominent cases, along the lines of Choucri with North (1972), in order to assess the full scope and applicability of this simple four-variable model.

Our results point out that future models of long-term American economic growth need to consider including the variables we have used. The confirmation for the relationships between leading sector growth rates, leading sector shares, global reach capabilities, and military mobilization also encourages us to explore the possibilities of expanding the empirical connections between and among economic growth, concentrations of power, and conflict preparations to other long-term domestic growth processes such as demographic growth, price fluctuations, investment, and the development of infrastructure. There are also other long-term politicoeconomic behaviors to examine besides interstate conflict. Protectionist tendencies and economic growth in the form of trade volumes and leading sectors dynamics, for example, apparently are linked, as we will demonstrate in subsequent chapters. There is also the long-term relationship

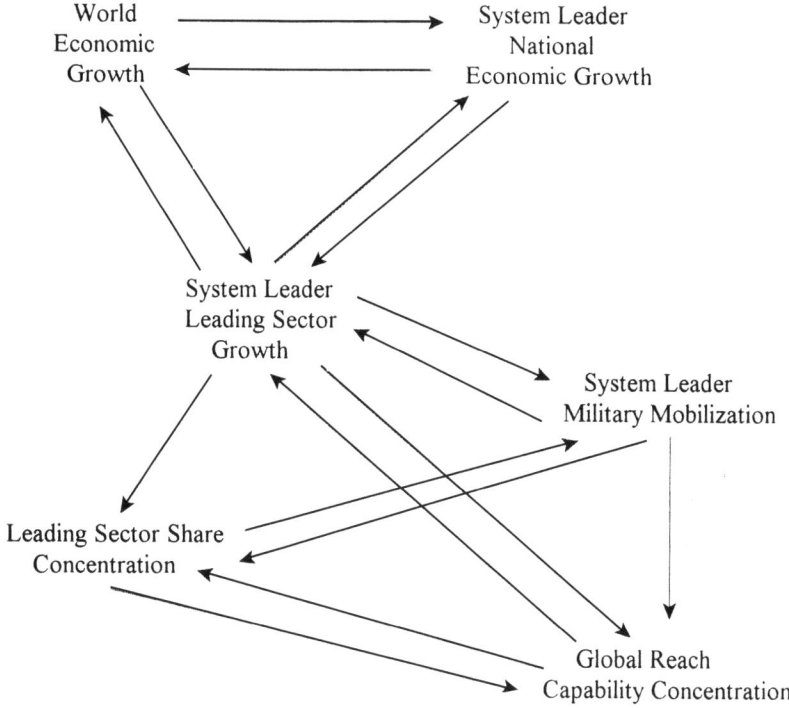

Fig. 3.3. Economic growth and the systemic leadership foundation

between discontinuous leading sector growth and relatively continuous, aggregate, economic growth at both the U.S. and world levels that was demonstrated in chapter 2. In this instance, if we combine figures 2.4 and 3.2, as is done in figure 3.3, we have already assembled a respectable proportion of the model first outlined in figure 1.1.

While there are a number of relationships yet to be worked out in modeling the political economy of structural change for the United States and other pertinent cases, we can at least be confident that the U.S. case, so often advanced as exceptional in one respect or another, does not appear to be exceptional in this regard. In stark contrast to classical realist assumptions about the separability of economic growth and interstate conflict processes, liberal assumptions about the inhibitory effects of economic growth on conflict propensities, and the orthodox economists tendency to compartmentalize economic growth processes away from international conflict processes, there are close links between economic growth and external conflict. This context of structural change may not determine exactly how decision makers make choices, but it may very well circumscribe the range of choices that are perceived to be available. Finally, one of the most successful and long-standing cases of liberal democracy achieved its systemic preeminence by concentrating economic and military power in the world system. There is an interesting irony here linking domestic political deconcentration to systemic politicoeconomic and military concentration. The irony deserves further exploration, especially inasmuch as it is quite likely that some portion of the democratic peace is traceable to the successive preeminence of the last two system leaders. At the very least, the impact of World Wars I and II on democratization would have been very different if the challengers had won. Our models of these various processes need to reflect better these long-term facts.

Having established the nature of the systemic leadership platform in chapters 2 and 3, the next part of this book turns its attention to protectionism and trading openness in our search for the effects of systemic leadership. Protectionism and new attempts at explaining that phenomenon are politicoeconomic topics that never quite seem to go away. In chapter 4, we examine seventeen perspectives on why protectionism occurs and demonstrate how they can be integrated with the help of a common denominator rubric combining long waves of economic growth and systemic leadership. We contend that most, if not all, of the seventeen explanations of protectionism are complementary. Equally strongly, we suspect that long waves in economic growth and systemic leadership are capable of tying these explanations together.

Part II. Protectionism

4. Explaining Protectionism: Seventeen Perspectives and One Long-Term Common Denominator

Protectionism is one of those politicoeconomic phenomena that never quite seem to go away. Nor do new attempts at explaining it. The centrality and salience of the topic seemingly help to account for its analytical popularity. Less obvious is why we continue to spin out new stories about why it occurs. Many of the stories are quite plausible, have ample face validity, and are frequently supported by some type of empirical evidence. Yet one would think if a score or more of explanations for a single phenomenon existed that they could not all be equally correct. Nonetheless, while we do not claim that all protectionism explanations have equal validity, we suspect that many of them do have some claim to validation. A primary reason for thinking this way is that most extant explanations seem capable of being interconnected and integrated. What we have, we believe, is another variation on the hoary elephant fable in which people poke and probe different parts of the animal and identify the ear, the snout, or the tail, without ever quite capturing the whole creature. Each approach to explaining protectionism tends to focus on some partial dimension of the phenomenon at hand. In the process of doing so, the overall contours of the protectionism elephant remain less than fully detected.

In this chapter, we look at seventeen perspectives on why protectionism occurs and demonstrate how they can be integrated with the help of a common denominator rubric combining long waves of economic growth and systemic leadership. The seventeen perspectives are first organized with the help of a 2 × 2 conceptualization contrasting intermittent versus persistent processes and protectionism supply versus demand. Each of these perspectives is then discussed within the context of the cell to which it is assigned. After establishing, albeit briefly, what these perspectives are about, we suggest how they can be further integrated by examining how they relate to long waves of economic growth and systemic leadership.

Thus, we have our main hypothesis for this chapter.

> H9: Systemic leadership and long waves of economic growth and trade impose fundamental constraints on protectionist behavior.

We do not argue that the interconnections work equally well for all political systems. In fact, they are strongly biased toward nineteenth-century British and twentieth-century American systems. The bias is especially appropriate because these two systems have had more than their fair share of influence on fluctuations in world protectionism. If they are treated as but two of perhaps two hundred existing political systems, all with variable propensities toward protectionism, a good proportion of the explanation for protectionism will have been sacrificed needlessly. On the contrary, these two nonordinary states have been critical in their own eras as leaders in shaping how much protectionism exists. They have not usually been able to coerce the rest of the world into following their example, but they have still had an unusual degree of influence, at least intermittently—and that is very much part of the larger protectionism story.

Categorizing Theories of Protectionism

A large number of factors and processes have been linked to increases and decreases in protectionism. What is needed is some organizing device that permits us to discuss approaches categorically—as opposed to tediously working our way through the many variations. One way might be to differentiate among short- and long-term factors. Another approach involves differentiating by level of analysis. Either or both approaches could be employed but not without problems in distinguishing short versus long or domestic versus international processes. For instance, a firm that is highly vulnerable to competition from foreign producers confronts the perceived need for some insulation in the immediate short run. Yet if there are a large number of vulnerable firms and their vulnerability persists, their demands for protection may become a long-term factor. Similarly, firms that have sought protection in the past, other things being equal, tend to continue seeking protection. What begins as a short-term impulse can become something much more long term in effect. We will return to the notion of short- versus long-term processes at a later point in our analysis but choose not to rely on it as a categorical device.

Level of analysis is another useful conventional device for distinguishing types of factors. Electoral processes and business cycles, for instance, customarily are thought of as national phenomena. A hegemonic concentration of power is thought to be a systemic factor. However, things become less neat when the same business cycles are being experienced throughout the world economy at roughly the same time, as in the case of a world depression. The impact of a hegemonic concentration of power may be felt more or less systemically, but where do we put the strategic logic of hegemonic decision makers if we are talking about the hegemon's protectionist stance? The effect may be systemic, but the logic, or some interpretations of it, may have more to do with the domestic politics of the hegemon than with its foreign policy. Arguments about interdependence encounter similar problems of placement. Firms are said to be more interdependent on an international basis if they operate multinationally and are highly dependent on exports. Greater interdependence is thought to lead to fewer demands for protection. Should we call this a system-level explanation, a firm-level interpretation, or both?

Perhaps the easiest way to skirt these conundrums is to develop an alternative categorization that leads to fewer problems of interpretation. We think a useful alternative can be constructed with a combination of emphases on relatively intermittent and persistent influences and emphases on the demand for, and supply of, protection. "Relatively intermittent" influences fluctuate between present and absent or strong and weak effects. Their influence comes and goes. "Relatively persistent" influences may also come and go, but they do so on a very long time-scale of several generations or more. They may also represent permanent shifts and thus be genuinely persistent influences. Emphases on supply factors relate to the political sources for protection (politicians, domestic and international institutions, hegemons), while emphases on demand factors encompass politicoeconomic developments that make claims for insulation more or less likely. As it happens, it is not uncommon for some analysts to emphasize supply and demand factors simultaneously. In such cases, we choose the emphasis that seems most prominent.

The combination of these two nominal variables, as in figure 4.1, generates four categories (cells in the 2 × 2 figure): intermittent-demand (cell A), persistent-demand (cell B), intermittent-supply (cell C), and persistent-supply (cell D). We do not claim that all categorical ambiguities are eliminated when employing such a scheme. Some intermittent elements can transform themselves into persistent elements, while what seemed to be persistent influences can revert to intermittent influences. We have also already noted the frequent bundling of supply and demand factors. Otherwise, though, the categorical problems appear to be minimized. The question then becomes one of whether the categorizations provide a useful ordering for an array of arguments without unduly distorting their explanatory value.

Figure 4.1 also shows our placement of seventeen explanatory emphases that we find useful in summarizing the rather broad literature on the fluctuation of protectionism levels and policies over time. We do not claim to treat every possible emphasis, but we think we at least touch upon a good proportion of them. Our goal is not to give extensive discussions of any of these topics but to provide just enough information that readers can better evaluate the claims of our own agenda: advancing the argument that many, if not all, of these emphases have value. But we think their value would be enhanced if their interconnections were brought out more strongly as opposed to the tendency for each emphasis to proceed as if it were a separate explanatory island.

Seventeen Perspectives on Protectionism

Intermittent Demand

The most popular image of protectionism is that of a threatened group seeking political insulation from foreign competition that is viewed as unfair or simply too formidable. The adjective that best characterizes the frequency of this sort of behavior is that it is *intermittent,* as opposed to constant. Whether the popular image is accurate or not, periods of greater and lesser protectionism have come in temporal clusters. It is usually assumed that something triggers greater demand for protectionism and that politicians respond to that greater demand. The question then is what triggers greater or lesser demands for protection from trade competition.

External Shocks. The most generic explanatory vehicle for promoting intermittent, increased demand for protectionism is some shock. Various economic shocks, as discussed later, are the most common referents. Fischer (1987) adds wars, or at least nineteenth-century wars, to economic depressions in his protectionist model. Since tariffs were once an important

Explaining Protectionism

	Intermittent	Persistent
Demand	External Shocks Business Cycles Surplus Capacity Leadership-Long Cycle	Structural Shifts Export Orientations Multinational Firm Alliances and Globalization
Supply	Electoral Behavior Endogenous Tariffs Foreign Policy Manipulation Alliances and Polarity Strategic Trade Theory Institutions Hegemonic Stability / Structural Incentives	Ideas / Ideologies Reciprocity Trade Regionalism

Fig. 4.1. Categorizing theories of protectionism

source of governmental revenues, expensive warfare encouraged postwar increases in tariffs.

Business Cycles.   Fluctuations in macroeconomic performance stimulate increased and decreased pressures for protection. Several authors have studied the effect of inflation, unemployment, and economic growth on trade policy.[1] Magee, Brock, and Young (1989) summarize these analyses by positing that inflation and economic growth reduce the demand for protectionism, while unemployment increases the demand for protectionism. The reasoning is economic. Inflation raises the prices of imports, but free trade reduces prices. Protectionism may reduce job losses in protected industries facing foreign competition. Economic growth raises the demand for imports and the supply of exports.[2] Other analysts emphasize economic booms and recessions. The business cycle influences the behavior of voters and interest groups and prompts them to demand free trade in good times or protectionism in bad times.[3]

Surplus Capacity.   As a variation on the business cycle theme, Cowhey and Edward (1983) and Strange (1979, 1985) argue that a persistent national surplus capacity, a situation in which domestic demand is too small relative to supply, may induce pressure for protectionism if it lasts long enough and is experienced by several sectors. Sectors with surplus capacity will press for protection from imports because imports are perceived as intensifying the problem. The more sectors are involved, and the greater is their economic significance, the greater is the probability that they will succeed in convincing politicians of the need for protection.

Leadership-Long Cycle. The leadership-long cycle model mixes elements of supply and demand, a point to which we will return in a later section. As we have noted in earlier chapters, analysts using this model assume that long-term economic growth is discontinuous and dependent on the development of radical innovations that produce new products or technologies with finite life cycles of high efficiency, productivity, and profit margins. The sources of these new products and industries tend to be spatially concentrated, which confers an enormous politicoeconomic advantage on the lead economy as the principal source and, initially, the principal beneficiary of the new technology. Even so, leads tend to be short-lived, thanks to imitation and diffusion. Yet each lead economy reigns predominant in at least two consecutive growth waves. In the first or ascent wave, the gap between pioneer innovators and other economies will be substantial. The gap also tends to be accentuated by bouts of systemic warfare fought in part over the implications of uneven growth. In the second or catch-up wave, some nonpioneering economies narrow the gap between the lead economy and the rest of the system.[4]

The implications for trade policy are several. When the returns from new products and technologies are high, the lead economy will unilaterally reduce trade barriers in order to reduce import costs. Other countries may also reduce their barriers to the new products until they, too, are capable of producing them. As the returns from the new product diminish, multiple producers will become capable of producing more than markets can absorb, and foreign trade will become more threatening. Collective action in pursuit of legislative protection will be more likely to be sought and more likely to be successful. More generally, downswings should be linked with decreases in openness while only every other upswing (catch-up wave) should be associated with increases in trade openness at the systemic level.[5]

Persistent Demand

Various aspects of the politicoeconomic landscape are depicted as either facilitating or discouraging the likelihood that groups will demand more protectionism. Incremental, longitudinal shifts are usually seen as working against the likelihood of protectionism.

Structural Shifts. Economies experience long-term changes in structural orientation that may influence the probability of protectionism. Perhaps one of the more basic shifts has been the movement away from agrarian economies toward more industrialized systems. Bairoch (1993) argues that this was critical in the nineteenth-century British case. Lowered tariffs accompanied the rise of industrial activities and elites and the relative decline of agricultural activities and landowning elites. While some European states followed the British lead for a few decades, the states that were first to revert to protectionism had remained highly agrarian in orientation and were reacting to the influx of less expensive American grain.

Export Orientations. Export-oriented sectors are expected to prefer free trade over protectionism because trade barriers at home increase the probability of trade barriers abroad. As the domestic significance of these firms increases, political elites might be expected to become increasingly sensitive to their preferences. Similarly, export-oriented firms will seek to support and influence politicians who share their internationalist concerns.[6] Milner (1988) takes this argument one step further by arguing that it is the interaction of export dependence and multinational firms that reduces protectionism. It is possible for exporting firms that do not operate multinationally to contemplate changing product lines and markets. It is also possible for some multinational firms to not be particularly dependent on exports. But for firms with both characteristics, the costs of protectionism will outweigh benefits. The argument takes two paths. While the 1920s and 1970s experienced economic vicissitudes, the latter period was markedly less protectionist than the former because more firms in the 1970s were export and multinationally oriented. In this respect, the world economy had become more interdependent. Systemic interdependence, then, works against the abandonment of free trade principles. The same expanding set of export-dependent multinational firms in the United States also provided the critical core domestic support for the open trading regime established by the Pax Americana after World War II.[7]

Multinational Firm Alliances and Globalization. In a vein related to the Milner argument, some authors note that modern production processes are becoming more global and mobile, with firms from different countries entering alliances to enhance their competitiveness. Modern trade includes the transfer of goods as well as technologies and knowledge among alliances and subsidiaries of multinational corporations. Richardson (1995) argues that globalization generates forces that may affect trade policy. For instance, if global alliances prove to be more capable than national firms, intensified international commercial rivalry may be one of the net outcomes. Such rivalries, in turn, may increase domestic pressures to increase trade barriers. But it is also conceivable that the alliance phenomenon could work in the opposite direction. If corporate alliances contribute to integration, freer trade becomes more likely.

Intermittent Supply

Protectionism does not simply appear on the scene. Some agent has to supply it. The question is which agents to choose and how best to capture what drives their behavior. Borrowing from Cervantes, O'Halloran (1994: 11) has suggested that the literature can be divided along a "giants vs. windmills" analogy. For her, the windmill models are predicated on the pressures applied by interest groups to bureaucrats and politicians demanding relief from trade competition. Periods of economic distress are especially important stimuli in provoking or escalating these demands. The giant models are focused on executives that pursue free trade as part of a more general foreign policy program, with some insulation from interest groups. While O'Halloran's perspective is geared exclusively toward domestic politics (and especially American domestic politics), the giant-windmill contrast can be extended to models that are not focused on domestic politics. The true giants of international relations are the hegemonic system leaders who, not coincidentally, are closely tied to protectionism arguments.

Electoral Behavior.   Perhaps surprisingly, this cell is not well stocked with many examples. Analysts, by and large, "assume" voters away from the active formulation of trade policy. An exception is Verdier (1994), who contends that voters have at least an important indirect role.[8] Depending on the degrees of salience and divisiveness that characterize trade issues in electoral politics, elections and voters determine who are the principal agents of trade policy formulation from a pool of three possibilities: pressure groups, parties, or executives. Why trade issues may be salient and divisive is a more open question and can be influenced by both internal and external processes. But once it is clear who the principal agents are, each one is primarily responsive to different sources of policy influence. Pressure groups are driven by the business cycle with the most organized groups making their preferences heard, party positions depend on which party wins the recent election and who the party represents, while executives are influenced primarily by international security considerations.

Endogenous Tariffs.   Endogenous tariff theory is predicated on the well-known Stolper and Samuelson (1941) theorem.[9] Stolper and Samuelson predict that protectionism will benefit the owners of the factor with which a country is poorly endowed. Assuming that the actors who stand to benefit from protectionist policies will be supportive, capital owners will demand protection in a country endowed with labor. Labor will demand protection in a country endowed with capital. Whether trade interests will achieve their goals depends on how much stronger they are and is not predicted by the theorem. The theorem only draws attention to who are the likely gainers and losers (Rogowski 1989).

Endogenous tariff theory postulates that trade barriers reflect the actions of maximizing, self-interested agents. Trade policies are the outcome of a struggle among those who gain from protectionism, those who lose from it, and the politicians who seek the support of these groups.[10] Actors that stand to lose from free trade (e.g., developed countries' labor-intensive industries, declining and rent-seeking industries, labor unions affiliated with such industries, nationalistic groups) demand protection. Actors that stand to gain from free trade (e.g., exporters, firms using imported inputs, consumer groups) demand free trade. Trade policy is supplied by politicians who seek support from voters, but not as individual decision makers. The more numerous, geographically decentralized, and politically powerful these interests are, the greater is the likelihood of their success. Thus, protectionist pressures and, therefore, policies should vary across industries (Krauss and Reich 1992). In general, sunrise, export-oriented industries will support free trade, while sunset industries producing for local markets will demand protection. In developed countries, industries that compete with developing countries are more successful in obtaining protection, and protectionism, once attained, generally exhibits inertia (R. Baldwin 1985; Krueger 1996; Salvatore 1997).

Foreign Policy Manipulation. The idea that trade policy reflects larger foreign policy goals dates back at least to eighteenth-century mercantilism, if not earlier. Modern treatments of this idea include the writings of economists (see, for example, Cooper 1968, 1987) and political scientists (most notably Gilpin 1987). In the literature on international political economy, the foreign policy–related determinants of trade policy are restated and reevaluated in terms of economic interdependence and vulnerability (Keohane and Nye 1977). Asymmetric interdependence (or dependence) implies a situation in which one trade partner needs the benefits of trade more than the other. Since both trade partners gain from trade, both lose when trade is interrupted, but the partner that values gains from trade more is more vulnerable to trade barriers, regardless of its politicoeconomic status (Knorr 1975; Baldwin 1979; Hirschman 1980). Along these lines, Paarlberg (1978) evaluates the use of trade in food and oil to coerce others, and D. Baldwin (1985) notes that trade policy in strategic goods is typically dictated by political goals. But Hufbauer and Schott (1990) and Martin (1992) conclude that trade policy is not an effective foreign policy tool and is therefore used as such only in very specific cases.

Alliances and Polarity. Akin to the foreign policy manipulation theme, Waltz (1979) argues that regional trade blocs and economic integration are more likely between states that are allied militarily. Similarly, Gowa (1994) predicts trade flows based on alliance patterns and several economic variables that appear in the standard trade gravity equation. Beginning with neoclassical trade theory, free trade enables a more efficient allocation of national input production. It follows, therefore, that free trade may enhance the military capabilities of potential rivals. Thus, Gowa argues that states will pay close attention to the division of trade gains among trading partners. Relative gain considerations will then lead to lower trade barriers among military allies and higher barriers with potential and actual enemies, as well as with neutrals. If alliances in a bipolar system are more stable and predictable than alliances in a multipolar world (Li and Thompson 1978; Duncan and Siverson 1982; Snyder 1984), the relative gains calculations associated with trade among allies suggests that trade openness is more likely to evolve in a bipolar world than in a multipolar world (Gowa 1994).[11]

Strategic Trade Theory. Also positioned within the general policy manipulation theme, new or strategic trade theory argues that unilateral competitiveness enhancing trade policies can be beneficial when countries compete in oligopolistic markets (Brander and Spencer 1985; Gilpin 1987; Helpman and Krugman 1989). This argument is in marked contrast to the contention of neoclassical trade theory that free trade is the best policy in terms of maximizing gain. One implication of the newer argument is that states potentially could expand their trade gains and rates of economic growth by initiating strategic trade policies. Authors such as Magaziner and Reich (1982), Tyson (1992), and Prestowitz (1995) combine elements from economic decline theses and new trade theory to argue that governments should promote winning industries and strive to acquire the largest systemic share of their export markets. It is also argued that strategic trade policies are becoming the norm for many industrialized countries (Richardson 1990; Laux 1991; Krugman and Smith 1994; Brander 1995; Salvatore 1997).

Explaining Protectionism

As exemplified by Borrus and Zysman (1992), some analysts link new trade theory to national security. Declining shares of winning sectors have implications for maintaining military superiority. To the extent that free trade is blamed for sectoral declines, an activist trade policy, it is argued, should enable former leaders such as the United States to regain their productive edges in winning sectors. During the Cold War, the United States was prepared to absorb the costs associated with the protectionist policies of allies (Krasner 1976, 1982; Lake 1988). The willingness to overlook such protectionism has eroded with the demise of the Cold War and the rise of economic competitors. The probability of reciprocal protectionist policies to the policies of other states on the part of the United States has thus increased (Mastanduno 1991; Vogel 1992; D. Baldwin 1995; Mastel and Szamosszegi 1997).

Institutions. No doubt some readers would put institutional changes in the persistent-supply cell. Indeed, some aspects of institutional changes may be enduring. However, the impact of the international institutional changes that usually receive the most attention may be less than enduring. That is particularly the case with institutional changes in U.S. trade policy-making. In the discussion of U.S. trade policy, considerable emphasis is placed on the inherent inability of legislators and legislative institutions to resist domestic pressures for protectionism. The central principle going back at least to Schattschneider (1935) is that the losers in an open economy are more motivated to seek relief than the winners because the burden experienced by the losers is more acute than are the benefits realized by the winners. To make it possible for more open policies to come about, the U.S. policy-making system had to be transformed in such a way that Congress had less influence on trade policy. Destler (1986, 1992) stresses that trade barriers became only a minor source of conflict in American domestic politics for a period of time due to several factors. The liberal consensus that the Hawley-Smoot Tariff Act of 1930 had been a mistake and the perceived necessity of rebuilding the economies of Cold War allies by opening U.S. markets, coupled with the good fortune of U.S. economic preponderance (which meant little in the way of genuine competition from abroad), all worked to downplay the salience of U.S. trade policy through roughly the 1960s.[12]

Some observers (e.g., Pastor 1980; R. Baldwin 1985) claim that the U.S. Congress had delegated away its trade policy-making role to the executive branch. If this had been a permanent shift, the institutional change would belong in the persistent category. But it was not permanent. One way to look at the phenomenon is to interpret it as something less than a surrender. O'Halloran (1994) stresses that for a period of time congressional control over trade policy became less direct. Moreover, as long as relations between the legislative and executive branches were not overly conflictual and/or different parties did not control different branches, the congressional role in trade policy could be expected to be relatively constrained. Neither institutional condition prevailed throughout the post–World War II era.

Another way to interpret what happened is that the confluence that worked to reduce the salience of trade policy gave way to a different type of confluence (Destler 1992; R. Baldwin 1995). U.S. economic preponderance and export competitiveness eroded. In the 1970s and 1980s, Congress began responding anew to injured interests. The U.S. economy had become much more internationalized than it had been in the 1950s and 1960s, thereby expanding the pool of potential losers to open trade policies. Finally, even the Cold War faded away. The national security rationalization for looking the other way as allies engaged in protectionist practices became more awkward. The liberal consensus about the value of free trade also suffered from the dramatic successes enjoyed by neomercantilistic policies employed by major economic competitors. In such a context, it was no longer possible to subordinate trade policy to foreign policy considerations as it had been earlier. Verdier (1994) has generalized part of this process by hypothesizing that executives are likely to assume control over trade policy when a country faces an inescapable, militarized external threat. But executive control will only persist as long as the electorate remains persuaded that there is such a threat. The general point remains that institutional interactions can influence the supply of trade policy and that the subordination of one type of institution to another, which may also influence the supply of trade policy, need not be permanent.

While the U.S. example has focused on domestic institutions, much the same can be said about international trade institutions. Ruggie (1982), among others, credits GATT with some contribution to the maintenance of an open trading system.[13] He argues that the economic institutions established after 1945 under American leadership externalized norms associated with "embedded liberalism," which encompasses both the principles of trade promotion and reducing the domestic costs of open competition. Once established, such regimes constrain domestic practices. Yet, the influence of international institutions is no less finite than that of domestic institutions. As Yarbrough and Yarbrough (1992) stress, the historical pattern of prevailing strategies toward trade policy institutionalization has been one of moving from initially unilateral to multilateral and, more recently, bilateral and regional arrangements. As one strategy loses its perceived efficacy, new strategies are sought.[14]

Hegemonic Stability and Structural Incentives. Krasner's (1976) highly influential approach focused on who gains or loses from international economic openness.[15] On the one hand, openness is thought to be beneficial to everyone's aggregate income levels. Yet the greater the exposure to external market fluctuations, the more frequent is the need to make internal adjustments that can threaten domestic stability. Larger and more developed states, because they have less exposure or an easier time making adjustments, are the least likely types of states to be vulnerable to this sort of problem. Small and less developed states are more vulnerable to the threat of trading system closure. This gives large and relatively developed states another edge in dealing with weaker states. But, to some extent, this edge is offset by the threat of technological information diffusing more rapidly in an open system. Large and relatively developed states should therefore lose interest in maintaining an open system once they have lost their competitive edge.

A hegemon, a state that is much larger and more developed than its trading partners, should favor openness as long as it continues to ascend or maintain or improve its lead. Small states have too much to lose from closure to stray from the openness preference camp. The interests of medium-sized states are the most difficult to predict and may ultimately depend on the degree of success achieved by hegemonic persuasion or coercion. The basic prediction that emerges is that the system will become more open as long as the hegemon is ascending and less open as the hegemon declines. But since trade structures do not respond quickly to changes in the distribution of power and consequent revisions in perceptions concerning state interests, major crises (e.g., depressions and world wars) are needed to overcome societal resistance to changes. Rising hegemons thus must overcome entrenched prehegemonic trade preferences before altering their trade policies. In periods of hegemonic decline, free traders retain their domestic clout and continue to press for the old policies that were linked to an ascendant phase. Some correspondence to the distribution of power remains discernible, but the timing of structural change in the trade and power spheres shows some tendency for the trade structure to lag behind changes in the economic power structure.

There are some variations on the basic hegemonic stability model.[16] In what we call the structural incentives model, Lake (1988) focuses on international economic structure in general, as opposed to hegemony per se. Rather than key the model to one large hegemonic actor's share of resources and trade, what matters is a mix of large and medium-sized actors, their respective trade shares and productivity, the dynamics of the system, and the levels of protectionism erected by states less involved in trade. The outcome is movement to and from phases of greater and lesser concentrations of trade control, but freer trade is not restricted to the phases of greater (hegemonic) concentration. Actors in less than hegemonic circumstances may also have incentives to reduce levels of protectionism.

More akin to the hegemonic stability model but proceeding at a different rhythm is Frederick's (1987) four-phased long cycle model. In phase one, which is characterized by a high concentration of resources, a new world power emerges from a period of global warfare, but a variety of factors militate against reductions in protectionism. Freer trade arrives in phase two as a consequence of technological diffusion until economic stagnation encourages protectionism among the non–world powers. The system becomes less liberal in phase three as non–world power protectionism increases. Phase four returns the system to a period of global war, which is hardly conducive to free trade.

Persistent Supply

Various facets of the politicoeconomic landscape are thought to facilitate the supply of protectionism. Persistent-supply facets are characterized by incremental changes that gradually make protectionism less likely. Still, just where one draws the line between intermittent and persistent, unfortunately, is to some extent a subjective enterprise. All three of the topics discussed in this section have intermittent dimensions but, if so, they are usually portrayed as protracted cycles. Ideas come and go, but not very quickly. Reciprocity is both an institutional device and a behavioral propensity that can be used to lower or increase protectionism. Regional bloc formation may be the most intermittent of the three, but the "new" regionalism is thought to work differently than the truly cyclical trading blocs of the past. Moreover, some propensity toward regional trading biases does persist as long as there are reasons for trading in the first place. As a consequence, we place it in the persistent-supply category.

Ideas/Ideologies. The ideational approach maintains that ideas have an independent influence on policy formation. Ideas do not simply cloak or rationalize post hoc underlying material interests. Actors come to accept various tenets or principles as beliefs that consequently constrain or bias their interpretations of reality and their subsequent behavior. In particular, proponents of free trade and numerous generations of economists gained a crucial ideological (and theoretical) foundation with the late-eighteenth-century and early-nineteenth-century writings of Adam Smith and David Ricardo. The largely unilateral movement toward free trade in early-nineteenth-century Britain is often seen, at least in part (Kindleberger 1975), as a result of this emergence of new doctrines about how best to organize trade and the international division of labor, and about the fundamental folly of protectionism.

Goldstein (1986) argues that the lessons of the 1930s Depression led to the acceptance of a set of policy-making rules and norms focused on the benefits of a liberal trade regime in order to avoid a repetition of severe economic downturns. Despite significant and threatening changes in the international structure and increased interest-group lobbying, the cognitive commitment to free trade has slowed a return to a more protectionist stance in the United States. The argument is not that there is a permanent ideological barrier to increased trade barriers, but that in the usual life cycle of the beliefs, once established, they are likely to outlive the extent to which they correspond well with reality. How quickly beliefs can be altered presumably depends to some extent on how abrupt the changes in economic realities are. If the negative shifts in economic position are incremental, so too is the erosion in free trade beliefs.

Reciprocity. The bilateral approach to trade policy was institutionalized by the U.S. trade agreement of 1934 that delegated to the president the authority to grant trade partners any reciprocal tariff reductions negotiated by the United States and other trade partners. Gilligan (1997) contends rather strongly that this delegation of presidential authority to engage in reciprocal arrangements is the principal key to explaining the U.S. movement toward free trade in the twentieth century. The basic thrust of this process was to make the supply of trade policy more autonomous from interest group pressures. Even so, the interpretative question would seem to remain whether it is more important to have an institutional device for negotiating freer trade or the incentives to create and make use of the device. As a behavioral propensity, trade policy reciprocity has received attention in the literature on optimal tariffs and trade wars.[17] It is also advanced as a general tendency: the trade policy of country A toward country B generally depends on the trade policy of B toward A. Several observers have described U.S. trade policy in the 1980s and 1990s as exhibiting definite reciprocal characteristics in the sense that U.S. policies appear to be conditioned on, and/or are a reaction to, the trade policies of others.[18]

Trade Regionalism. Analysts disagree on whether trade blocs imply a rise in protectionism. For example, Gilpin (1987), Bhagwati (1991, 1993), Krugman (1991), and Garten (1992) stress the negative consequences of trade blocs. Oye (1992) and McDonald (1998) argue for positive consequences, while Viner (1950), Lawrence (1996), Grilli (1997), Haggard (1997), and Mansfield and Milner (1999) fall in between the two ends of the continuum.[19] Lawrence (1996), among others, argues that trade blocs reflect the successful lobbying of exporters. Exporters' appreciation for free trade is linked to inexpensive imported inputs, the expanded ability to make resources available for export production, and the possibility for lower trade barriers abroad on the basis of reciprocity. Since these processes are not thought to be widely appreciated by the publics, unilateral trade liberalization is difficult politically. In the late twentieth century, liberalization through multilateral agreements may not be as attractive as trade blocs to exporters who see, via GATT and the WTO, all members automatically receiving the benefits of most favored nation status. Multilateral agreements may also reflect compromises that do not always match the specific needs of a single economy. These objections are less likely to be prominent in trade blocs inasmuch as the benefits are more visible and less diffused (Bhagwati and Krueger 1995).

General Observations

We have reviewed a considerable number of emphases that seek to explain changes in trade protectionism. The different approaches are often couched in more interdependent contexts than our survey might suggest. That is to say, we do not argue that scholars associated with any one perspective are unaware of the other perspectives or that they do not acknowledge the existence of other perspectives. Occasionally, efforts are made to integrate one or more perspectives to others. We are unaware, though, of much in the way of attempts to integrate large numbers of protectionism emphases simultaneously.[20]

Many of the multiple emphases have received some empirical support in the form of either statistical studies or case analyses. In statistical studies, however, the goodness of fit (in the wider sense) is never such that other explanations are completely ruled out. What this observation implies is that trade policy is probably not caused by one force but is rather the consequence of the combined operation of a number of forces operating at several levels of analysis. The observation also implies that a unified theory of protectionism will not be arrived at easily. While parsimony may be a virtue in some areas of research, it may not be of much use in the case of trade policy.

But how can one integrate such seemingly disparate approaches as hegemonic stability and endogenous tariffs? On the face of it, at least, these two examples appear to invoke different sets of influences working at different levels of analysis. One answer is that none of the emphases are necessarily wrong; they may simply be incomplete. What we need are common denominators to tie them together.

In principle, we may be able to cultivate some common denominators by attempting to answer questions that each approach, when taken alone, does not seek to answer. For example, hegemonic stability emphases are based on the on-off presence of a systemic hegemon. But why do systemic hegemons appear and then decline? Another on-off premise reviewed here is focused on surplus capacity and other distressful macroeconomic conditions emphasized by a number of authors. Granted, hard times encourage protectionist pressures, but what are the sources of hard times? Similarly, emphases on free trade ideas and ideologies and the development of pro–freer trade institutions at the domestic and international levels link the advent of ideas and institutions to changes in protectionism policies. But do these ideas and institutions emerge randomly? Or, is it probable that they have something in common with fluctuations in system leaders and hard times?

In the next two sections we suggest one way to integrate the preceding theories in a logically consistent manner. We then evaluate the implications this approach has for future empirical work.

Long Waves and Systemic Leadership as Common Denominators

We contend that underlying much of the analytical variety in the theories of protectionism displayed in figure 4.1 are the long-term common denominators of long waves of economic growth and systemic leadership. No doubt this basic premise will be deemed controversial, at least for some observers, as the existence of long waves of economic growth and systemic leadership is itself an issue that is not accepted in all academic circles. Long waves, however, have received much attention in the international political economy literature. By now, there is considerable empirical evidence in support of long waves, which leads us to conclude that, at least historically, such waves exist. Minimally, all this claim means is that the prospects for economic growth and prosperity have not been constant over time. Periods of strong growth are followed by periods of weak growth, and vice versa. Minimally, claims for systemic leadership reduce to the observation that one state has tended to lead in the intermittent generation of economic growth and prosperity. When willingness and resource opportunities have combined, the lead economy tends to play an especially prominent role in the world's political economy. Hence, we refer to specific eras as a Pax Britannica or a Pax Americana.

In point of fact, these minimal claims are not very controversial. The claims only become more controversial when we assert, more maximally, that it is the lead economy that generates the world economy's waves of growth via temporal clusters of technological innovation. Yet it is interesting to note that some of the claims of long wave politicoeconomists have found their way into the recent, more mainstream, economic growth literature.[21]

Figure 4.2 portrays our conception. We suggest that long waves of economic growth and systemic leadership contribute strongly to the setting of the context in which supply/demand, intermittent/persistent, and international/domestic politicoeconomic processes function. These common denominators do not determine exactly how the factors in the various perspectives operate, but they do exert strong, politicoeconomic, structural influences. Another way of asserting this general set of relationships is to suggest that system leaders and the long growth waves that produce them establish a systemic set of constraints that create the contexts and establish boundaries within which the other perspectives and their chosen emphases operate (hypothesis H9).

H9: Systemic leadership and long waves of economic growth and trade impose fundamental constraints on protectionist behavior.

Our approach assumes an unconventional interpretation of the systemic level of analysis. Most analysts think of the system level as the aggregate of lower levels. We are not denying that systemic properties can be constructed mechanically by the aggregation of variables from lower levels. However, we are asserting that systemic properties, processes, and structure are affecting the variables at the lower levels. Moreover, systemic properties are influenced mightily by specific national agents—namely,

Explaining Protectionism

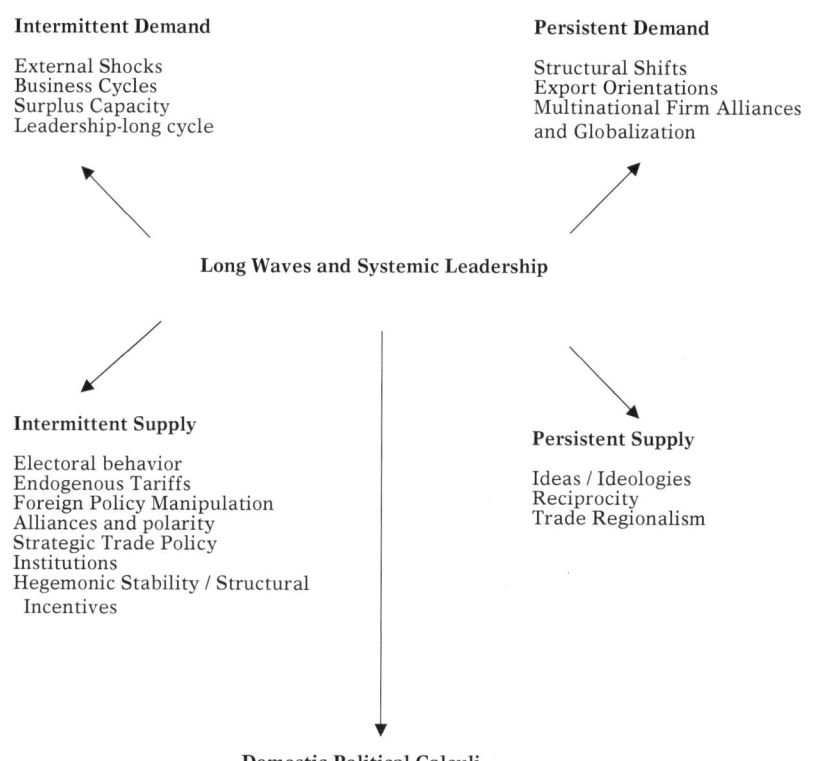

Intermittent Demand

External Shocks
Business Cycles
Surplus Capacity
Leadership-long cycle

Persistent Demand

Structural Shifts
Export Orientations
Multinational Firm Alliances
and Globalization

Long Waves and Systemic Leadership

Intermittent Supply

Electoral behavior
Endogenous Tariffs
Foreign Policy Manipulation
Alliances and polarity
Strategic Trade Policy
Institutions
Hegemonic Stability / Structural
  Incentives

Persistent Supply

Ideas / Ideologies
Reciprocity
Trade Regionalism

Domestic Political Calculi

**Fig. 4.2. Long waves, systemic leadership,
and protectionism processes**

the system leader. In their respective time periods, system leaders are the initial sources and principal beneficiaries of waves of long-term economic growth, predicated on commercial and technological innovation. Their economic edges in the new ways of doing things aggravate international conflict patterns and have led to major and intensive bouts of global combat in which one state has emerged as the victorious coalition leader with a preponderant lead in material and politicomilitary resources.

A system leader's life cycle has a specific trajectory. They rise, they reign (but do not rule), and they decline, roughly in correspondence with the life cycles of the technological paradigms on which their leadership depends. At the same time, there is no reason to assume that system leaders and long waves are immune to reciprocal influences from the subjects they influence.

In this respect, all of the arrows in figure 4.2 might easily be drawn as double-headed. However, since we are less familiar with all of the complexities of potential reciprocal influences than with the ways in which leadership-long wave influences work, it is best to confine ourselves for the present to one-way causal influences. We could also draw more causal arrows between and among the clusters of explanations, but that would only clutter the point we are trying to make in figure 4.2.

In the context of this chapter, our core argument is that long waves and systemic leadership are primary drivers (but certainly not the exclusive drivers) of many of the trade policy processes delineated in figure 4.2. Beginning in the upper left corner with intermittent-demand processes, not all these shocks are long wave driven, but the most serious of these shocks are. Major depressions are brought about by the transition from one economic growth wave to the next. The longer the transition and reconfiguration needed, the more severe and protracted the depression.[22] Global wars, the other type of major shock most frequently mentioned by authors, are brought about in large part by the destabilization introduced by new long waves of economic growth and the consequent struggle for systemic leadership.[23] Recessions are not more long wave driven than are all other conceivable shocks, but the frequency of recessions has been said to increase in the downturn of long economic growth waves.[24] Surplus capacity is a problem that emerges when too many producers create more products than consumers are in a position to buy. One way in which this comes about systematically is after new economic production techniques have been diffused to a number of advanced economies, and producers learn that the world demand for steel, or autos, or computer chips is more finite than was once thought.

Obviously, structural shifts can go on in all sorts of economies, but the major examples are those undergone by the respective system leaders, Britain and the United States, as both moved away from agrarian to industrial systems. One of the consequences was leadership in reducing trade barriers. Similarly, Britain became the "Workshop of the World" in the nineteenth century, and the U.S. overall industrial lead still endures. Being able to produce something the rest of the world cannot yet (or not as inexpensively or with equal quality) is a strong basis for trade and export incentives. That Britain and the United States were, for certain periods of time, the world's leading exporters was neither coincidental nor random. Neither was the tendency for American firms to dominate the spread of multinational corporation (MNCs) in the second half of the twentieth century. These were all outcomes of spearheading new economic innovations and systemic leadership. As more British and American firms became export oriented and multinational in operations, they became less interested in protectionism.

Any government can contemplate manipulating trade policies for foreign policy purposes. The most prominent example is the U.S. Cold War concern that allies be allowed to protect their economies while, at the same time, having access to the U.S. economy—all in the name of national security. In fact, the evidence for allies engaging in freer trade within bipolarized alliances rests almost exclusively on the contrast between international relations before and after World War II and the postwar bipolarization of U.S. and USSR allies.[25] We also do not find it coincidental that strategic trade theory has emerged in a context of Cold War beliefs breaking down and competition renewing among erstwhile allies.

The leading example of a shift of trade policy control from the legislature to the executive branch is again the United States. In this case, the 1930s shift was strongly influenced by the deep Depression (which, in our perspective, was due fundamentally to a long wave transition between technological paradigms) and the need to try something different in responding to a crisis. The U.S. institutional shift was then aided and abetted by the postwar sense of emergency and the security threat posed by the Soviet Union. Once these crises receded, in conjunction with the playing out of the postwar economic growth wave, institutional conflict over trade policy resumed in the U.S. political system.

Internationally, the postwar trade institutions were also a product of U.S. systemic leadership. The international institutions have not disappeared with the subsequent decline of the American role, but their effectiveness has eroded. The links among long waves, systemic leadership, and hegemonic stability are even more obvious. In our view, hegemonic stability is another term for systemic leadership at or near the peak of a long economic growth wave. Instabilities, as in the case of institutional inefficacy, begin to appear after the peak is passed and systemic leadership goes into relative decline.

It is not difficult to fit in free trade ideology, particularly with its strong Anglo-American flavor. As Kindleberger (1975) has observed, free trade is a most convenient belief system for political systems that also happen to be the world's leading producers and exporters. As the preponderant status is lost, the beliefs become more awkward to maintain, but that does not mean that they will not be characterized by substantial inertia. In this context, trade policy reciprocity is simply an institutional device and propensity that facilitates the lowering of protectionist barriers when negotiators on both sides seek such an outcome. How they lower the barriers is not as important as why they choose to do so.

Finally, the current movement toward regional free trade areas (FTAs) appears to be not so much a reversion to the closed regions of the 1930s as they are perceived antidotes to the problems encountered in developing freer trade on a global, multilateral basis. The global, multilateral approach was effective in reducing trade barriers to a point, but it depended on an underlying foundation of long wave economic diffusion, the prospects of catching up with the growth leader, and strong systemic leadership. As we enter a new long wave phase without strong systemic leadership, regional pacts are a product of attempting to cope with a combination of current problems and the uncertainty of the future. Whether regional FTAs advance the cause of freer trade worldwide or encourage the opposite remains to be seen.

Of the preceding seventeen selected topics, we have so far omitted electoral behavior and endogenous tariff arguments. We do not claim that domestic political calculi are always straightforward outcomes predicated on long wave and systemic leadership dynamics. But domestic political calculi are not aloof from these dynamics, nor are they immune to the other processes delineated in figure 4.2. However voters, interest groups, firms, and politicians interact, they do so within the politicoeconomic context established by the multiple processes that have already been discussed. They respond to stimuli such as shocks, business cycle downturns, and security emergencies. Their responses, which may be conditioned by gradual shifts in economic orientation and interdependence, may change protectionism but can also change institutions, ideas, and, in general, strategies for coping with politicoeconomic problems. Agents are influenced by structural change, but they also can bring about structural change.

Of course, it is easy to proclaim that everything is interconnected via a long wave-systemic leadership context that does not determine behavior but does strongly shape it. Do we have any evidence to support such a story? We have demonstrated empirically in chapter 2 that U.S. leadership in technological innovation has systematically contributed to world economic growth. The remainder of this book will provide additional evidence. We will find in chapter 5 that systemic leadership and long waves are respectable predictors of the actual fluctuations in the protectionism of the major economic powers and of the international system of the last two centuries. Moreover, from a causal perspective, it is more fluctuations in trade that drive protectionism in the long run rather than the other way around. This finding (chap. 6) suggests that intermittent economic growth is more responsible for the intermittent attempts at political intervention. We often assume the contrary—that political intervention is primarily responsible for downturns in trade. In addition, we will also demonstrate that, historically, world economic openness has been driven by systemic leadership (chap. 7).

These findings do not fully establish our claims that protectionism is embedded in an economic long wave-systemic leadership context, as noted in hypothesis H9, and that analyses of protectionism might benefit by recognizing this fundamental context for efforts to open and close the world economy. But the findings will go some way toward reinforcing the assertions that have been made.

The Long and the Short of It

Our review of the protectionism literature indicates that there is an ample mixture of supply, demand, and timing elements and levels of analysis. But there are also short- and long-run dimensions to these theories, which may assist us in further integrating the multiple perspectives. First, however, we need to be more exact in defining what we mean by short and long term. A short-term process is not necessarily one that lasts a shorter period of time, but rather a process whose dynamics appear to be relatively faster than a long-term process. By suggesting that the best common denominators are long waves of economic growth and systemic leadership, or the leadership-long cycle approach of this book, we are postulating a certain type of long-term change as the fundamental bed for a variety of other long-term changes, as well as for a variety of short-term changes.

Thus, long-term changes, generally, are slower moving than short-term changes. One metaphor is to view the shorter, faster dynamics riding the backs of longer, slower dynamics. Imagine the world economy as a collection of several hundred vessels (countries) afloat and widely spaced on a vast sea (the international system). If the ships are sufficiently dispersed, they will be subject to different winds, weather, and currents. The ships also come in all sizes and types of propulsion. Some are sail-rigged, others steam-powered, while a few have nuclear reactors. Different principles of command chains exist. Some ships are run very hierarchically; others almost seem to steer themselves. The quality of the officers and crews also varies. Some are experienced sailors, while others are less so.

Continuing the metaphor, periodically the sea generates huge waves that propagate to all parts of the ocean, and the ships must survive as best as they can. Facing these waves, each ship and crew may react somewhat differently, depending on their means of propulsion, location, skills, resources, and good fortune. Some ships sink. Some are badly damaged but survive. A few other ships benefit immensely from the experience, and one in particular, the leading economy, moves to the head of the flotilla. Much of what this particular ship learns is ultimately passed along to some of the other members of the flotilla, and they begin to close the gap between the lead ship and the rest of the vessels.

The real point of the metaphor is that the sea represents a long-term dynamic process that evolves at one pace. At the same time, each of the ships is also confronted with various short-term dynamics of changing weather, crew mutinies, men overboard, broken masts, and leaking ships. These long- and short-term dynamics interact just as any single country's economic growth over time may resemble a linear trend upward until one looks more closely and sees the short-run troughs and downturns that are intermixed with the more general upward progression.

Metaphors are, of course, tricky analytical devices, and we do not mean to dwell too long on all the ships at sea. One problem with this metaphor, for instance, is that in the long wave story it is one of the ships that actually generates the big waves. But no matter. What we are attempting to get at with the metaphor is that protectionism (a strategy for dealing with inclement "maritime" conditions) involves processes that literally work in different time frames and speeds, with the short-run forces generating perturbations around the long-run trend line.

We have previously noted that there is value in all of the reviewed perspectives on protectionism. It is conceivable that they all could muster some empirical support. Hence, they may all be correct to some extent. Their "errors" most likely relate to forces that they omit from the full story and the effect of those forces on the processes that they choose to privilege in their particular versions. There are, no doubt, multiple short-run dynamics at work, and they likely play themselves out differently in different national contexts. There may also be several long-run dynamics at play as well. Our contention, though, is that there is one basic long-run dynamic that influences the other processes in ways that can hardly be evaded. Yet while the nature of this influence may be singular, there is no reason why the national responses to the stimuli of the long waves and systemic leadership need be identical.

Implications for Further Analysis

We have fallen far short of developing an explicit theory in this chapter interrelating the multiple perspectives with long waves of economic growth and systemic leadership. Instead, we have really only suggested some apparent linkages that deserve more exploration. Implicit to this suggestion is the idea that we might do well to cease and desist from the future development of single-emphasis perspectives on protectionism. Fully integrating all seventeen in one fell swoop would be a rather daunting and overly ambitious project. It would be far more prudent to begin the theoretical integration process slowly. One strategy would involve commitments to working with or within two to three perspectives simultaneously. Analysts could examine multiple perspectives as if they were competing explanations, but we think it would be even more profitable to explore the possibility that many of these perspectives are complementary. The question then is, How much explanatory power is attained with the incremental addition of complementary perspectives? At some point, the explanatory return is likely to become increasingly marginal. But the point remains that we do not know where that explanatory tipping point is located.

A second strategy involves focusing more closely on the asserted common denominators—long economic growth waves and systemic leadership. We claim that these processes provide the fundamental context for fluctuations in protectionism (hypothesis H9). They are not the sole shapers of long-term context, but they may prove to the be the most significant ones. Many of the other perspectives listed in figures 4.1 and 4.2 are thus supply and demand intermediaries between context and protectionism outcomes. From this point of view, we might consider two approaches. One strategic path combines long-term context with one or more of the intermediate processes. Initially, this path might best be investigated in case studies. Rather than, say, exploring the evolution of ideas in relative isolation, we are suggesting that they be explored in the context of systemic changes in political and economic structure. If changes in ideas precede the changes in structure, what intervening processes are necessary for ideas already in existence to become predominant? Does it require elite and generational shifts? Does it require new technologies and systemic leadership? Similarly, if there is also a lag between structural change and consequent ideational shifts, is more elite and generational shift required? Must new technologies become routine and systemic leadership decline?

Alternatively, do the lags in the rise and fall of prevailing ideas work the same way coming and going? That ideas matter has now been established. The next step is to better establish the context in which they matter and how their life cycles are patterned.

Another analytical path involves eliminating the middle men. If long waves and systemic leadership are fundamental contexts for protectionism, can we successfully model protectionism as a function of long waves and systemic leadership? This particular path has two attractions. One is that it empirically tests the assertion that we are making about the centrality of long waves and systemic leadership. If these processes are as central as we claim, we should be able to observe systematic relationships over the last two centuries or so. If the relationships are observed in a statistically significant fashion, our assertions will not have been fully established. But the assertions would be transformed into something other than casual observations.

The second attraction of this path is that it is one way to proceed empirically in the interim. The interim that we have in mind refers to the complexities associated with attempting to model long- and short-term dynamics simultaneously. How can one test a theory that implies an intermingled structure of long- and short-term dynamics? We do not have the magic answer about how to do this, and the technical issues involved may well require new statistical methods and measures. One way of illustrating the problem is to assume, for the moment, that the only accurate perspectives on protectionism are those of business cycles and hegemonic stability. The business cycle perspective tells us that interest groups are more likely to lobby for protection in recessions than in booms. The hegemonic stability perspective tells us that periods of hegemonic ascendancy are characterized by freer trade than are periods of hegemonic decline. But the periods of hegemonic ascendancy and decline will also encompass years of recession or boom in different times and places. In this example, we again encounter short-run, faster-moving forces (recession) riding on long-term, slower-moving processes (the rise and fall of system leaders or hegemons). The outcome is likely to show different propensities toward protectionism at different times and places even though there may exist long-run common denominators.[26]

Even when considering all the complexity associated with this example, it is clear that it greatly simplifies the complexity associated with simultaneously juggling a large number of perspectives (as opposed to but two) in varying national contexts. The number of possible permutations quickly assumes high figures as more and more variables are introduced. Still, that is not an argument for avoiding the analytical task altogether.

We see a number of empirical problems that would require solution prior to modeling relatively fast and slow dynamics simultaneously. Non-linear techniques may be necessary to capture long waves. Yet these long waves are not only irregular in intensity and timing, they may also change their form over time. If one has long time-series to capture the long-term fluctuations, equally long series are necessary for the shorter-term factors. Business cycles and polarity may be relatively easy to measure. Surplus capacity, institutional effects, multinational alliances, and prevailing ideas are less so. For that matter, changes in trade policy raise various problems for long-term measurement. Different trade policy instruments (e.g., tariffs, subsidies) have enjoyed different favor at different times. All of these series, however measured, may entail measurement error and noise that may require data transformations. There is also the awkward issue of model specification. Figure 4.2's causal arrows might be understated. More arrows could be drawn, and some of them might need to be double-headed reflecting reciprocal influences. This last problem is a reminder that more theoretical specification is in order before something very ambitious could be undertaken empirically.

Consequently, we fall back on a plea for less ambitious integration until we learn how to resolve these many problems of theory, methods, and data. Our bottom line is that we now know many ways to explain protectionism. We suspect strongly that most, if not all, of these explanatory routes are complementary. Equally strongly, we suspect that there are some underlying common denominators that are capable of tying these explanations together. It is time to put these suspicions to the test.

In chapter 5, the development of a new data set on the 1800–1990 average nominal tariff rates of five of the system's most important traders (Britain, France, the United States, Germany, and Japan) permits a new empirical examination of alternative explanations of protectionism. Seven models, with various emphases on hegemony, business cycles, war shocks, and economic growth, are used to generate nine schedules of expected changes in the direction of tariff rates. Correlations of the expected schedules with the observed directional shifts demonstrate clearly the timing superiority of explanations based on long waves and external shock emphases.

5. The Timing of Protectionism

There are any number of ways to explain the waxing and waning of protectionism, as we have seen in chapter 4. For example, ideologies, business cycles, elite orientations, surplus capacities, structural economic shifts, technological shifts, polarity structures, and the presence or absence of economic and political leadership have all been promoted as offering critical explanatory clues.[1] Many of the arguments seem quite plausible, and some have been advanced with variable amounts of supporting empirical evidence. However, most of the efforts to explain protectionism, as well as the efforts to test their implications, tend to be country- and temporally specific. Only a few attempt to span the entire world economy, or its most important actors, and even fewer offer explicit protectionism timetables encompassing the past two centuries.

Moreover, none of these more ambitious efforts to span centuries has managed to match theory and data fully. Either they have tried to do so and failed, or they have left more rigorous testing of their contentions to future undertakings. An important dimension of this problem is the awkwardness of the available data on protectionism. Prior to this time, it has been impossible to generate long series capable of directly capturing the fluctuations in the level of protectionism, either at the systemic level or for a number of the most important economic actors. Thus, whatever testing was accomplished had to rely on fairly crude, indirect information if the goal was to examine systemic trends historically.

During the nineteenth century and through the first half of the twentieth, protectionism was manifested primarily through tariffs. Beginning in the early 1970s, the use of nontariff trade barriers (NTBs) increased significantly, while the reliance on tariff barriers declined. The development of a new data set encompassing the 1800–1990 period, tariff and nontariff trade barriers, and focusing in part on five of the most important trading states in the world system permits a new examination of the vexing question of the timing of changes to barriers to trade. The new data also enable us to examine and compare the relative accuracy of the models that have attempted to explain trends in protectionism over long terms and multiple economies. Thus, in this chapter we will reexamine some of the assertions of Krasner (1976), Fischer (1987), Frederick (1987), Lake (1989), McKeown (1991), Thompson and Vescera (1992), and Bairoch (1993) that were introduced earlier in chapter 4. We will try to determine which, if any, correspond reasonably closely to observed intervals of increasing and decreasing tariff rates and nontariff barriers over the past two centuries.[2]

Multiple Protectionism Logics

The seven models that we focus on in this chapter possess different drivers. We have discussed briefly these arguments in chapter 4. Here we elaborate on each one for the sake of testing their predictions. In addition, we add one more argument (referred to as the import/GNP model) that also predicts patterns of openness.

The most well-known model stresses hegemonic stability (Krasner 1976) and is predicated in large part on the size and technological lead of the hegemonic leader. Openness may be beneficial to everyone in some respects, but it is most beneficial to states that are large and well developed. As the state with the largest and most well-developed economy, the hegemon not only benefits the most, it also suffers the least from the vicissitudes of external market fluctuations—one of the major liabilities of trade openness. Thus, as long as the leader continues to maintain its lead it will favor openness, and so will small economies that are too weak to resist hegemonic preferences. The actions of states with medium-sized or large but relatively underdeveloped economies are difficult to predict within this framework. Nevertheless, Krasner argues that the system's openness hinged on whether the hegemon is ascending or descending.

Krasner's argument is linked to a particular schedule of hegemonic rise and fall, but there is in fact no great consensus about the precise timing of hegemony. For example, two other well-known interpretations of hegemony suggest somewhat different periodicities even though they do not link the presence and absence of hegemony to a particular schedule of fluctuations in protectionism. As utilized in Mansfield (1994), Wallerstein (1983) views British and American hegemony as having been present in the 1815–73 and 1945–67 periods. Gilpin (1987) dates these hegemonic interludes as 1815–1914 and 1945–80. We view these disagreements about the timing of hegemonic decline as variations on hegemonic trajectory. While Krasner provides a concrete logic relating hegemony to trade openness, his dating of the trajectory of hegemony is a separate issue. He might have the right logic but the wrong dates. Thus, we will examine three hegemonic trajectory models (Krasner, Wallerstein, and Gilpin) with each one differentiated by the variation in trajectory timing.[3]

Fischer's (1987) loosely articulated external shock model has several components: war, depression, trade propensity, legislative political influence, and public mood. States that are heavily involved in trade tend to be and remain more free trade–oriented than states that are not. Wars and serious depressions tend to trigger swings toward higher tariffs. In the nineteenth century, customs revenues were highly significant as sources of governmental income. Wars raised the need for governmental income. Thus, tariffs were apt to be raised in wartime and in the postwar period to help pay government debts.

The impact of depression and war is similar in that economic downswings increase the perceived need for protection against international competition. Thus Fischer associates the three largest swings toward protectionism with depression onsets (1815, 1875, and 1929) and suggests that the 1970s were no different except that international institutions (GATT) have prevented the movement toward protectionism from being fully realized. Economic upswings, on the other hand, may facilitate swings back to free trade, but the likelihood seems to depend on the length of the upswing. Longer upswings are more likely to change public moods than short ones.

Finally, effective legislatures add an aggravating factor. As legislatures become more effective, so do pressure groups. Depending on the economic climate and the ensemble of interests within a particular national economy, legislatures in democratic political systems, in contrast to authoritarian systems, can constitute an institutional push toward or away from greater protectionism.

Frederick's (1987) long cycle model links trade rules directly to the rise and fall of global political leadership. With the exception of the principal winner, rivals are exhausted by the struggle over which state will emerge from a period of global war as the new world power. However, trade barriers remain high in the immediate postwar period (world power) due to the legacy of the global war period, tariff revenue considerations, and the need to protect recovering economies. In the next phase, delegitimation, the system leader and its rivals gradually turn toward freer trade as a function of diffusing competitiveness. The system leader lowers its barriers faster than the other major economies until a period of economic stagnation brings a halt to the liberalization trend. In the deconcentration phase, the leader continues its pattern of liberalization because its closure costs are too great, while its major competitors turn toward increased protectionism. Overall, the trading system becomes less liberal. In the fourth phase (global war) all actors turn toward less liberal trading policies as part of the more general struggle for leadership succession.

Lake's (1988) structural incentives model develops a phased schedule for structural shifts in the international political economy that alter actor strategies on trade liberalization due to changes in the number of competitive actors that lead in economic size and productivity. Five types of phases are observed to have characterized the past two hundred years: hegemony (late eighteenth century—1897), hegemonic decline (1897–1912), bilateral opportunism (1912–32), unilateral opportunism (1932–45), hegemony (1945–65), bilateral opportunism (1965–75), and multilateral opportunism (1975–present).

In Lake's model, hegemony may produce free trade, but it does not necessarily do so. Free or freer trade may also be produced in nonhegemonic phases. What is most important is the type of international economic structure prevailing at any given time. Types of international economic structures are differentiated by the number of large and medium-sized actors (measured in terms of world trade share) present in the system and the mix of strategic types of actors (leaders, opportunists, spoilers, and several varieties of free riders) operating in the system. Actor types, in turn, are a function of trade share and relative labor productivity. For instance, a hegemon is a state with 15 percent or more of world trade and high productivity. An opportunist is a state with more than 5 but less than 15 percent of world trade and high productivity.

According to these definitions, Lake finds that the world economy has moved back and forth between phases of hegemony and opportunism. The high productivity of opportunists and hegemons gives them positional interests in free trade. Whether they pursue this interest depends in large part on the degree of international economic instability, the consequent protectionist behavior with which they are confronted by other states, and changes in their own relative size. While space does not permit a detailed exploration of the anticipated behaviors, opportunistic phases in which the actor or actors in question have strong structural incentives to encourage moderation in protectionism are more likely to result in free trade than are phases of hegemonic decline or unstable periods of unilateral opportunism. Thus, Lake argues, both hegemonic and collective leaderships may contribute to the development of more liberal trade systems.

The problem for our analysis is that Lake's focus is on predicting individual actors' trade strategies and not on applying his modified hegemonic stability theory to aggregate protectionism outcomes. Therefore, it is awkward for us to translate his arguments into the terms of the current examination. However, we believe that his theory might be interpreted as predicting the following protectionism pattern for the system leader and probably the system as a whole: decreasing from the 1790s to 1897, 1912–32, and 1945–to the present; and increasing in 1897–1912 and 1932–45. We hasten to add once again that this schedule is entirely our own interpretation of Lake's argument. But even if we have erred in our interpretation, we can still assess the extent to which Lake's phases capture different types of protectionist behavior.

McKeown's (1991) imports/GNP model is not really an explanatory model in the sense that the others are, so it was not among the seventeen approaches we reviewed in chapter 4. While McKeown does test some aspects of hegemonic and business cycle explanations of trade openness in one part of his analysis, the section that is most relevant for our purposes is his contention that the ratio of the growth of system imports to the growth of system income provides a simple indicator of the world trading system's openness (1991: 154). The rationale is that, holding transport and insurance costs, import prices, and protectionism constant, one would expect imports to fluctuate more or less in tandem with national incomes. Imports growing faster (slower) than national incomes would suggest an opening (closing) trading system.

In addition to some bivariate regression analysis of the relationship between national income and imports, McKeown reports mean annual ratios of import values to nominal GNP in industrial capitalist countries for seven intervals in the 1880–1987 period: 1880–1900, 0.127; 1901–13, 0.134; 1921–29, 0.100; 1930–38, 0.078; 1948–58, 0.084; 1959–72, 0.088; 1973–87, 0.151. His conclusion is that the post–1945 period unquestionably has been more open to trade than in the 1930s, but the late 1940s through the early 1970s were not all that much more open than the 1930s. It is only after 1973 that the openness ratio registers scores signifying more openness than in the decades immediately prior to 1913.

The Timing of Protectionism

Price fluctuations seem to have something to do with McKeown's openness ratio pattern. If one examines import volume as opposed to value (McKeown 1991: 158), the first four period means move in the same direction as with the value index, but the change from period to period is not very great (0.124, 0.133, 0.130, 0.128). However, the mean volume series troughs in 1948–58 (0.101) instead of the 1930s before continuing to rise through the 1980s (0.154, 0.217). Thus the contemporary "freer trade" era is even more sharply delimited to the period after the late 1950s.

McKeown infers nothing about the timing of protectionism per se from his data analysis, but the ratio of import volume to real GNP could be viewed as suggesting the intervention of increased domestic protectionism after 1913 and decreases after 1958. To make this inference, we must assume according to McKeown's argument that transport and insurance costs fluctuations are relatively insignificant and that the import volume index controls appropriately for import price changes. Overlooked by McKeown but seemingly equally applicable to the analysis of long trade volume series are the assumptions that World Wars I and II were not major factors and that domestic protectionism actually influenced trade volume. If either of these last two assumptions is inappropriate, it is difficult to infer that protectionism has been a principal culprit in decreasing trade volumes. But, as McKeown reminds us, we are only looking for clues to structural changes and not seeking to delineate precisely how the system works.

The leadership-long cycle model (Thompson and Vescera 1992), which is fundamental to this book's theses, keys its explanation to successive waves of radical innovations that fuel spurts of economic growth. To recapitulate the implications for trade, the radical innovations tend initially to be concentrated within one lead economy. To the extent that trade is strongly influenced by lags in the ability to adopt new technologies, nonpioneers will initially lower their barriers to the new products until they can produce them independently. The pioneers, who have little in the way of competition at the outset, have incentives to lower their own barriers if only to reduce import costs. As the new technologies and the ability to produce them diffuse throughout the system, follower incentives to raise protective tariffs will increase, the output of multiple producers will oversupply markets, and competition will become more intense, especially if there is also some possibility of competing for the system's lead economy status. Thus, the basic rhythm is one of alternations in greater and lesser amounts of protectionism depending on the pace established by one state achieving a substantial lead over other states. This lead is established twice (immediately before and shortly after global wars).

During the first innovation peak, liberalization is likely to be more asymmetrical, with the lead economy enjoying the most incentives to lower trade barriers. It is in the second of each long wave set that other economies genuinely begin to catch up with the leader. Freer trade is more likely on the upswing than it is on the downswing of each long wave but particularly so in the catch up wave.

The model that is most limited temporally is the structural shift approach advanced by Bairoch (1993). Indeed, his approach is really more a commentary than a fully developed model. Domestic pressures against high levels of protectionism were slow to develop, even in liberal and system-leading Britain. A main reason is that it took time for the national balance between agrarian and industrial economic activities to shift decisively from agrarian to industrial activities, despite the early-nineteenth-century industrial production leadership enjoyed by Britain. As the first major economy to make the shift from a primarily agricultural to primarily industrial economy, Britain led the way in lowering its trade tariffs. For political reasons, other European states eventually followed the British lead for one or two decades until agrarian pressure groups, in economies still oriented primarily to agrarian production, were able to reverse the liberalizing trend thanks to the development of hard times for agrarian producers. Twentieth-century protectionist tendencies are not discussed by Bairoch, but, presumably, other factors must come into play after the shift to industrial economies has been more or less completed.

Evaluating Previous Empirical Examinations

One may choose to quarrel with the assumptions and earlier analyses of these models in any number of ways. We do not see our current role as one of providing specific critiques of each interpretation. Instead, our approach here will be simple. One of the primary bases for evaluating the explanatory utility of the seven models is their relative accuracy in capturing significant fluctuations in observed levels of protectionism. Each of the seven analyses we selected for comparison generated (or could be manipulated into generating) nine schedules of anticipated fluctuations in protectionist levels. Each of the seven models either assumes or actually discusses the degree of correspondence between its expectations and the observed behavior. But, for the most part, previous analyses either have been descriptive or have relied on indirect indicators. None of the seven models has really been evaluated in the context of an adequate information base on tariff levels and nontariff trade barriers. Moreover, none of the previous examinations has been equally attentive to each of the analytical levels (system, leader, "others") to which references are made in the models viewed collectively.

Fischer (1987) and Bairoch (1993) provided only a few years' worth of information on tariff levels, and their use of tariff data is entirely descriptive. Lake's (1988) empirical focus was aimed at hypotheses concerning matters other than protectionism levels. Krasner (1976), Webb and Krasner (1989), and McKeown (1992) preferred to rely on more indirect measures of trade openness and closure, such as the ratio of trade to national income, regionalization proclivities, or imports as a proportion of GNP. Thompson and Vescera (1992) examined the ratio of customs revenues to imports, another indirect index of protectionism sometimes used by social scientists (Lindert and Kindleberger 1982; Kuderle 1985; Verdier 1994). Yet these measures do not address levels of trade protectionism directly even though they may reflect the results of increasing and decreasing protectionism levels. Only Frederick (1987) looked at nominal tariff data, but her series were less than complete and restricted to unweighted British and American data. Even so, none of the earlier efforts devotes much attention to the increasing reliance on nontrade barriers since the early to mid-1970s. Nor does any of these earlier efforts attempt to measure the shift from tariffs to nontrade barriers.

The general problem with the indirect indicators is that while they may reflect the results of increasing or decreasing protectionism levels, they do not address these levels in a straightforward manner. They may also reflect the effects of other economic and political variables. For instance, expanding imports stimulated by accelerated rates of economic growth but unaccompanied by any changes in tariffs could lead to the same empirical outcome as a situation involving decreased tariffs and relatively constant rates of growth. Ratios matching imports (or exports) to national income in both cases would suggest greater trade openness when only the second case actually involved a decrease in protectionist tendencies. Alternatively, the ratio of trade to national income could decline while the absolute value of trade was actually increasing but not as quickly as increases in national income. In such a case, we might infer that protectionism levels had increased while in fact they might not have changed at all, or might even have decreased.

Obviously, we would prefer more direct, serial measures of protectionist tendencies, if at all possible. We also would prefer to calculate the relative weight of tariff and nontariff barriers in order to combine them into one series. Only then could we be sure that the data addressed protectionist behavior, as opposed to other sorts of politicoeconomic activities. Similarly, if we ignore nontariff barriers altogether, we may entirely miss significant changes in the way actors prefer to restrict trade. An old problem associated with examining longitudinal data is that the meaning of the indicators may change over time. Even if we had complete tariff series, it would be unwise to rule out the possibility that nontariff barriers have become more important than tariffs in assessing the level of protectionism.

A second type of problem pertains to some ambiguity as to the appropriate unit of analysis for empirical tests of protectionism models. Some authors focus primarily on the system as a whole, while others link their models to leader behavior or some variable combination of the system leader, the system, and selected other states. In some cases, data for the system leader is assumed to reflect the entire system or to address a systemic model's predictions. In other cases, it is implied that systemic data are representative of all types of actors' behavior. Much different expectations are generated by the models that are very explicit about the reasons for different types of actors responding differently to similar cues.

Our question is whether the correspondence between observed protectionism levels and the predicted levels, if any, applies equally well to the system and to its leader. There is no theoretical need to insist that all states follow an identical protectionist schedule. Such a stipulation would be highly unrealistic. But since the seven models focus on different levels of analysis, it would be equally unrealistic to assume that each model should do equally well at all conceivable analytical levels. A pure leader model should correspond to leader behavior; it need not predict the behavior of the rest of the system equally well. Similarly, a pure systemic model may not do as well in capturing the behavior of the leader as it does in charting general systemic tendencies. Attempting, on the other hand, to test the fit of these models to several specific nonleader countries should be a separate undertaking because the more specific the spatial application, the less fit we should anticipate with a general schedule of protectionism fluctuations. The less the anticipated fit, the more noise we would be introducing about our more general question of which model drivers seem to do best at the macrolevel.

Nine Protectionist Level Schedules

Table 5.1 represents our attempt to use the seven models to generate specific expectations at different levels of analysis (system and leader). At first glance, table 5.1 may seem to suggest a fairly high degree of agreement. All of the authors have some element of alternation between phases of trade opening and closing. Thus, some shared synchronization in phase clusterings is evident, with somewhat more disagreement emerging in the twentieth century. Nonetheless, the level of agreement is less apparent in the identification of specific phases that are keyed to different processes. Fischer emphasizes the external shocks of war and depression and their interaction with domestic institutions. Krasner's, Gilpin's and Wallerstein's timing are linked to perceived hegemonic ascent and decline. Lake's focus is on structural incentives for the most important actors. Frederick's clock is predicated on a four-phase conceptualization of the long cycle of global leadership (global war, world power, delegitimation, and deconcentration), taken from Modelski (1981, 1982). Thompson and Vescera's protectionist timetable is based on Freeman and Perez's (1989) technological long wave schedule. The Fischer and Bairoch time frames are predicated on their historical examinations of differential behavior among Britain, Europe, and the United States. McKeown's schedule is oriented toward trade openness, and only by inference can it suggest something about protectionism. Since these approaches emphasize different processes, it is perhaps not surprising that there is continuing disagreement about the periodicity of protectionism.

Other things being equal, one would think that hegemonic trajectories, long cycles, wars, business cycles, and long waves should be overlapping phenomena, and, indeed, it is not difficult to make a strong case for their overlap.[4] It is the primacy accorded to different variables that produces different expectations. Krasner's emphasis is on the rise and fall of the leader and its perceived self-interest, as is Lake's emphasis, but the former's focus is almost entirely on the leader's lead status while the latter considers the closing and widening distances among the major trading countries' market shares. Frederick stipulates some degree of deconcentration and the rise of competition as important to liberalization interludes, but, as in the case of the hegemonic trajectory models, her interpretation is strongly geared to the leader's status.

TABLE 5.1. Anticipated Intervals of Protectionism

		Protectionism	
Model	Interval	System	Leader
H.T., variation A	1820–79	decreasing	decreasing
(Krasner timing)	1879–1900	increasing	increasing
	1900–1913	increasing	increasing
	1918–39	decreasing	decreasing
	1945–60	decreasing	decreasing
	1960–	increasing	increasing
H.T., variation B	1815–73	decreasing	decreasing
(Wallerstein timing)	1873–1945	increasing	increasing
	1945–67	decreasing	decreasing
	1967–	increasing	increasing
H.T., variation C	1815–1914	decreasing	decreasing
(Gilpin timing)	1914–45	increasing	increasing
	1945–80	decreasing	decreasing
	1980–	increasing	increasing
External shock	1790s–1820s	increasing	increasing
	1820s–1873	decreasing	decreasing
	1873–1930s	increasing	mixed
	1945–1970s	decreasing	decreasing
	1970s–	increasing	unclear
Long cycle	1816–48	high	high
	1849–80	decreasing	decreasing
	1881–1913	increasing	decreasing
	1914–45	increasing	increasing
	1946–1973	high	decreasing
	1974–	increasing	decreasing
Structural incentives	1790s–1897	decreasing	decreasing
	1897–1912	increasing	increasing
	1912–32	decreasing	decreasing
	1932–45	increasing	increasing
	1945–65	decreasing	decreasing
	1965–75	decreasing	decreasing
	1975–	decreasing	decreasing
Imports/GNP	1880–1900	decreasing	—
	1901–13	decreasing	—
	1921–29	increasing	—
	1930–38	increasing	—
	1948–58	high	—
	1959 72	decreasing	—
	1973–87	decreasing	—
Leadership–long cycle	1800s–1820s	increasing	increasing
	1830s–1860s	decreasing	decreasing

TABLE 5.1.—*Continued*

Model	Interval	Protectionism	
		System	Leader
	1860s–1890s	increasing	increasing
	1900s–1910s	decreasing	decreasing
	1910s–1930s	increasing	increasing
	1940s–1960s	decreasing	decreasing
	1960s–1990s	increasing	increasing
Structural shift	1815–1844/46	high	high
	1844/46–1858/60	decreasing	decreasing
	1858/60–1877/79	decreasing	decreasing
	1877/79–1890/92	increasing	decreasing
	1890/92–1913	increasing	decreasing

Note: H.T. denotes Hegemonic Trajectory. In most cases, it is possible to describe protectionism behavior as moving in one direction or the other. However, some authors use more static descriptors such as "high" for some periods. We interpret these phases as ones of increasing tariffs. When authors point out that actor behavior varied by state, region, or type of economy, we use the "mixed" descriptor and exclude that period from the analysis.

Thompson and Vescera's model envisions technological gradients and discontinuities as fundamental to trade and protectionist incentives. Bairoch emphasizes the structural shifts involved in agrarian economies becoming increasingly industrialized, and therefore elites and populations become more sensitive to hindrances in the exchange of manufactured goods and raw materials important to manufacturing processes. Fischer sketches a picture of protectionist pendulums swinging back and forth in tune to pushes from external conflict and the deterioration of the business cycle.

Expected Results and Qualifications

Given the different foci and emphases, we might expect either the hegemonic trajectory or structural incentives model to perform best in the leader behavior column. Whether other actors and the system as a whole follow the lead of the leader is a separate question that we do not pursue at this time. The long cycle, imports/GNP, and long wave models ostensibly are systemic models and should do best in the first column. However, Frederick's interpretation of the system is strongly flavored by a focus on the system leader and, therefore, should be expected to do well in that column as well. Fitting the agrarian-industrial structural shift and external shock models into the system/leader categories is awkward. To fully test these models, we would need additional information on the pace of the structural shifts in different economies and the differential timing of national business cycles. It is also difficult for another party to aggregate the systemic implications of descriptive statements about the behavior of different states. Table 5.1, therefore, should be seen simply as an interpretation of what the seven models and their authors might have said if forced to work within our categorization of systemic and leader behavior. The question, then, is, Which of these approaches is best corroborated by the actual history of protectionism?

It is important to keep in mind that any tests of the seven models are subject to a variety of qualifications because each model comes with various caveats. For instance, Krasner's (1976) own examination of the hegemonic trajectory model did not fare quite as expected. Several phases were misidentified. The shocks of major external crises and the lags associated with vested interests were introduced to help account for the poor fit of the model, with the idea being that trade structures respond slowly to changes in the distribution of power. The amended hegemonic trajectory model thus contains an unspecified institutional lag that can be overwhelmed in the context of world wars and depressions, not unlike the later-developed Fischer model. But since world wars and depressions can also characterize periods of hegemonic transitions, it is unclear how much credit we should attribute to institutional lags, external crises, and leadership transitions. Nor do we know how to translate these considerations into a revised timetable for trade closure. Hence, we have elected to focus on the original hegemonic trajectory explanation and timetable.

Similar qualifications apply to the other models. Thompson and Vescera's focus on long waves acknowledges the role of generational shifts and ideational lags. External crises are also seen as providing unusual opportunities for altering governmental policies. Bairoch's emphasis on structural shifts certainly pays attention to how internal developmental processes interact with external changes such as the increased export of North American wheat to Europe in the 1870s. Frederick's categorizations depend a great deal on behavioral lags from the preceding phase.

These various qualifications notwithstanding, there is still the question of how useful the basic drivers of each model are in generating grounds for explaining and anticipating, as well as postdicting, changes in tendencies toward greater or lesser protectionism. The point is not to set the models up for failure by stripping them of their elaborations and amplifications. Rather, the question is, How close can we come to capturing protectionist reality with rival simplifications of what matters most in creating that reality?

The Timing of Protectionism

The Protectionism Data

The question of how best to measure protectionism is not an easy one to answer. However, one obvious criterion is that the index not be subject to potential biases introduced by indirect means of assessment. Otherwise, one can never be quite sure that the protectionism measure is specifically measuring the level of trade barriers as opposed to other phenomena such as trade volume.

For most time periods in our study, the most direct measure of protectionism is the average nominal tariff rate for a national economy. No claim is made that this index is without liabilities. Three threats to its validity and reliability are trade fluctuations, effective tariffs, and the existence of nontariff barriers to trade. In principle, it is possible that the average tariff could fall or rise without any change in the nominal tariff schedules. If the composition of trade were to change structurally so that the ratio of high to low tariff imports decreased or increased significantly, average tariff rates could be affected. To know just how serious a threat this possibility is would require quite a bit of knowledge about import commodities, their tariffs, and their fluctuations. In the absence of specific information about such shifts in types of imports, we are forced to ignore this potential threat.[5]

The idea of effective tariffs takes into account the possibility that nominal duties for a final product, simply the statutory rates, may differ from those applied to the inputs used in its manufacture. Therefore, the rate of protection on the value added in the production process could differ from the statutory rate. Moreover, it can be shown that, for most goods, effective rates are higher than nominal rates. But the question remains whether the political economy of protectionism is more concerned with nominal or effective tariffs. Chen (1974) contends that nominal tariffs probably are more relevant for three reasons. First, in trade negotiations, the concept of effective tariffs is virtually absent. Second, in practice it is easier for pressure groups to seek changes in their own nominal rates than to seek changes in the rates of all their production inputs. Third, effective tariffs are simply difficult to compute and, therefore, have limited practical meaning.

Even though the notion of effective tariffs may not be understood as clearly as statutory rates, there are arguments promoting the utility of effective, as opposed to nominal, rates for the measurement of protectionism levels. Barnett (1976) argues that the concept was understood clearly by Canadian policymakers as early as 1858. Some evidence that both producers and governments were aware of the concept is also demonstrated by Taussig (1931). Still, the quantitative analyses of Caves (1976), Helleiner (1977a), Finger and DeRosa (1979), and Lavergne (1983) indicate that no different results emerge when effective and nominal rates are substituted for one another in regression equations. The likelihood of a high correlation existing between nominal and effective rates also suggests that it should not make too much difference which indicator is used in hypothesis-testing exercises. There is also the important question of data availability. Since national information on the inputs used to produce a variety of different commodities and their respective tariffs is not available for the lengthy period of time in which we are interested, the computation of a historical time-series for effective tariffs is almost an impossible task.

Nontariff barriers (import quotas, voluntary export restraints, restrictive licensing, discriminatory governmental procurement, antidumping and countervailing procedures, escape clauses, surveillance, safeguards, government production subsidies, tax incentives for exporters, the imposition of domestic standards on imports) are a different story. After the late 1960s and early 1970s, these nontariff protectionism measures became more common. While extremely resistant to easy measurement, they appear to have become too important to dismiss on the ground of mere inconvenience. Moreover, the available evidence indicates quite strongly that the significance of the many forms of nontariff barriers increased in the 1970s and 1980s and that they affected an increasing portion of the trade volume of the industrialized countries.[6]

Two problems are associated with measuring the extent of NTBs and their incorporation into our analysis. The first problem is how to compare information based on different metrics of nontariff trade barriers—as, for example, in the case of percentage of imports affected by quotas and the number of unfair trade cases. The second problem is one of combining information about nominal average tariffs and NTBs into one coordinated time-series of protectionism. What is the average nominal tariff equivalent of each of the many types of existing NTBs, and how should NTBs be aggregated?[7]

We have no direct answer to the question of how to combine NTBs and nominal tariffs. For our present purposes, however, we need only to be able to label a given time period as one of increasing or decreasing protectionism. There appear to be three ways to combine our information on average nominal tariffs and NTBs to generate what might be called "net trade barriers." If average nominal tariff rates are not changing much but NTBs are increasing, net trade barriers would seem to be increasing, albeit at an uncertain pace. If average nominal tariff rates are declining rapidly but NTBs are increasing rapidly, we would be inclined to label such a period as one of increasing protectionism. If average nominal tariff rates are clearly increasing and NTBs are increasing as well, there should be little hesitation in describing this time period as one of increasing protectionism.

Combining different NTB measures into one meaningful aggregate has been addressed in several analyses. In principle, these methods do not try to answer the direct question we posed earlier. Instead, they measure the percentage of trade covered by NTBs in different time periods. Several sources (GATT 1979, 1980; Page 1981; Laird and Yeats 1990b) compute the proportion of different countries' and world imports that are covered by NTBs for periods beginning in the late 1960s and ending in the late 1980s. Their definition of the several types of NTBs is based on the classification scheme currently employed by the UN Conference on Trade and Development (UNCTAD) Data Base on Trade Measures as described by Walter (1972) and by UNCTAD (1988).[8] Using these data sources we developed several arrays of information on the spread of NTBs in the countries in our study, between 1966 and 1986.[9]

The top half of table 5.2 reports the estimated proportion of all imports of the United States, France, Germany, the United Kingdom, and Japan that are covered by NTBs. The bottom half of the table reports the same information for manufactured goods. Table 5.3 contains data on the percentage of the world's total imports and manufactured imports covered by NTBs. The general tendency suggested by this information is one of increasing NTB use, both for each of the countries in our study and for the world as a whole. The data on manufactured commodities demonstrate this tendency most dramatically. The total import numbers include large fuel components, the price of which industrialized countries try to keep as low as possible, especially if they do not produce fuels domestically in large quantities. In all, the data on NTBs indeed suggest that protectionism of these more subtle types is on the rise starting sometime in the late 1960s.

In order to calculate the periodicity of protectionism at several different levels, we develop eight series of average nominal tariffs for the 1800–1990 period, calculated in five-year intervals. Five of the series are national and encompass the most important national economic actors of the past two centuries: Britain, the United States, France, Germany, and Japan.[10] The raw data were collected from several sources. In the case of Britain and the

United States, the available data were quite extensive. For Germany, France, and Japan, there were time periods in which it was only possible to identify the direction, but not the precise amount, of nominal tariff changes. These instances required estimation, subject to the following rules.

1. When nominal average tariff data were not available, tariffs on manufactured goods, when available, were used as proxies.
2. Unless information was available that suggested some specific type of change, brief gaps in the series were filled through linear interpolation.

TABLE 5.2.   Imports Covered by NTBs

States	1966	1974	1979	1980	1986
All Imports					
United States	36.0	36.2	44.4	45.8	45.0
France	16.0	*	*	*	82.0
Germany	24.0	*	*	*	41.0
UK	16.0	*	*	*	38.0
Japan	31.0	56.1	59.4	59.4	43.0
EC	21.0	35.8	44.5	44.8	54.0
Manufactured Imports					
United States	39.0	*	*	45.1	71.0
France	6.0	*	*	36.5	61.0
Germany	12.0	*	*	27.5	51.0
UK	9.0	*	*	25.7	44.0
Japan	48.0	*	*	23.8	50.0
EC	21.0	*	*	*	54.0

Source: Laird and Yeats (1990b), data from GATT (1979, 1981), and Page (1981) as summarized in Lew (1987:3).
Note: Unavailable data points are indicated by an asterisk.

TABLE 5.3.   Systemic NTB Coverage

	1966	1980	1986
All imports	25.0	47.8[a]	48.0
Manufactured imports	19.0	31.0[a]	58.0

Source: Laird and Yeats (1990a), GATT (1979, 1981), and Page (1981) as summarized in Lew (1987: 3).
[a]Weighted average of U.S., U.K., Germany, France, and Japan NTB coverage (utilizing world trade shares as weights).

3. When the sources indicated only that nominal tariffs went up or down, the estimation approach depended on the availability of additional information.[11] For instance, the most extreme example is associated with German nineteenth-century data. In 1820, Germany's (Prussia) tariff equaled 12 percent. No further specific information on German tariffs was available until 1875 (6 percent). However, Isaacs (1948) and Ashley (1911) discussed German tariff tendencies for the 1820–75 interval. Since no tariff changes are noted for the 1820–43 period, we assumed that tariff levels did not change. Isaacs (1948) states that German tariffs rose in 1843 and again in 1846. Based on the information that German tariffs in the nineteenth century never exceeded 20 percent, we assumed that the peak level was attained in 1845. Linear interpolation was then used to compute the five-year points between the assumed 1845 level and the reported 1875 level. Fortunately, the other interventions required much less heroic assumptions.

The estimated national series are reported in table 5.4. In addition, a systemic index was calculated by aggregating these five national series, appropriately weighted by their share of world trade.[12] A seventh series, the tariff levels of the system's leader, was created by splicing the national series of Britain and the United States at 1945, which is the point at which, among other developments, the United States' trade share surpassed the British trade share.[13]

Figure 5.1 compares the systemic customs revenue/imports series used by Thompson and Vescera with the systemic protectionism data.[14] Both indicators seem to capture the same two-peaked phenomenon. The customs revenue–based indicator does less well in the twentieth century, as indicated by the sizable gap between the two second peaks. Nor does it detect the protectionism dynamics observed in the tariff data during the 1860–1900 and 1945–55 periods. Nevertheless, the correlation between the two series is a high 0.89. By definition, the nominal tariff indicator is a more direct and therefore more desirable indicator of protectionist barriers, but the customs revenue/imports indicator appears to outline roughly the same long-run shape of protectionist fluctuations. In this respect, they serve to cross-validate each other. However, we hasten to add that this observation pertains only to the systemic level of analysis. At the national level, the discrepancies between changes in proportional customs revenues and changes in nominal tariffs are greater.

TABLE 5.4.   Estimated Nominal Average Tariff Rates (in percentages)

Year	UK	FR	GE	US	JA	SY	SL
1800	29.5	23	*	*	*	28	29.5
1805	34.2	27	*	*	*	33	34.2
1810	40.7	39	*	*	*	40	40.7
1815	45.1	50	15	*	*	40	45.1
1820	43.8	86	12	45	*	44	43.8
1825	53.1	90	12	50.5	*	51	53.1
1830	47.2	90	12	61.7	*	50	47.2
1835	40.5	90	12	40.4	*	46	40.5
1840	30.9	90	12	34.4	*	41	30.9
1845	32.3	90	20	34.5	*	43	32.3
1850	25.3	90	17.7	27.1	*	40	25.3
1855	19.5	76	15.3	26.8	*	32	19.5
1860	15	30	13	19.6	*	18	15
1865	11.5	15	10.7	47.6	5	17	11.5
1870	8.9	16.3	8.4	47.1	5	15	8.9
1875	6.7	17.5	6	40.6	5	17	6.7
1880	6.1	22	2	43.5	5.8	16	6.1
1885	5.9	23.5	6.3	46.1	6.6	17	5.9
1890	6.1	25	12.5	44.6	7.4	19	6.1
1895	5.5	29.5	18.8	42.2	8.2	20	5.5
1900	5.3	34	23	49.5	9	23	5.3
1905	7	34	19	45.3	16	23	7
1910	5.9	40	19	41.6	23	23	5.9
1913	5.8	20	13	23.7	30	15	5.8
1920	6.9	15	13	16.4	35	14	6.9
1925	9.3	21	20	37.6	40	23	9.3
1930	11.6	30	21	44.7	45	26	11.6
1935	34.8	35	64	42.9	50	42	34.8
1938	37.4	40	64	53.6	50	44	37.4
1945	40	40	44	28.2	46	33	28.2
1950	30	19.8	25	13.1	42	22	13.1
1955	25.8	25.2	15	11.9	34	20	11.9
1960	21.7	23.3	11	12.2	25	18	12.2
1965	17.5	22.9	8	11.9	16.1	15	11.9
1970	13	13.6	12	12	14	13	12
1975	9.5	8.3	8	8	12	9	8
1980	8.3	7.7	8.3	6	9.9	9	6
1985	5.3	8.6	6.3	5.5	5	6	5.5
1990	5.9	5.9	5.9	5	5.3	5	5

Note: Unavailable data points are indicated by an asterisk. UK denotes United Kingdom, FR, France, GE, Germany, US, United States, SY, System, and SL, System Leader.

The Timing of Protectionism

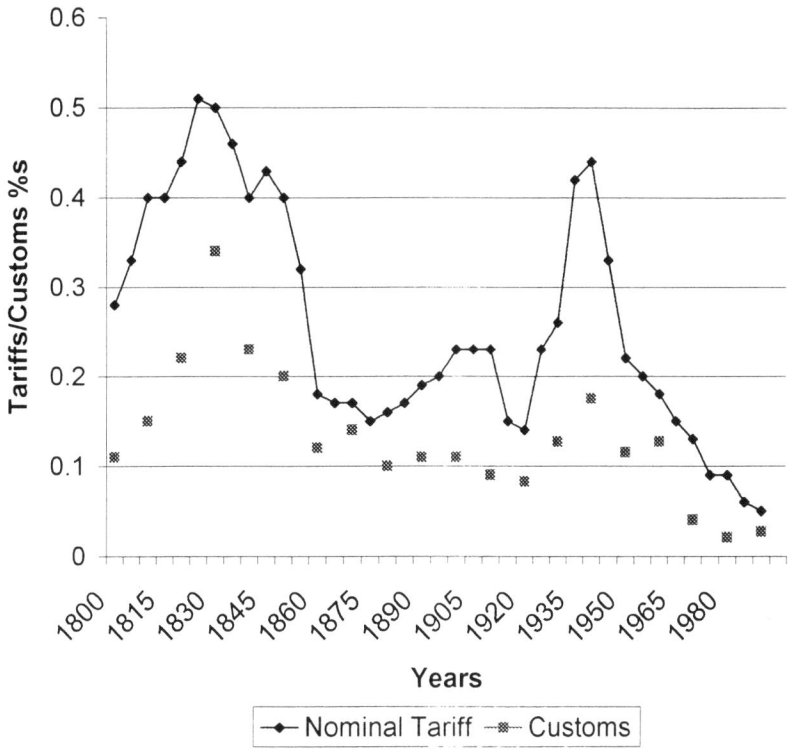

Fig. 5.1. Systemic measures of nominal tariffs and customs revenues/imports measures

Interpreting the nominal tariff rates is a reasonably straightforward process until the most contemporary period. In all three columns, the average tariff rates have declined from highs around the World War II period through 1990. However, the rate of decline slowed discernibly from the second half of the 1970s onward. Since the nominal tariff rate numbers are approaching zero, some slowing in the pace of tariff liberalization was mathematically inevitable. However, we view this period as one in which tariff levels, while decreasing, did not change all that much. In addition, if we were to express the numbers more precisely (including changes to the right of the decimal point), some very slight increases would be recorded in 1990. Thus, in view of the apparent increasing significance of NTBs, the last two decades may be seen, from our perspective, as a period of at least

131

moderate movement away from trade liberalization.[15] Nonetheless, we recognize that this view remains controversial and, therefore, will treat the issue empirically as an open question.

Matching the Models to the Data

Our current approach is not the more conventional one that seeks to determine how much of the variance in protectionism can be captured by the various models under review. Most of these models would be difficult to operationalize in a direct manner. We propose a less direct approach. Our question is which model's historical protectionism schedule most closely approximates the observed fluctuations in protectionism data. To match the nine protectionism timing schedules to our newly developed measure of actual protectionism, we applied the following procedures. First, we coded the observed protectionism behavior by assigning a value of 1 to each five-year period during which tariffs decrease (opening the economy for international trade). The one exception to this procedure are the intervals 1915–1919 and 1940–44, which were excluded from the empirical tests as abnormal periods of world war. Second, we coded the systemic and leader's timing predictions, for the same five-year intervals, by assigning a value of 1 (opening) or 0 (closing). Since the timing schedules rarely coincide with our neutral five-year intervals (e.g., 1800–1804, 1805–9, 1810–14, and so on), some five-year intervals were predicted to encompass mixed protectionist behavior. For instance, a timing schedule might have 1838–43 as opening and 1844–55 as closing. In such cases, we used a majority year rule. A five-year interval in which three years are predicted as opening (closing) is coded as 1 (0). In our example above, 1840–44, 1845–49, and 1850–54 would be coded as 1, 0, and 0 respectively.

Finally, we computed the cross-correlations between each of the predicted and observed series as well as separately for the systemic and leader behavior. In computing the cross-correlations we computed up to one lag and lead period on the tariff series in case the predictions were close but not precisely on target. We also experimented with two lag and lead periods but found that it failed to enhance any schedule's predictive accuracy significantly.

Combining nontariff trade barriers and average nominal tariffs into a single quantitative protectionism measure is not a straightforward task. Since we cannot resolve the dispute about the direction of protectionism in recent years, we computed the cross-correlations in three ways: 1800–1974 (nominal tariff data only), 1800–1989 with 1975–89 coded as a period of decreasing protectionism, and 1800–1989 with 1975–89 coded as a period of increasing protectionism. We focus here on the 1800–1974 results and report pertinent information from the 1800–1989 analyses as necessary.

Table 5.5 reports the cross-correlations between actual and predicted movements in systemic protectionism, while allowing zero and one lag (lead) of nominal tariff levels. According to this table, four schedules (Krasner's hegemonic trajectory, long cycles, structural incentives, and import/GNP) offer no significant assistance in capturing the timing of systemic protectionism. The other five offer some explanation, with the long wave and external shock approaches generating the highest cross-correlations. The overall winner without introducing lags is the long wave schedule. The external shock schedule does slightly better if tariffs are lagged one five-year interval, but the difference in the two leading cross-correlations is not statistically significant. Hence, viewing the leadership-long cycle and external shock models as "tournament" co-winners, the outcome suggests that long-term, Kondratieff waves, major economic depressions and booms, technological innovations, and the residual effects of major wars are reasonable places to look for assistance in explaining the vicissitudes of systemic protectionism. Thus, we have found additional support for hypothesis H9. Still, it is obvious that there are limitations to the

TABLE 5.5.   Cross-Correlations between Tariffs and Protectionism Predictions at the Systemic Level, 1800–1974

Models	Lag(–1)	Lag(0)	Lead(+1)
Hegemonic Trajectory			
Variation A	0.071	0.118	0.140
Variation B	0.452	0.443	0.535
Variation C	0.314	0.438	0.353
External shock	0.733	0.645	0.584
Long cycle	0.293	0.261	0.079
Structural incentives	0.187	0.006	−0.092
Imports/GNP	0.051	0.054	0.003
Leadership-long cycle	0.564	0.723	0.564
Structural shift	0.251	0.360	0.161

Note: The hypothesis that the cross-correlation is 0 is rejected at the 5 percent level if the sample cross-correlation is greater than 0.274, and at the 10 percent level if it is greater than 0.215. However, the full 1800–1974 time span applies only to the external shock, structural incentives, and leadership-long cycle models. Statistically significant cross-correlations need to be higher for the other models that encompass shorter time spans.

explanatory power of both models. Neither one accounts for more than 50 percent of the variance.

Does adding the 1975–89 period alter these findings? Not much, although the exact outcome depends on which way the most recent period is coded. If this period is seen as one of increasing protectionism, thanks to increases in NTB activity, the leadership-long cycle and external shock models do equally well and at the same coefficient level. The only real difference is that the Gilpin and Wallerstein hegemonic trajectory coefficients improve (to about the 0.5 level with no lag), elevating their performance to second place. If the 1975–89 period is viewed as one of decreasing protectionism, the external shock and leadership-long cycle models still do best with slightly lower coefficients (0.667 for external shock with one lag and 0.6 for leadership-long cycle at zero lag). The runner-up is the structural shift model (0.469 with zero lag).

Table 5.6 summarizes the relevant cross-correlations for leader behavior, less any coefficients for the averaged imports/GNP predictions that, in our view, cannot be expected to address systemic leader behavior. Only four models produce significant cross-correlations for leader behavior: Gilpin's hegemonic trajectory, external shock, long cycles, and leadership-long cycle. Moreover, all of the reported cross-correlations are smaller than those obtained at the systemic level. Once again, the differences between the winner of the tournament (Gilpin's hegemonic trajectory with no lag) and

TABLE 5.6. Cross-Correlations between Tariffs and Protectionism Predictions at the Systemic Leader Level, 1800–1974

Models	Lag(−1)	Lag(0)	Lead(+1)
Hegemonic Trajectory			
Variation A	0.087	−0.062	0.087
Variation B	0.226	0.219	0.232
Variation C	0.374	0.510	0.399
External shock	0.343	0.324	0.263
Long cycle	0.329	0.315	0.224
Structural incentives	0.076	0.080	−0.144
Leadership-long cycle	0.372	0.286	0.312
Structural shift	0.087	0.139	0.119

Note: The hypothesis that the cross-correlation is 0 is rejected at the 5 percent level if the sample cross-correlation is greater than 0.274, and at the 10 percent level if it is greater than 0.215. However, the full 1800–1974 period applies only to the external shock, structural incentives, and leadership-long cycle models. Statistically significant cross-correlations need to be higher for the other models that encompass shorter periods.

the next two runners-up (leadership-long cycle with a one interval lag and external shock with no lag) are not statistically significant

Differentially coding the most recent period (1975–89) does not alter table 5.6's leader outcome any more than the systemic level outcome was affected. An increasing protectionism stance leaves Gilpin's hegemonic trajectory in first place and moves the long cycle model into second place, followed by the leadership-long cycle and external shock schedules. A decreasing protectionism interpretation leaves table 5.6's initial outcome completely unchanged.

Since the cross-correlations at the leader's level of analysis are less favorable to all of the tested models, the leader's protectionist behavior presumably is subject to influences that none of the individual models captures all that well. Alternatively put, the models do much better at the aggregate level. Various factors such as business cycles, free trade ideology, and domestic politics are unlikely to work in a uniform fashion in different national settings. This observation applies to the last two systemic leaders with their protectionist behavior characterized by long and well-known lags in the sense that their economic lead within the world economy preceded the decision to significantly reduce tariff levels by roughly a generation. Both have also displayed an overt reluctance to abandon their free trade stance despite the erosion of their leading positions. It follows as well that the models that do best at the systemic level and less well at the leader level are apt to perform even more poorly in attempts to predict the tariff behavior of other states in the world economy. Whether the converse holds—that models that do poorly at the systemic and leadership levels do better with the fluctuations of certain states—remains to be seen. It is clear that the models that do best at the systemic leader level (e.g., Gilpin's hegemonic trajectory) do not necessarily fare equally well at the systemic level.

Assessing the Results

Why should the leadership-long cycle and external shock models perform better, at least at the systemic level, than the others? One provisional conclusion, argued explicitly in chapter 4, is that the processes they emphasize are important to the dynamics of protectionism. Whichever model performed best, other things being equal, would appear to offer the superior, if not necessarily a completely comprehensive, explanation. It is also not coincidental to the outcome that the leadership-long cycle and external shock models are related. The real difference between them is that the shock model views wars and depressions as exogenous and relatively random processes. In the leadership-long cycle model, wars and depressions are endogenous and cyclical. Nor are the shocks equally "external" for all actors. In the leadership-long cycle model, the external shocks originate in one economy's success in developing radical innovations and diffuse outward in a regularized fashion. Some of the major wars are closely related to the instability in the systemic pecking order fostered by the periodic economic revolutions. The major depressions (such as those beginning in 1873, 1929–30, or 1973) are the troughs of the long wave.

The outcome in table 5.5 probably is more understandable if we also keep in mind that the leadership-long cycle model claims to incorporate or be able to incorporate several of the other postulated dynamics (hegemonic trajectories, long cycles, structural incentives, and economic growth), as well as encompassing some of the other arguments in the protectionist literature (such as surplus capacity and even ideology to a lesser extent). Parsimony need not always be a virtue in seeking to explain the complexities of international political economy. In this sense, the leadership-long cycle model is a truly multivariate model of protectionism.

Long wave models also have a built-in explanation for partial explanatory failures. Long waves of economic growth, unlike some other systemic attributes and processes we discussed, clearly have differential impacts. Economies on different parts of the technological gradient will not be affected identically by growth discontinuities generated at the upper end of the gradient. It is the general systemic context with which all actors must all cope in some way that changes. Actors in different circumstances may choose to respond in different ways with different levels of protectionism to roughly identical long wave impacts, depending on their access to resources, their institutions, their political leadership, and their ability to exploit opportunities for movement along the technological gradient. Good examples are the rich variety in politicoeconomic responses to the worldwide depressions of the early 1870s and 1930s discussed by Gourevitch (1986).

A third reason for the superior leadership-long cycle performance is that it avoids some of the major weaknesses of its rivals by not assuming: (1) that the system and other states will always respond to hegemonic preferences voluntarily or with the help of coercion (as in the hegemonic trajectory model); (2) that protectionist impulses are contingent solely on the interaction between idiosyncratic changes in the external environment and structural shifts within the internal environment (as in the structural shift model); (3) that major wars and depressions are random occurrences (as implied in Fischer's external shock model); or (4) that behavior is strongly contingent on permissive systemic attributes without anchoring the systemic changes to changes in domestic processes (as in Frederick's long cycle model). Additionally, the leadership-long cycle model, like Frederick's long cycle model but unlike Krasner's hegemonic stability model, Bairoch's focus on unilinear economic development, or Fischer's nontreatment of hegemonic leads, includes two peaks in the leader's performance. A double-peaked hegemonic trajectory does a better job of explaining the fluctuations in protectionism of the last two centuries than does a single-peaked view of ascent and decline, because the double-peaked approach is seeking to capture the fundamental motors of change underlying ascent and decline while the one-peaked approach accepts it as given. Another way of putting these observations is that the leadership-long cycle model has a greater capacity for encompassing the complexities of the politicoeconomic phenomena that determine protectionism.

Long Waves and External Shocks at the Microlevel

Our empirical results show that the leadership-long cycle and the related external shock models of protectionism can encompass the complexities of systemic politicoeconomic interactions and structural change. However, these models, while still outperforming many of the other models, do less well at the leader level. Presumably, the politicoeconomic processes associated with the structure of international trade at disaggregated levels are more complex and not necessarily uniform across different actors. Their explanation probably requires elements that are not present in the models that do best at the systemic level.

Another complexity associated with the leadership-long cycle and external shock models of protectionism concerns the variable responses to similar cues within the general context of external shocks and long wave up- and downswings. While knowing the rhythm of the economic growth long wave or the timing of the shocks is useful information, it is not enough to account fully for, or to explain, all the variance in observed protectionist behavior. Different actors may respond differentially to the same long wave/external shock.

The weaker performance of the long wave/external shock approaches to protectionism at subsystemic levels may be linked to the incentives they relate to actors that are less than fully microgrounded. Three examples focusing on the leadership-long cycle model should help illustrate this observation. First, according to the leadership-long cycle model, when the returns from technological innovations are high, the innovating pioneer should reduce its trade barriers unilaterally in order to reduce its import costs. However, traditional trade theory contends that a country with monopoly power can maximize its welfare by imposing an optimal tariff that is greater than zero. In the real world, the lead economy is slow to reduce its trade barriers, but it also eschews the optimal tariff path. There must be additional intervening variables at work here, perhaps along the lines of Krasner's institutional lags or Bairoch's structural shifts, that need further theoretical attention.

Second, the leadership-long cycle model predicts that when the returns from the new technologies diminish, production overcapacity develops. But diminishing returns should be a market signal to reduce production. Why do producers choose to ignore these signals? Must we assume that producers are nonrational or that markets fail to clear with some regularity? The leadership-long cycle model's implicit assumption about overcapacity requires further consideration, elaboration, and possibly some alteration.

Third, the leadership-long cycle model is predicated on specific approaches to economic growth and trade. Long-term economic growth is postulated as occurring in spurts driven by radical innovations. International trade is then based to a great extent on lags in technology diffusion from the lead economy to other parts of the world economy. But there are certainly a number of other models of economic growth and trade that might have some relevance. More theoretical and empirical work is necessary to explain why the effects predicted by other models, some of which are competitive while others may be complementary, are either secondary or absent. More attention to the growth and trade motors of the leadership-long cycle model might lead to richer explanations of leader and follower behavior.

To fully capture the different state-level responses to the signals of the long wave, one must be prepared to deal differentially with preferences and incentive structures affected by the discontinuities inherent to the nature of long-term growth processes, along with the derivative changes in leadership structure. To capture the oscillations in leader-follower behavior, for example, it is necessary to theorize at a lower level of analysis than the current long wave model of protectionism. What we need is theory construction centered around the following issues: (1) How, why, and when do domestic agents and institutions respond to long-term economic fluctuations? (2) What determines differential responses to similar systemic signals? (3) Why does the aggregated response to long wave signals differ from leader and follower responses?[16]

We do not argue that all actors should be expected to react to long wave/external shock perturbations in precisely the same way and at the same time. Differences in geographical location, technological gradient position, resource endowment, and politicoeconomic structure presumably intervene. This is precisely why the many different models of protectionism extant in the literature continue to appeal. They highlight various aspects of a complex problem. The theoretical challenge is to integrate these parts into a compelling whole. Now that we have additional empirical reason to suspect that explanations involving long waves and other external shocks are on the right track, the trick is to develop more precise theoretical generalizations about, and appropriate empirical testing of, the variance in protectionist behavior within the systemic context of long-term economic fluctuations.

Chapters 6 and 7 undertake this task—to wit, to develop more precise theoretical and empirical testing of the relationships between protectionist behavior and long-term fluctuations in economic processes. Chapter 6 tackles this subject head-on by investigating whether increases or decreases in tariff protectionism influence the expansion or contraction of trade in the long term. We suggest two perspectives to understand the relationship between protectionism and trade. In the standard, short-term economic analysis, protectionism reduces trade. In the long term, chapter 6 argues that the causality flows primarily from trade expansion and contraction to protectionism. Empirically, the chapter finds that changes in tariff levels can make a difference in the short run—either encouraging or discouraging trade depending on their direction. But, in the long term, a more fundamental economic growth process influences the political seductiveness of tariff-level increases and decreases. A fair amount of evidence is found to show that in the long term, trade antecedes protectionism, and it does so especially at the systemic level and in the histories of the system leaders.

Part III. Protectionism, Trade, and Openness

6. Tariffs and Trade Fluctuations: Does Protectionism Matter as Much as We Think?

A respectable proportion of the theoretical and empirical concern in international political economy over the last twenty-five years has revolved around questions pertaining to the relationships among power concentration and its behavioral implications (hegemony/leadership), political intervention in economic processes (for example, tariffs), and fluctuations in economic growth, trade, and systemic openness.[1] Invariably, it is assumed that political intervention makes some measurable difference in economic activity. But is this a reasonable assumption? In particular, can we really be confident that increases and decreases in tariff protectionism influence the expansion and contraction of international trade?

The principal influences on tariffs were found to be long waves and external shocks (chap. 5). It could be that long economic growth waves drive both trade and tariffs. If so, it may be that the influence of tariffs on trade volumes is only minor, with the real link being between growth and trade. Then again, it is also conceivable that tariffs have an additional impact on trade volumes that compounds the extent of fluctuation.

The question of whether tariffs impact trade may seem nonsensical to some readers. The safest assumption one might think entertainable is that tariffs are imposed to constrain the volume of imports by increasing their cost to domestic consumers. Therefore, the higher the tariff barriers, the greater the intended effect in decreasing the amount of trade—ceteris paribus. Partially as a consequence, we have arguments about whether and how the presence of hegemons or system leaders is conducive to lowering tariffs and stimulating freer trade. Alternatively, we ask, How does one go about maintaining open trading regimes in the absence of a powerful system leader?[2]

To a considerable extent, these debates presume that protectionism is a powerful threat to the stable functioning and prosperity of the world economy. It is often assumed, for instance, that the remarkable prosperity of the post–World War II era is in part attributable to an expansion in trade linked, in turn, to the GATT-led significant lowering of tariffs. The threat of increased protectionism therefore invokes the specter of tariff wars and retaliatory spirals that would lead directly to dramatically reduced levels of trade and economic growth rates.

But what if the instinctive assumptions are wrong in some respects? The argument here is not that changing tariffs are unlikely to have some short-term effects on trade volume. It would be illogical to assume otherwise. Yet the underlying assumption regarding this short-term behavior is that political decision makers use tariffs to intervene in ongoing economic processes to protect national production from external competition when they feel that legislative barriers are necessary or appropriate. It seems equally unlikely that such political intervention occurs randomly or in a vacuum.

However, from a longer-run perspective, it can be argued that protectionism tends to be as much, if not more, a political response to long-term, declining economic growth possibilities than a short-term way of gaining an advantage over the competitive field. For instance, increasing protectionism in the early 1930s may have made the Depression worse but it is not usually cited, at least by economic historians, as a primary cause of the deteriorating economic conditions.[3]

We have already discussed a short-term/long-term interpretation of protectionism (chap. 4) in which we suggested that the leadership-long cycle perspective serves as a common denominator unifying all the theories and models that we reviewed. The contrast drawn here between short- and long-term perspectives continues this approach. In the short term, we should expect changes in the levels of protectionism to influence the volume of trade, or tariffs $\rightarrow$ trade (that is, tariffs influence trade), just as we might expect short-term declines in economic growth due to business cycles to encourage protectionist lobbying.[4] In the long term, however, we think it is declining growth and trade prospects that stimulate protectionism, or trade $\rightarrow$ tariffs. Our question is, Which way does the causal arrow point? Does trade drive protectionism, or is it the other way around? Of course, it may be that different circumstances warrant different answers to this question. That is, the systemic or aggregate answer may not be mirrored exactly in the experiences of all national subsystems—some of which will be responding to different sets of incentives. There is also ample room for reciprocal behavior—that is, trade $\rightarrow$ tariffs *and* tariffs $\rightarrow$ trade.

Tariffs and Trade Fluctuations

We elaborate two interpretations—one for the short term that seems compatible with a number of approaches to protectionism questions and one for the long term. For us, short-term dynamics are fairly quick and manifest themselves within at most five to ten years. The long term, in contrast, is measured in decades and is characterized by relatively slow dynamics. Economics and political science, by disciplinary inclination, are more oriented toward capturing the former, relatively more static, types of dynamics than they are the latter. Analyses of trade policy provide particularly good examples in that long-term analyses, or even examinations of long time-series of pertinent data, in both economics and in political science, are rare. The question that remains open is whether we are missing something by confining our attention exclusively to short-run windows on the phenomena of interest.

The short- and long-term perspectives lead to testable predictions about the relationship between trade and protectionism. Empirical tests of these expectations are executed using serial trade and protectionism data (1854–1990) from the five leading economic powers of the past two centuries: Britain, France, the United States, Germany, Japan, and the interdependent system they create in the aggregate. The test results support the interpretation that argues that trade $\rightarrow$ tariffs or protectionism. It is by no means clear that in the long run protectionism matters as much as most scholars assume. At the very least, expanding the window for observation reveals trade-tariff dynamics that might go undetected otherwise.

Short- and Long-Term Theoretical Perspectives

Neoclassical trade theory espouses free trade as the preferred approach to international economic competition. If each state acknowledges its endowment-based comparative advantage and focuses on producing and exporting the commodities in which it enjoys an edge in efficiency, the resulting division of factors of production and international exchange of goods will produce a collectively optimal welfare outcome in which each state makes absolute gains relative to no trade. That does not mean that the gains from trade for every state will necessarily be the same, or that the relative gains from trade may not differ among traders. By "cheating" on their endowment base, nations may increase their trade gains, assuming others continue to follow the policy of free trade.

This argument is predicated on the assumption that it makes sense for all actors to accept their natural endowment fate and to not attempt to improve upon it. Of course, if this were the case, the world economy might still be predominantly agrarian in nature. Things change, and people often disagree on what is optimal. Uneven development leads to some economies outperforming others. Situations are created in which domestic producers can no longer compete with more technologically advanced rivals. Uneven endowments, a late start, and/or the fear of falling behind in international economic competition can lead to political resistance in the form of political coercion and/or national barriers to free international economic competition. Political agents work to set trade barriers as their interests dictate. Depending on the argument, system leaders, small states, and export-oriented firms support free trade, non–system leaders tend to free ride, large states are apt to rely on economic muscle to get what they want, late developers need protection for their infant industries, and domestically oriented firms and labor in sunset industries seek legislative protection from external competition.

We are not interested in penetrating too deeply into the theoretical labyrinth of competing interpretations of trade behavior in international political economy. The bottom line of these arguments is that political agents seek to raise or lower tariffs to protect their interests. Whether tariffs get raised or lowered depends on whose interests and political clout are paramount. If tariffs are raised, it is presumed that the threatened interests are protected to some extent and that trade volumes will decline. The more numerous, widespread, politically powerful, and organized the threatened interests, the greater will be the consequent decline in trade volume.

A dependence on political agency is not in question, as political actors do attempt to raise and lower tariffs. The question is to what degree the context in which these attempts are made matters. Some analysts peg tariff changes to short-term, national business cycles. Short-term economic deterioration leads to increased attempts to protect threatened economic interests. In contrast, where there is economic prosperity there are fewer threatened interests and, therefore, fewer attempts at protection. Other analysts think that the presence (absence) of a hegemon/system leader should directly, perhaps subject to some lag, translate into lowered (increased) protectionism and greater (lesser) trade openness because free trade serves the hegemon's interests. These perspectives tend to identify relatively straightforward contexts in which behaviors operate. Economic prosperity comes and goes. When it goes, particular interests are roused into action. So, too, with hegemons. When they are present, the system is expected to respond to their preferences. When they are absent, national actors may act on their own preferences, which, often as not, means more restrictions on trade.

While short-term contexts may complicate the causal diagram, the expectation is that contextual changes alter the immediate incentives for raising or lowering tariffs, which leads to trade contraction or expansion. Although none of these models is implausible, a longer-term perspective on the impact of economic growth suggests a different model—one in which trade fluctuations either precede tariff fluctuations or in which tariffs do not have much impact on trade.

Focusing on these two causal chains, it is possible to generate long-term expectations that contradict the short-term hypotheses. The long-term expectation (economic growth fluctuations → trade fluctuations → tariff fluctuations) assumes that changes in long-term economic growth and trade prospects are the contextual source of stimulation for tariff lobbying and adjustments. If economic growth is relatively random—a few good years are interspersed with a few bad years in no set pattern—the short-term perspective seems plausible. If, on the other hand, economies experience longer-term phases in which prosperity or depression tends to predominate, as illustrated by the vivid contrast between the two decades following World War II and the decade immediately preceding that same war, we might anticipate economic growth and trade to Granger cause tariffs as agents react to the changing prospects for long-term growth.[5]

Other things being equal, in phases of prosperity, trade should be expanding, and in phases of depression, trade should be contracting. Such a relationship suggests that protectionism policies that did not address long-term economic growth prospects should not be expected to intervene in the linkage between long-term economic growth and trade. That is, it would seem unlikely that countervailing tariffs (e.g., tariff cuts in years of depression) alone would be likely to have all that much impact on growth and trade, or even to be politically conceivable. The more likely expectation is that tariffs would follow the long-term trend in growth/trade. In terms of causality, we would expect the trade → tariff relationship to be stronger than the tariff → trade relationship.

Other things are not always equal, and some exceptions come immediately to mind. One exception would be the Listian protectionism sought by late developers when it is thought that development cannot be attained without substantial political insulation.[6] Another exception is the case of small economies that are highly dependent on trade. High trade dependency, conceivably, weakens the political temptation to tamper with tariff levels. In cases in which tariffs did not vary much across time, there is no reason to anticipate a significant trade → tariffs, or tariffs → trade relationship.

A third major exception is the case of system leaders who have espoused and "internalized" free trade ideas after developing a technological and industrial lead. Some lag should be expected between the initial emergence of technological predominance, expanding trade, and the political triumph of free trade advocates. Similarly, when that technological lead is no longer in evidence, the free trade ideology may have become so firmly entrenched that there should also be a lag between relative decline and the abandonment of free trade policies. If these phases are examined as a unit, the different subphase relationships (trade expanding, high tariffs; trade expanding, decreasing tariffs; trade contracting, low tariffs; trade contracting, high tariffs) may cancel one another's effect. Thus, we might expect a lesser likelihood of a systematic relationship between trade and tariffs to emerge in the case of system leaders than might otherwise be the case. Given the crucial effect of the lead economy on the system, we anticipate that systemic trade will behave along the same lines that characterize the system leader cases.

Finally, followers, those economies that have the most potential for emulating the system leader's innovations, will react both to the success of the pioneering leader and to long-term economic growth fluctuations. They may attempt to emulate the system leader's free trade approach, but they also learn that lowered tariffs weaken their defenses from the leader's spectacular economic success and increasing competition from other follower economies. Thus, the incentives for follower protectionism should oscillate and lead to fluctuations in tariff levels that are sometimes consonant with trade expansion/contraction and sometimes opposed to it. While this suggests that tariffs may cause trade in these cases as tariffs are set to induce growth, it may also suggest another case in which the trade-tariff relationship is weakened by mixed behavior over time when those phases are analyzed as one unit.[7]

In sum, over the long term, protectionism is less likely to drive trade in the leader cases and more likely to do so in the follower cases. It is conceivable, however, that no trade-protectionism relationship will emerge in the leader cases. The seesawing long-term processes in follower economies may also tend to weaken the long-term relationship between trade and protectionism. Long-term systemic trade is expected to behave, vis-à-vis the trade-protectionism relationship, along the lines of the system leader cases. Our approach to capturing the long term in this chapter will stress opening the window of observation. Instead of looking at a few years, as in the spirit of comparative statics analysis, we will use relatively long time-series to better allow the long-term dynamics to display themselves.

But Where's the Microdynamic?

Echoing the onetime commercial/political complaint "where's the beef?" it has become customary to insist upon an explicit microdynamic explanation of politicoeconomic phenomena. In its absence, many analysts would deny the presence or possibility of an explanation. While this supposition remains dubious, it is worthwhile to contemplate the conceivable micro-dynamics associated with the relationship between trade and protection-ism. What we need is a long-run dynamic, because a long wave explanation does not necessarily conflict with short-term dynamics (as in the case of protectionism driven by business cycle fluctuations) that can be encom-passed by longer-run tendencies.

It is not necessary to look far. At first glance, Ronald Rogowski's (1989) well-received adaptation of the Stolper-Samuelson theorem seems to fit the bill in terms of supplying a long-term dynamic for trade-driven, political reactions to the appeal of protectionism. Nevertheless, problems emerge when we attempt to link this approach to the long wave perspective.

Rogowski's formulation has four parts.

1. Technological innovation in transportation and hegemony lower the costs of trade.
2. Lowered costs of trade increase trade.
3. Increased trade alters domestic political alignments/cleavages (as filtered by factor endowments).
4. Domestic political alignments/cleavages produce differential pro-tectionism preferences.

The first leg of this argument is compatible with a long wave interpretation, even though the interpretation regarding the significance of innovations is more selective than we would prefer. Rogowski chooses to emphasize inno-vation in transportation forms (railroads, steamships, canals, oil tankers) and their effects on lowering transportation costs and expanding trade. Some long wave analysts prefer to emphasize the transitions to and from energy eras, as in the movement from wind to coal/steam and petroleum as the defining characteristics of long waves of economic growth. Even if more emphasis is put on technology, it is difficult to miss the connection between sequential clusters of new technology and their changing demands on raw materials and energy sources. Railroads in the nineteenth century and automobiles in the twentieth bestowed premiums on steam and petroleum respectively. But these energy/technological transitions do more than merely lower the costs of doing business. They also fundamentally alter who does business best and what types of transactions are conducted.

Rogowski's lowered protection costs associated with periods of hegemony, or in our terms, systemic leadership, are described as having similar, cost-reducing impacts on trade expansion. Such a perspective suggests that the hegemon's primary function is to lower protection costs. But that overlooks entirely the reason why one state becomes hegemonic. It does so because it generates new technological innovations that transform the world economy. Not only is the hegemonic pioneer transformed into a preponderant economic powerhouse, the patterns of trade are also transformed. Automobiles and petroleum, for instance, were not major trading items in the nineteenth century. Computer hardware and software were not major components of international trade in the first half of the twentieth century.

Rogowski does argue, as do we, that trade fluctuations can influence political behavior as opposed to focusing only on how political behavior influences trade. How various political systems react to trade expansions and contractions, from his perspective, depends primarily on the way in which national factor endowments are combined. The Stolper-Samuelson theorem, which is a direct implication of the Heckscher-Ohlin theory, stipulates that protection will benefit (harm) factor owners and producers associated with factors that are relatively scarce (abundant). Thus, a political system characterized by abundant labor and capital and scarce land should lead to an urban-rural cleavage, with the urban coalition (labor and capital) favoring less protectionism. A different political system in which labor is abundant and capital and land are scarce should lead to a fundamental class cleavage with upper-class land and capital owners favoring more protectionism.

Who wins or loses these politicoeconomic struggles is not predicted by Rogowski. Interestingly, he regards the outcomes as short-term phenomena that are also subject to variables exogenous to his theory, and he treats the Stolper-Samuelson dynamic as long-term in effect. But if the Stolper-Samuelson logic is a long-term dynamic, we should be able to make equally long-term predictions about protectionism outcomes. Political systems characterized by dominant coalitions that favor more (less) protectionism should move toward a more (less) protectionist stance in the long term, other things being equal. And we might extrapolate, using the assumptions employed by Rogowski, that more (less) protectionist stances lead to greater (lesser) protectionism impacts on trade—again, ceteris paribus. But here is where one begins to encounter translation problems in attempting to apply the Rogowski framework to our interest in the long-run protectionism-trade relationship.

To be sure, there are operational problems in distinguishing between the relative scarcity and abundance of factors of production. Just where the appropriate thresholds should be is not clear. But the most serious problem is that the Stolper-Samuelson theorem is conceivably useful for long-run predictions only if the factor endowments and the production technologies are correctly specified. It is blind to the distinction between pioneers and followers (or uneven development) and assumes they are fairly static in their distribution. These are not minor obstacles from a long wave perspective, or, for that matter, from other, purely economic, dynamic perspectives such as the product cycle and technology gap models in international trade and endogenous growth theories.

One problem with distinguishing classically among capital, labor, and land is that the distinctions may simply be too gross to be all that useful. For instance, a long wave interpretation would stress the distinction between sunrise and sunset capital and their differential orientations toward protectionism. Rogowski's framework incorporates a corollary that is somewhat similar but still not quite the same thing. It emphasizes the abundance of capital as opposed to its multiplier effects on the economy. If capital is scarce, industries will be as protectionist as they are capital intensive. If capital is not scarce, industries will be as free trade–oriented as they are capital intensive.

From our perspective, the problem is that new, leading sectors may or may not be more capital intensive than older sectors. But even if new leading sectors are capital intensive in their formative stages, the capital scarcity problem (for major economies at least) is more likely to involve investment trade-offs between old and new sectors. The lure of high profits should benefit new industries over old. It should also make some difference where the capital is located. What should be significant for attitudes toward protectionism is whether sectors are new and leading at home and abroad. New and leading sectors in follower economies are more likely to prefer protection initially than are new and leading sectors in lead economies that face little competition initially as pioneers. Hence, the dynamic of the scope, type, and geographic location of economic activity leading to trade is crucial in our perspective.

The static problem is also captured implicitly by Rogowski's capital scarcity corollary. What is scarce or abundant changes over time, especially once the observation window opens to include long periods of time (as in our study). For instance, German land was considered relatively abundant (by Rogowski) until the North American grain-growing areas entered the world economy in the last quarter of the nineteenth century. In the long-run explanation of protectionism, it is these evolutionary trajectories that are probably more important than how we characterize capital-labor-land distributions at any given point in time. Thus it is movement toward some particular distribution that may be more predictive in the long run than knowing how to characterize an economy at time t and then expecting its political behavior to align eventually with this characterization by time $t +$ 1. Hence when Rogowski argues that there is complete consensus on whether the Stolper-Samuelson theorem holds for the long run, we must demur. It derives from the Heckscher-Ohlin theory, which is itself static. The Stolper-Samuelson logic can be a long-term dynamic only if everything that counts is stable. Otherwise, it is in fact a short-term dynamic. Moreover, it is probably the differential pace of the trajectories over time that makes it so difficult to predict political outcomes in the short term as well. Hence, it is difficult to guess which way the evolving trajectories are heading without the benefit of hindsight.

Rogowski was not particularly interested in predicting short-term political outcomes, nor are we. At the same time, it seems fair to say that Rogowski was more interested in the forms that domestic cleavages/alignments may take than we are, while we are more interested in the trade-protectionism relationship outcome than he was (at least in 1989). This is not the appropriate place to test the relative effects of general commercial/industrial innovations, innovations in transportation costs, and the political order wrought by system leaders on trade expansions—although it is certainly an interesting question. Nor do we have any disagreement with Rogowski's theoretical assumptions: (1) victims (beneficiaries) of change will seek to retard (accelerate) it; (2) groups with expanding (contracting) wealth will be able to expand (forced to relinquish) political influence; and (3) political entrepreneurs are capable of overcoming obstacles to change as political preferences evolve. That leaves "only" the Stolper-Samuelson theorem as a microdynamic sticking point.

We acknowledge and appreciate the seductive insights about coalition formation that can be derived from the Stolper-Samuelson-Rogowski framework. But our explanatory interests are less ambitious. It suffices for our purposes to argue that pioneering innovation in the lead economy (the leader in technological development) privileges the relative place of capital within its national factor endowment. This privileging process is gradual or dynamic and has been facilitated in the past by civil warfare that worked toward deemphasizing the political clout of land ownership. These changes facilitate the gradual emergence of political coalitions that favor and initiate decreasing levels of protectionism for extended periods of time.

The ascendancy and maintenance of political coalitions based to some extent on new, leading commercial/industrial sectors and favoring reduced levels of protectionism in follower economies is a less straightforward process. Technological change in follower economies will need protection from the earlier technological change in the pioneer economy. The political influence of older sectors is also more likely to prove resistant to change, especially if the new sectors are slow to emerge. Historically, the land factor, in particular, is less likely to have been subordinated in civil warfare. Old capital is also more likely to possess strong staying power. These characteristics suggest that protectionism battles are more likely to resemble a seesawing process, with follower economies moving back and forth between stronger and weaker protectionist stances in reaction to waves of technological change originating elsewhere.

Accordingly, we anticipate less effective protectionism in the cases of system leaders and more effective protectionism to be manifested in the cases of follower economies. We think, therefore, that trade is more likely to drive protectionism in the former cases and the reverse relationship should be more likely to prevail in the follower cases. The one caveat to this prediction is that the seesawing processes in follower economies may result in periods of trade → protectionism and protectionism → trade that, when examined over long periods of time, could tend to cancel out the different types of relationships. The statistical outcome may simply be no relationship between trade and protectionism. More generally, since systemic trade in our perspective is considerably dependent on the successes of the system leader, we would expect the trade → protectionism relationship to be stronger at the aggregate or systemic level than the protectionism → trade relationship.

In making this argument, we are doing three things to the Stolper-Samuelson-Rogowski thesis. First, we effectively privilege capital or new, innovative capital over land and labor considerations, which are all given equal significance. Second, we insert and give considerable weight to the role and timing of uneven development. We are not suggesting that the logic of coalition-making works differently in leaders and followers. Rather, the timing of technological innovation makes different coalitions, in addition to whatever factor-endowment differences may be significant, more likely in follower economies than in lead economies. Third, we attempt to avoid the static, snapshot-like, cul-de-sac of the Stolper-Samuelson-Rogowski factor-endowment argument in favor of explicitly emphasizing the evolution of technological innovation over time.

Our microdynamic argument can be summarized thus.

1. Technological innovation expands trade.
2. Expanded trade influences domestic political cleavages/alignments as filtered by leader/follower status and by weighted relative domestic factor endowments.
3. Domestic political cleavages/alignments, leader/follower status, and weighted relative factor endowments lead to differential protectionism preferences.
4. Differential protectionism preferences generate differential trade-protectionism relationships.

In this chapter, we do not test all of the aspects of this protectionism argument. The specific hypotheses that we examine here are restricted to the following two.

H10: In the short term, protectionist behavior influences the volume of trade; in the long term, declining growth and trade influence the probability of protectionism.

H11: The long-term influence (trade → protectionism) is stronger than the short-term influence (protectionism → trade).

We limit ourselves to these more obvious outcomes of our argument not because they are easily observable but so that our present findings can feed into the model-building process at work in the other chapters of this analysis. An alternative approach, focused on cleavages/alignments, would require a much different methodology (case studies) and would take us fairly far afield of our current concerns. A more ambitious exploration of our amendment of the Rogowski argument must await a different and future venue.

Testing Considerations

Research Design Considerations

Since part of our question amounts to determining whether or to what extent protectionism antecedes trade or trade antecedes protectionism, we employ Granger causality tests. As we have explained in chapter 2, causality is of course a controversial topic in the social sciences, but a minimal assumption underlying the statement that X "causes" Y is that X precedes Y. If they are coterminous in time and both change values at the same time or if changes in Y actually precede changes in X, we would be unlikely to insist that X impacted on Y. In this respect, Granger causality tests can be useful in delineating and/or ruling out (in)conceivable patterns of antecedence—that is, establishing which variable, if any, came first. At the same time, Granger causality tests are unlikely to generate the last word on the protectionism-trade question. The statistical outcomes that are produced should always be viewed as preliminary to the development of more fully specified models. However, our immediate goal is not one of creating a fully specified model of the variables related to protectionism and trade. Therefore, the preliminary statistical outcomes associated with Granger causality tests should suffice for our more modest questions pertaining to antecedence patterns linking trade and protectionism.

Several technical issues, about which econometricians continue to debate, are important in that they could have some influence on the Granger causality results. These issues include the choice of a distributed lag length (Geweke 1984; Kang 1985), the stationarity of the time-series (Pierce and Haugh 1977; Feige and Pierce 1979; Nelson and Kang 1984; Kang 1985; McCallum 1993; Hamilton 1994), the adequacy of the test's specification (Pierce 1977; Feige and Peirce 1979; Granger 1980), and the role of ARIMA processes (Freeman 1983) (see chap. 3 and app. A). In our view, the significance of these various issues, for the most part, continues to be contested, but acknowledging them alerts us to the several possible limitations of Granger testing and our need to be sensitive to their possible impact on analyses such as ours. Limitations notwithstanding, we feel that Granger causality testing retains considerable utility in empirically assessing theories and generalizations about patterns of antecedence.

Our specific research design is conservative. We determine whether time-series include unit roots according to the results of a majority of the tests. To deal with possible nonstationarity, we employ first differences of trade and protectionism series and report causality results only when the error terms are white noise. Finally, since the literature on the appropriate lag lengths to be used in a Granger test is subject to continuing discussion and multiple preferences, we systematically try many lag lengths.

Data and Indicators

We assume that the actions of some countries exert a greater politicoeconomic effect on the world economy than do others. We have constructed a longitudinal trade data set that encompasses five of the most significant traders (Britain, France, Germany, the United States, and Japan) and allows us to create an aggregation that approximates the world trading system.[8] In many years, these five states represent more than 60 percent of world trade. But we need to be careful in assuming that the trade behavior of a few of the most powerful states can stand in for the rest of the world's.

Accordingly, we have gone to some pains to collect data on imports and exports among the five as opposed to simply relying on their total trade volumes. Otherwise, we would be including some behavior that needs to be kept separate because it is part of the overall protectionist-trade historical story. For example, in the second half of the nineteenth century Britain shifted some of its trade away from increasingly protected European markets to its own imperial markets. Such a shift would not necessarily be detectable in total trade volume but should be observable in a series restricted to trade among the major economic powers. While some bilateral trade data are available before 1854, only after that date are we able to obtain sufficient serial information identifying the specific trade partners that we seek on an annual basis. Thus, our six trade series (one for each country and an aggregated one) extend from 1854 to 1990.[9]

Trade data are known to be noisy, reflecting the effects of inflation, economic recessions and growth, commodity price changes, and fluctuations of exchange rates. To simplify our conversion problems, we normalize each annual trade datum by gross domestic product. Assuming that recessions, economic booms, and inflation affect GDP and total trade in similar ways, missing variables are less likely to influence our results. Assuming competitive markets, price fluctuations will similarly affect GDP and trade, and therefore their impact on the trade ration should be small.[10]

To construct an aggregate index, we first computed each of the five countries' share of world trade and then recalculated the proportional shares based on a new denominator that is derived from the five-country total. Since there is a variety of dyadic imbalances in exports and imports at any given point in time, we rely exclusively on total trade (the sum of imports and exports) among the five. Next, the ratio of trade to GDP of each country is weighted by the recalculated "world" trade share and then summed over the five countries for each year in the series, thereby generating a weighted, five-power trade series that we believe captures a respectable proportion of world trade behavior.

The protectionism measure we use in this examination is based on an 1800–1990 average nominal tariff series previously generated for the five major trading states (chap. 5). As was explained there, the basic argument is that while no perfect measure of protectionist barriers exists, more direct measures are superior to more indirect measures such as regionalization proclivities or imports as a proportion of national income. In principle, the validity of average nominal tariffs is threatened by the possibilities that effective tariffs may be much different from nominal tariffs and that goods subject to very high tariffs receive little weight in this index.[11] The analyses of Caves (1976), Helleiner (1977), Finger and De Rosa (1979), and Lavergne (1989) indicate that similar results emerge when effective and nominal tariff rates are used interchangeably in regression equations. Similarly, the analysis of Lerdau (1975) points out that average nominal tariffs and those computed from using weights from the wholesale price index are highly correlated. Moreover, calculating effective tariffs or using weights as in Lerdau would require a tremendous amount of data on the inputs of production used to produce different commodities or on wholesale price indices. Such data are not readily available for the long time periods in which we are interested.

The tariff data are reported as observations every five years. Since our trade data are annual, we assume that the tariff series are smooth within each five-year interval and linearly interpolate these data to arrive at annual tariff levels. Given the nature of the availability of protectionism data and Granger analysis's requirement of large degrees of freedom, we assume that this interpolation will not unduly influence our results. As emphasized by McKeown (1991: 154), inquiries of the type examined here seek clues to the nature of the relationship between trade and protectionism; highly precise delineations of this relationship must await further analysis and, no doubt, an improved database.

Nontariff trade barriers are difficult to handle since they include various measures that are not easy to assess such as discriminatory procurement, quotas, restrictive licensing, voluntary export restraints, antidumping, escape clauses, surveillance safeguards, subsidies, domestic standards, and countervailing duties.[12] While we are prepared to assume that NTBs have increased since the late 1960s, we and others have yet to successfully combine NTBs and tariff levels in a single series. In this examination, we will focus exclusively on tariff levels as a consequence. However, to test the robustness of our results concerning this issue, we attempt to model crudely the effect of NTBs by adding a dummy variable (zero for 1854–1967 and one for 1968–90) to our test.[13]

We have noted that bivariate Granger investigations run the risk of ignoring relevant variables. On the other hand, it is impossible to include all of the conceivably relevant variables, assuming we knew which ones these were. We suspect that for the nineteenth and twentieth centuries, the most important variables to include information on for the purposes of our long-term Granger analysis are wars and recessions.[14] To mark periods of systemic recession, we set a dummy variable to one when the overall weighted GDP of the five countries declines. In national tests, we include a dummy variable indicating times of national recessions according to the approach suggested and used by Maddison (1992). For wars, we include only those conflicts fought among the five included states: the Franco-Prussian War (1870–71), World War I (1914–18), and World War II (1939–45).

A final design consideration concerns the temporal structure of the tests. We have two reasons for examining periods of time shorter than the full 1854–1990 period. First, we suspect that system leader behavior is different from follower behavior. No single state led consistently in the 1854–1990 period: Britain led prior to World War I, and the United States led after World War II. To be able to assess whether their protectionism-trade relationships changed in accordance with their changing roles, more discrete time periods are necessary. A second reason for examining shorter periods of time is the question of robustness. Robust findings should be fairly consistent across time. We need to check whether this is in fact the case. Just because two states could be said to have played similar roles in two different centuries does not mean that their tariff-trade behavior will be identical in all respects. Their approach to other matters, such as investment, corporate structures, and alliance behavior, was not.

The two different considerations suggest that we should concentrate the focus of our tests within three time periods: 1854–1913, 1914–45, and 1945–90. In the first period, Britain was the system leader while the United States has that role in the third period.

Granger Causality Specification

The final Granger test implemented in this chapter is based on F-tests derived from the following equations.

$$T_t = T_0 + \sum_{i=1}^{L_T} \alpha_i T_{t-i} + \sum_{i=1}^{L_p} \beta_i P_{t-i} + \gamma t + \delta W_t + \theta R_t + \psi N_t + u_t \tag{7}$$

$$P_t = P_0 + \sum_{i=1}^{L_T'} \alpha_i' T_{t-i} + \sum_{i=1}^{L_p'} \beta_i' P_{t-i} + \gamma' t + \delta' W_t + \theta' R_t + \psi' N_t + u_t' \tag{8}$$

In these equations, T_t is the first difference of our trade indicator at time t, while T_{t-i} is the same indicator i years ago. Much the same description applies to P_t the first difference of our protectionism indicator. T_0 and P_0 are intercept terms, and a linear trend component is denoted by t. W, R, and N are dummy variables respectively for wars, recessions, and nontariff trade barriers. L_p, L_T, L'_p, and L'_T are the number of annual lags of protectionism and trade. We use u_t and u'_t to denote error terms, which are assumed to be white noise. All Greek symbols denote regression coefficients.

If the coefficients β_i in equation (7) are significantly different from zero, the inclusion of past values of first differences in protectionism will yield better forecasts of future trade than the use of past trade alone. Hence, one would conclude that *changes in protectionism Granger cause changes in trade.* The roles of changes in protectionism and trade are then reversed in (8) to test if *changes in trade Granger cause changes in protectionism* by determining whether the coefficients α'_i are significantly different from zero. If both β_i and α'_i are significantly different from zero, *the causality between protectionism and trade is reciprocal* (both variables Granger cause each other).

Data Analysis

The results from our Granger investigations are presented in tables 6.1 and 6.2.[15] In table 6.1, we present the best statistical significance level from F-tests per country/system by the appropriate time period. For our present purposes, the best F-test outcome is defined as the lowest significance level for rejecting the null hypothesis of no Granger causality in a certain direction within the lag structures examined. Since the precise dynamics of trade and protectionism are unknown and may be relatively slow for changes in one variable to register in the other variable, up to eight annual lags are inspected for each actor. In all, thirty-two Granger tests are performed for each of our six units of analysis. The results are reported only if the error terms in our equations are white noise.

Yet even though we can reduce the summary outcome to forty-eight numbers, it is still difficult to interpret the outcome without the assistance of a guide. Table 6.2 provides a further simplified guide by indicating which time periods were significantly associated with a specific Granger causal pattern. Readers are invited to rely on either one or both tables in assessing independently the nature of the statistical outcome.

As suggested by the need for two tables, the Granger causality results vary by actor and time period. For the whole time period (1854–1990), no pattern emerges for the system, Britain, or Japan. The United States' pattern is one of trade anteceding protectionism. France shows the opposite pattern with protectionism anteceding trade. Summarily then, we find no

TABLE 6.1.   Best F-Test Significance Levels in Looking for Antecedence in the Protectionism-Trade Relationship

Unit	1854–1990	1854–1913	1914–45	1945–90
	Trade → Protectionism			
System	0.554 (1)	0.011 (3)	0.005 (4)	0.000 (6)
Britain	0.445 (3)	0.576 (4)	0.082 (1)	0.004 (1)
United States	0.006 (5)	0.121 (3)	0.036 (4)	0.007 (6)
France	0.448 (1)	0.485 (1)	0.080 (8)	0.005 (7)
Germany	—	0.139 (6)	—	0.273 (1)
Japan	0.435 (1)	0.303 (1)	0.518 (4)	0.497 (2)
	Protectionism → Trade			
System	0.539 (3)	0.015 (4)	0.378 (8)	0.176 (7)
Britain	0.176 (8)	0.594 (7)	0.536 (8)	0.010 (1)
United States	0.445 (5)	0.027 (7)	0.041 (8)	0.408 (1)
France	0.000 (7)	0.424 (8)	0.000 (7)	0.380 (6)
Germany	—	0.532 (8)	—	0.508 (8)
Japan	0.402 (6)	0.577 (1)	0.472 (1)	0.157 (2)

Note: Entries denote best (lowest) significance levels for rejecting the appropriate null hypothesis (trade does not Granger cause protectionism for T → P and protectionism does not Granger cause trade for P → T). The numbers in parentheses are the lag lengths associated with the best F-test outcomes. The German (1880) and Japanese (1890) tests begin later than 1854 due to missing trade information. Missing information for Germany in the 1914–45 period also precludes an examination of that interval and the 1880–1990 period.

evidence of reciprocity (trade $\leftrightarrow$ protectionism) and no evidence that protectionism influences trade outside France.

But, as we indicated earlier, it is not clear that the 1854–1990 results are likely to represent the most meaningful tests of our arguments. When we turn to the more discrete time intervals, more evidence for reciprocity emerges at the system level (1854–1913), for the United States and France (1914–45), and for Britain (1945–90). Stronger evidence for the predominance of the trade $\rightarrow$ protectionism pattern also emerges. In addition to the four periods characterized by reciprocity, the system (1914–45 and 1945–90), the United States (1945–90), Britain (1914–45), and France (1945–90) are associated with trade anteceding protectionism. Only one additional case (besides the reciprocal ones) of protectionism anteceding trade is found (the United States, 1854–1913).

How do our more specific predictions fare? At the system level, and relying primarily on evidence from the three consecutive time periods, the pattern is primarily one of trade anteceding protectionism—the long-term pattern suggested in hypotheses H10 and H11. It is unfortunate that we have been unable to extend the data back earlier than 1854. The reciprocal pattern associated with the system-level data prior to 1913 might have been even stronger, as suggested by figure 6.1. Alternatively, the post–Napoleonic War trade expansion in the 1820s through 1840s might have been shown to have clearly preceded the tariff reductions, begun by the British only in the 1840s, thereby yielding a possibly even stronger trade $\rightarrow$ protectionism relationship.[16]

For the two system leaders in the sample, Britain and the United States, the evidence is not quite as clear-cut but still largely supportive of the long-term emphasis. As predicted, no causal pattern is found in the nine-

TABLE 6.2.   A Summary of Significant Granger Causality Patterns

Unit	1854–1990	1854–1913	1914–45	1945–90
System		T $\leftrightarrow$ P	T $\rightarrow$ P	T $\rightarrow$ P
Britain		T $\rightarrow$ P	T $\leftrightarrow$ P	
United States	T $\rightarrow$ P	P $\rightarrow$ T	T $\leftrightarrow$ P	T $\rightarrow$ P
France	P $\rightarrow$ T		T $\leftrightarrow$ P	T $\rightarrow$ P
Germany	—		—	
Japan				

Note: The threshold for statistical significance is the 0.10 level. However, all but two cases (T $\rightarrow$ P for Britain and France, 1914–45) are significant at the 0.05 level as well. Missing information precluded an analysis of German data in the 1914–45 and 1854–1990 periods. Empty spaces in table denote a nonstatistically significant relationship.

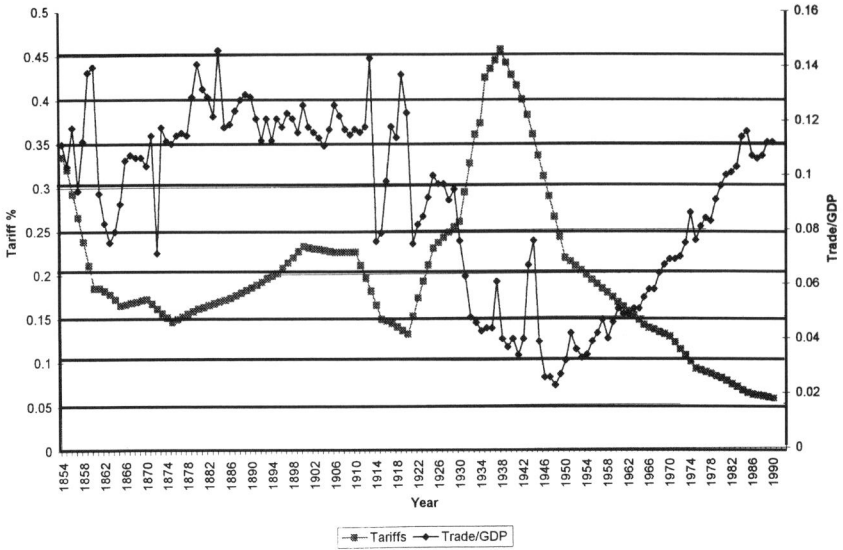

Fig. 6.1. Systemic trade and tariffs

teenth-century British case. This finding may be due to the truncated nature of the data noted earlier in the sense that being forced to begin in 1854 eliminates much of the initial British tariff reductions that commenced immediately prior to the 1850s and the presumed expansion in trade of the first half of the nineteenth century. Yet, the inclusion of the earlier period might only reinforce the absence of a causal pattern. As suggested in figure 6.2, the pre-1854 data missing from the figure would most likely resemble the post–World War II period in which trade expansion preceded declining tariffs. In contrast, figure 6.3 captures the post–Civil War rise in U.S. tariffs and the contraction in trade growth. After World War I and into the 1930s, tariffs began a dramatic rise that was not accompanied by equally dramatic decreases in the trade/GDP ratio. Nor can it be said, based on the visual evidence and the Granger outcome, that the marked decline in U.S. tariffs after World War II produced a corresponding trade expansion.

A comparison of the movement in British and U.S. causality patterns diachronically reveals an explicable evolution with each state moving in opposite directions. In the nineteenth century, protectionism influenced U.S. trade but not, apparently, Britain's. In the interwar period, the inter-

162

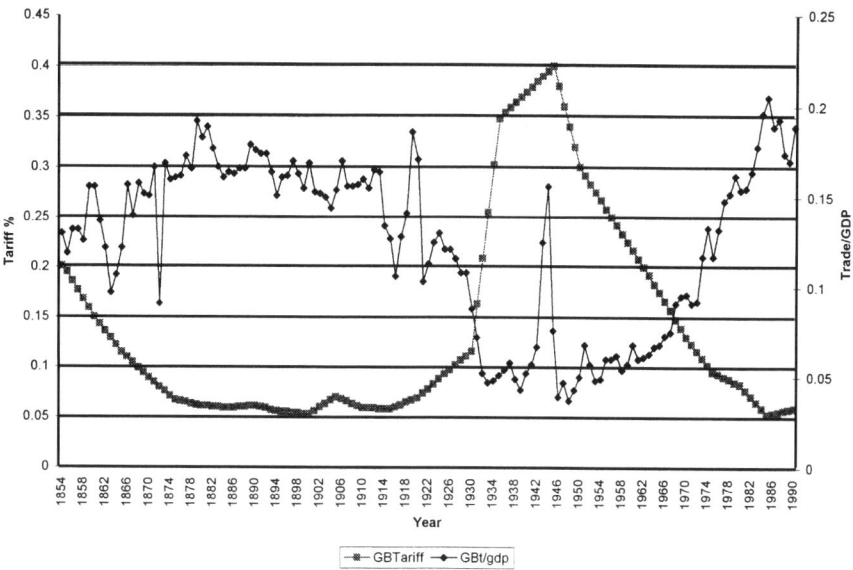

Fig. 6.2.   British trade and tariffs

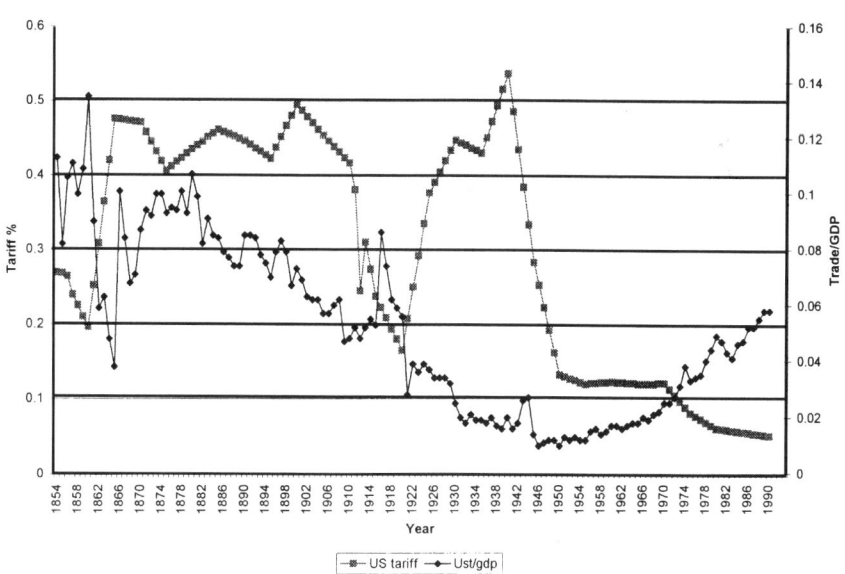

Fig. 6.3.   U.S. trade and tariffs

action becomes more reciprocal in the United States, while Britain's protectionism responds to trade contraction. In the post–World War II era, it is U.S. protectionism that is responding to trade—in marked contrast to the nineteenth century—whereas the British protectionism-trade interaction has become reciprocal. We read this movement as suggesting that protectionism has become gradually less influential in the U.S. case as it moved into the system leader role and more influential in the British case as it moved away from the system leader role. By and large, the system as a whole has also moved along lines more similar to the pattern displayed by the United States—with protectionism becoming a less influential causal factor over time, and trade becoming a more influential causal factor for protectionism.

How to interpret the other country outcomes is less obvious. No pattern ever emerges in the Japanese case. The data plotted in figure 6.4 are supportive of the no relationship outcome. Japanese tariffs climb to a peak in the 1930s and then gradually decline to a low in the 1980s. The climb of the tariffs long precedes the Depression-war trade contraction in the 1930s and 1940s. Similarly, the long descent of Japanese tariffs in the second half of the twentieth century appears to have little to do with Japan's trade/GDP ratio. Of course, this case may be one of the more egregious instances of NTBs interfering with an interpretation of the data analysis. But even if that is the case, it is not the measurable tariff levels that matter in the Japanese case.

The German record is very similar to the Japanese case. Figure 6.5 shows an initial rise (through the 1890s) in tariffs that does not appear to have an impact on the German trade/GDP ratio. The immediate pre–World War I situation was characterized by a moderate decline in tariffs without much change in trade. The German interwar period, characterized by Nazi attempts at autarky, is suggestive of a case in which tariffs can make some noticeable difference. Yet the clarity of the relationship appears, for the most part, to be restricted to the 1930s interval. The steep decline in tariffs after World War II did not lead to a corresponding strong increase in trade/GDP. The trade expansion accelerated only in the late 1950s and 1960s by which time tariffs were already relatively low.

The French outcome is more complicated. The overall result suggests that protectionism is more predominant than trade. But the more discrete time periods suggest movement along a path more similar to the U.S. pattern. Although no clear causality pattern emerges in the nineteenth cen-

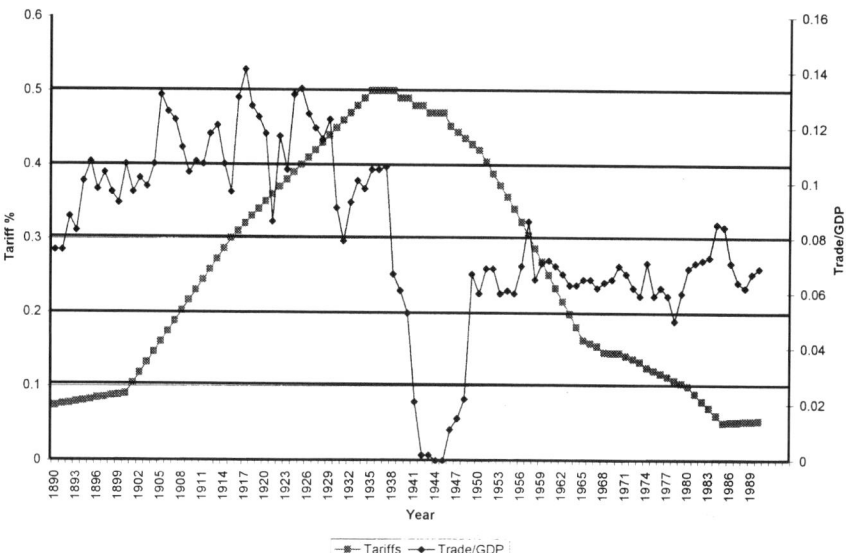

Fig. 6.4.   Japanese trade and tariffs

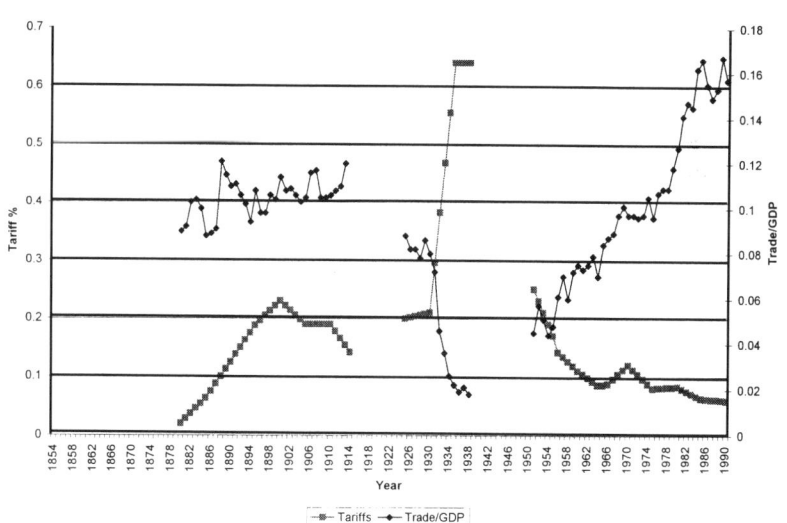

Fig. 6.5.   German trade and tariffs

tury, either statistically or visually as indicated in figure 6.6, the interwar years are associated with tariff-trade reciprocity and the postwar years with trade predominating over protectionism. Appropriately, figure 6.6 shows a marked drop in tariffs and a very strong increase in its trade/GDP ratio in the period immediately prior to the 1920s and then reversals of movements in both series into the 1920s and 1930s.[17] The interwar tariff-protectionism reciprocity seems genuinely portrayed by the respective serial fluctuations recorded in figure 6.6. And, after World War II, the expansion of French trade clearly preceded the movement toward tariff reductions.

So far we have been silent about the outcomes associated with the various controls administered for war, recessions, and NTBs. It is worth emphasizing that our Granger modeling falls well short of what might be viewed as developing a sophisticated model of tariff-trade relationships. One implication is that we should not give too much weight to the specific coefficients of the dummy variables. Still, they are not without interest in their own right and deserve some summary attention.

The recession dummies were significantly different from zero in nine cases. When statistically significant, the recession variable was associated with a decrease in trade and an increase in protectionism, just as one might anticipate. These results are more pronounced in the cases of the system as a whole, the United States, and Britain, and less so for the other countries.

The war variable was significant in fifteen cases. With two exceptions, war is associated with decreases in trade and tariffs. The two exceptions are not surprising. The U.S. data (1854–1913 and 1914–45) yield a positive relationship between war and trade, reflecting the geoeconomic advantages enjoyed by the United States in provisioning European allies in the two world wars of the twentieth century. As in the case of recessions, the war outcome is more apparent in the examinations conducted on the systemic, U.S., and British data, and less so for the other cases.

Finally, the dichotomous controls for the NTBs apply only to the 1854–1990 and 1945–90 time periods since the NTB dummy is coded 1 after 1967. Out of eleven trade → protectionism regressions, the NTB dummy was statistically significant (and negative) in two cases (Britain 1945–1990, France 1945–1990). Of eleven protectionism → trade regressions, the NTB dummy emerged significant (and positively signed) in only one case (Britain 1854–1990). However, the scant results may say more about the crudity of the NTB dummy than about whether NTBs make some difference in the antecedence patterns.

Tariffs and Trade Fluctuations

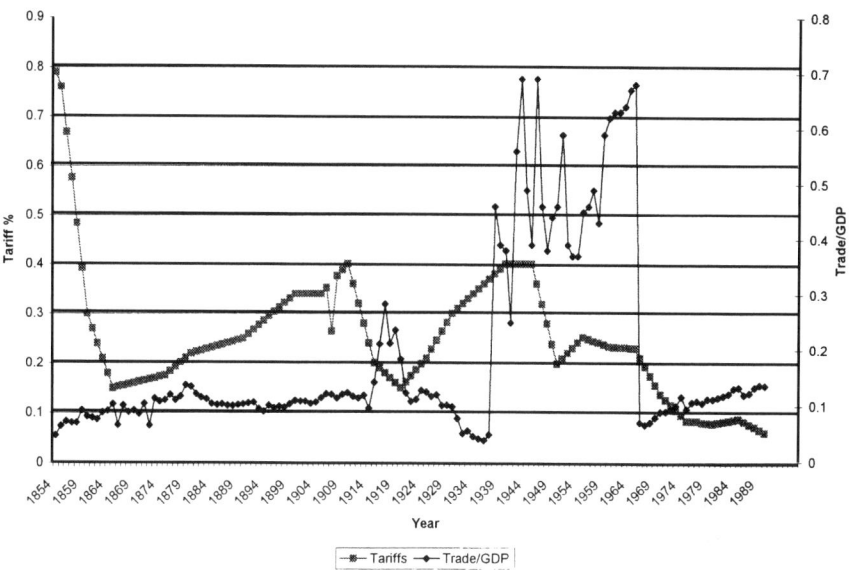

Fig. 6.6.   French trade and tariffs

Conclusion

The evidence appears to corroborate the argument derived from long-term reasoning that the antecedence of trade on protectionism predominates over the reverse causal pattern (hypotheses H10 and H11). Changing tariff levels can make a difference in the short term—either encouraging or discouraging trade—but, in the long run, more fundamental economic growth processes influence the political seductiveness of tariff level increases and decreases. Nonetheless, the evidence is not without ambiguities. Nor do we claim that there is only one way to assess the outcome. However, and even though there is evidence for protectionism influencing trade, we do find substantial and proportionally more evidence that the influence of protectionism is not as strong as some might think. Causality patterns with protectionism predominant turn out to be quite rare in tables 6.1 and 6.2. Moreover, we also find a fair amount of evidence that trade antecedes protectionism, and it does so especially at the systemic level and in the histories of the system leaders. Most interesting is the sug-

167

gestive pattern of a gradually receding influence for protectionism in the most recent system leader case (the United States) and an increasing influence in the older case (Britain).

Still, the strong absence of uniformity in the statistical outcomes underscores the need for theoretical caution. It also reinforces the metaphor suggested in chapter 4 and the conclusion we reached in chapter 5 in examining the correspondence between the predictions of a number of models of protectionist behavior and the observed record of fluctuations in tariff levels. The long-term interpretation is helpful in elucidating trade and protectionism behavior, but there are limits to its explanatory power. Just as an emphasis on the long term need not preclude a substantial role for short-term considerations, there is no imperative to eliminate the need for explanations more geared to short-term national and domestic processes. Long-term economic growth is reacted to in different ways by different actors. While a few states may ride the long-term tendencies most profitably, and a few others react most violently to its implications for who wins and loses, most other states are caught somewhere in between. The interaction between their trade and protectionism strategies may also be expected to fall somewhere in between.

Formalizing the metaphor introduced in chapter 4, a long-term perspective offers only a general frame of reference or context within which a variety of behaviors may take place. The question is whether we can dispense with the long-run context and rely exclusively on developing an understanding of short-term dynamics. In the case of tariff interactions with trade, we suggest the answer would seem to be no. Otherwise something important is left out of the equation.

Chapter 7, therefore, keeps the long-run context in the relationships between systemic leadership and economic trading openness. Studies of hegemonic stability tend to specify periods when hegemony is present or absent in the world system. Periods in which hegemony is present are expected to exhibit openness for trade. Periods in which hegemony is absent should be associated with trade closure. Partially as a consequence of this nominal measurement strategy, scholars continue to be unsure whether hegemony and systemic leadership are linked to the openness of the world's trading system. We contend that analysts need to devote more attention to the sources of preponderance and less to its arbitrary presence or absence.

Tariffs and Trade Fluctuations

Focusing on the United States from 1870 to 1990, we first articulate a leadership-long cycle theory linking certain politicoeconomic systemic leadership variables to world trade openness, making sure to specify the direction, signs, and diffusion speed of the causal links. We then estimate Granger causality and distributed lag models to test our predictions empirically. The empirical results support our theoretical interpretation. The Granger causalities between world trade openness and the systemic leadership variables are found to be reciprocal, with the effects of systemic leadership on world trade openness working faster than those of world trade openness on the hegemon. World trade openness exerts a negative effect on systemic leadership, while systemic leadership declines as the world economy becomes more open.

7. Systemic Leadership and World Trade Openness

We have established a foundation for systemic leadership in the form of leading sector growth, leading sector concentration, and naval capability concentration (chaps. 2, 3). We were also able to demonstrate that the foundation for systemic leadership was important to world economic growth. Subsequent chapters explored fluctuations in protectionism and tariffs, just as the previous chapter looked at the relationship between trade volume and tariffs. Now we are ready to investigate the connections between the foundation for systemic leadership and world trade openness. Chapters 4 through 6 suggest that the relationship should be quite significant.

It seems almost axiomatic to connect systemic leadership with the drive for freer world trade regimes. The apparent periodicity of fluctuations in protectionism—high in the first half of the nineteenth century, then decreasing only to rise again in the last part of the century, decreasing again and then rising in the 1930s, declining after 1945 and then rising again since the 1980s in the form of nontariff barriers—gives the impression of some degree of perceived fit with the high-water marks of British and American politicoeconomic systemic leadership. Both system leaders have also helped to make the connection by moving unilaterally away from high levels of protection to much lower levels at some point well into their respective ascent trajectories. After these thresholds are attained, their decision makers have also become among the most dedicated and visible free trade supporters.

Despite all these apparent fits, scholars remain uncertain just how systemic leadership and world trade openness are related. We think there are at least two reasons why this might be the case. One is that the field of inquiry has been dominated by hegemonic stability analysis. This research program began with an emphasis on the notion that politicoeconomic hegemony was related to world economic stability and openness. Two things then happened. Over time, the two dependent variables (stability and openness) took over the inquiry to such an extent that the hegemonic part of the equation faded away. A second characteristic of hegemonic stability analysis was a tendency to emphasize the political nature of the hegemon's free trade policies. The implication was that the system's trade became freer primarily because the hegemon wished it to be freer and worked to make it so. As it became clearer that the hegemons' embrace of free trade did not correlate well with their stints as leaders, and that hegemons had less of an impact on what other states chose to do than was initially presumed, analytical resistance to a strong equation of structure and behavior arose. Ultimately, these tendencies seem to have encouraged analysts of international political economy to move away from the hegemonic stability program.

A second reason scholars remain uncertain about how systemic leadership and world trade openness are related is that the few empirical efforts to test the linkage between them have yielded decidedly mixed results. For instance, Krasner (1976; see also Webb and Krasner 1989) delineated five periods of hegemonic presence and absence (1820–1970) but found that trade openness behaved as anticipated in only two of the five periods. McKeown (1991) examined several indicators of systemic concentration (in naval power, national income, and trade), but the only indicator that emerged with statistical significance in an analysis of 1881–1987 trade openness was the percentage of world imports accounted for by five leading economies—an indicator that is not easily related to hegemony. Mansfield (1994) examined the ratio of global exports to global production as a function of two alternative, binary (i.e., on-off) timing specifications of hegemony. One had British hegemony extending from 1815 to 1914 and U.S. hegemony beginning in 1945 (with no end date specified). The second one dated British hegemony as 1815–1873 and U.S. hegemony as 1945–67.[1] The first indicator produced a positive linkage with the export ratio while the second one produced a statistically insignificant linkage.

We think previous results pertaining to hegemony are based on fairly static conceptions of leadership. System leaders (hegemons) are either present or absent, without regard to whether they are ascending or declining. Every year of presence or of absence receives equal weight even though the initial identifications of hegemonic tenures are fairly subjective estimates in their own right.[2]

If the arguments on hegemonic stability have validity, what is needed are analyses that can link systemic leadership to world trade openness without relying too much on hegemonic coercion. We also need to move beyond the limitations of dichotomous, time-based indicators of hegemony. We believe that systemic or hegemonic leadership is predicated on a resource foundation that creates the underpinnings for a high degree of systemic capability concentration. We might talk about the presence or absence of leadership if we could identify explicit thresholds of concentration necessary for leadership. Since the explicit threshold path has not been pursued much in the past, an alternative approach is to focus on the resources thought to be the most important proxies for leadership. Both of these objectives are pursued here.

We first summarize the hegemonic stability arguments and then recapitulate the theory of world trade openness predicated on structural technological change (chap. 1). We then test some of the theory's derivations by examining the directions, signs, and diffusion speed of causal links among trade openness and three indicators of the capability foundation that we contend are critical for systemic leadership, namely, the hegemon's leading sector growth rates, leading sector global production share, and global reach capability share.

The empirical tests provide support for our theory. Systemic leadership is found to promote world trade openness. An anticipated reverse causal arrow from world trade openness to systemic leadership is also found to be at work. World trade openness hastens systemic leadership decline. Given that in the nineteenth and twentieth centuries, system leaders promoted openness for trade, one might ask why, in hindsight, they were so irrational as to contribute to their own downfall. The answer is not very complex. System leaders, like most other political actors, operate in the present and discount future losses—and even that statement assumes that decision makers spend much time evaluating the long-term costs and benefits of their current actions. Somehow, we doubt that such evaluation occurs with great frequency.

The Hegemonic Stability Literature

Lake (1993) and others who have surveyed the hegemonic stability literature stress two main themes. One focuses on hegemonic stability. Economies need mediums of exchange, liquidity, property rights, and lenders of last resort to function well. The world economy is no exception.

Systemic Leadership and World Trade Openness

The question is whether, and to what extent, hegemony is necessary to create and maintain the prerequisites of a functioning world economy. Kindleberger (1973, 1981) is noted for his argument that hegemony is necessary (although he professes that was never his intention). Others (Krasner 1983; Keohane 1984; Snidal 1985; Lake 1988) have noted that, from a logical if not historical perspective, hegemony is not necessary to either the creation or persistence of a functioning world economy.

The second cluster of hegemony literature revolves around differential trade policy preferences that stem from a country's position in the world's economic hierarchy. Hegemons prefer free trade and will use their coercive advantages to force other states to open to trade. One approach (Krasner 1976; Gowa 1989a) argues that large, developed actors that are less dependent on trade prefer open systems for their relative gains in terms of welfare and/or security. A second variant (Gowa 1989b) stresses that trade policies are associated with specific industries and that different economies possess different mixes of industries. Hegemons encourage foreign producers to focus on supplying, as opposed to competing with, the hegemon's more advanced economy. Or, it may be that the most capital-abundant economies seek to encourage the retention of capital-intensive industries and that the hegemon's lead means that it does not have to try as hard as other economies to protect its industries (Lake 1988). A third thread (Frieden 1988; Rosecrance and Taw 1990; Brawley 1993) emphasizes the emergence of domestic groups within hegemons with incentives to foster free trade. If those groups become sufficiently powerful, they will encourage their governments as well as other governments to pursue free trade.

In some respects, then, the hegemonic stability research program is reducible to the statement that hegemony can produce economic stability and free trade. However, this statement does not specify how hegemony or systemic leadership works. In principle, systemic leadership can be linked to stability and trade openness, but it also can be linked to conflict, technological innovation, global reach capabilities, political innovation, democratization, economic growth, debt crises, inequality, and North-South polarization, among other processes. That there has been a tendency to delimit analyses to stability and openness need not be necessarily interpreted as implying that these are the only dependent variables of interest. Moreover, with a few notable exceptions such as Gilpin (1975, 1987), most hegemonic stability analysts do not study the origins of hegemony. The emphasis often has been placed on the question, Given the demise of the incumbent hegemon, should we expect the world economy to become increasingly dysfunctional? Less evident is an interest in the circumstances that are propitious for hegemons to emerge as system leaders. These circumstances, in many respects, are the focus of this chapter.

In our leadership-long cycle interpretation of trade and protectionism dynamics, we begin with the idea that technological innovations are introduced in a twin-peaked flow by economic developments in the system's lead economy. In the first growth peak, the productive gap between the leader and competitors widens as the new industries emerge. The lead economy may move toward opening its own economy, albeit subject to overcoming resistance at home, because it has little to fear from competitors and much to gain if it can encourage market opening elsewhere. Reduced import costs are also viewed as highly desirable. Still, the slow start of the lead economy's conversion to free trade doctrines and the differential incentives involved in a situation in which nonlead economies are far behind the lead economy's productive edge suggest that we should not expect a direct and consistent link between the appearance of new industries and world openness.

While there may be some positive response to the leader's unilateral initiatives, marked gains in trade expansion and the opening of markets are more probable in the second, catch-up growth wave because more actors have more to gain from participating fully in the world economy. More competitiveness generally means less demand for protectionism. The system leader will have been preaching free trade for some time. More people will be prepared to listen as their own relative productive status improves. If the system leader has also just completed an intensive, trial-by-combat test of its leadership, its powers of persuasion will be all the stronger as it attempts to reorganize the world economy in its own image.

One of the ironies of freer trade is that it both reflects and encourages the diffusion of industrial competitiveness. Genuinely competitive economies should be more relaxed about the temptations of making imports more expensive. Yet the proliferation of genuine competitors also hints at prospects for slower economic growth ahead. As the productive edge of the system leader erodes, its own growth prospects begin to diminish. Its share of leading sector production must shrink (if others are improving their shares). Its surplus for funding leadership overhead activities, including maintaining its global reach capabilities, is also likely to shrink. Freer trade is not necessarily the direct agent of leadership decline. Those honors go to the impossibility of suppressing the diffusion of technological edges once attained and the propensity for some inertia and complacency in the face of gradual relative decline. But freer trade is one of the mediums through which relative decline travels. As such, it bears some indirect responsibility for the eventual negative consequences of economic success.

Expansion phases tend to give way to periods of contraction. The diminishing returns associated with fading leading sectors that have become increasingly routine, diffused throughout the world economy, and subject to overproduction by multiple economies are especially prone to initiating slowdowns in economic growth. Slow economic growth encourages protectionism (chap. 6). Even the system leader may eventually succumb to domestic demands for insulation from external competition if the world economy becomes sufficiently depressed and if the incumbent lead economy has lost its productive edge.

These arguments suggest this chapter's three hypotheses.

H12: After some lag, world trade openness will be positively influenced by systemic leadership, as reflected in the leader's leading sector production superiority and global reach capability.

H13: The influence of leading sector growth in the lead economy on world trade openness is likely to be weak.

H14: After some lag, systemic leadership and the leader's leading sector growth, leading sector production superiority, and shares of global reach capability will be negatively influenced by world trade openness.

Research Design

The standard approach to systemic analysis is to aggregate all of the variables in question. We think, however, that one of the motors of the system is the lead economy. As a consequence, we model processes measured at the system leader's national level with the expectations that these processes affect, and are affected by, the behavior of the system. Thus, we regard this as a systemic analysis, while others may classify it as examining the interaction between the system and one of its actors. Essentially, in order to test hypotheses H12 through H14, we need to answer two questions: (1) Has systemic leadership preceded or anteceded world trade openness? (2) What is the sign and the speed of the effects that systemic leadership and world trade openness exert on each other?

Growth, Trade, and Systemic Leadership

Spatial and Temporal Considerations

Our temporal domain continues to be geared to the past century or so. This approach is taken because, empirically, it is quite difficult to treat the British era of systemic leadership in the same way one can deal with the U.S. era. With the U.S. case, one can begin quite early in its ascent. What is sacrificed is complete information on its relative decline trajectory (which is not yet fully known). In the British case, it is difficult to obtain a full range of serial information that encompasses its eighteenth-century ascent phase. The available British data and the appropriate system data involve mostly the British decline phase. There is also a tendency in the IPE literature to argue over whether Britain was hegemonic in the late nineteenth and early twentieth centuries, but most analysts will concede the U.S. credentials as a twentieth-century system leader. From our perspective, if we were to focus on British data from the late nineteenth century onward (because of the availability of data), we would be biasing the examination toward years in which Britain was least likely to affect world openness—either in terms of its politicoeconomic leadership or its capability platform for leadership. If forced to choose between the U.S. and U.K. cases, we prefer to focus on the fuller empirical variance associated with the U.S. case.

Another way of looking at this approach is to note that in our perspective, leadership capability platforms come into place long before the periods normally associated with behavior labeled as "hegemonic." The U.S. leadership platform began to emerge in the late nineteenth century. Since we assert that capability concentration is critical to leadership, our analysis needs to be geared to the timing of concentration and not restricted to conventional assumptions about when the U.S. case for leadership was most obvious. Consequently, we focus on the United States as it emerged in the years prior to 1945 as the system leader, as well as in the years after 1945 when most researchers would agree that it performed as the leader. We do this not because we are operating under the illusion that the United States was a system leader in the nineteenth century, but because we wish to trace its gradual emerging into preeminence in the twentieth century, and to avoid focusing too heavily on what may be the tail end of its leadership.

Given limitations on the availability of data, we start in 1870. In general, the period before World War I is a decline phase of Britain as a system leader, while the U.S. leadership was still emerging. The period between the world wars was one in which the U.S. leadership was forming.

The period after World War II, at least until the mid-1970s, is one in which the United States clearly was the lead economy and politicomilitary system leader. Hence, no single state led consistently in the 1870–1990 period, thereby making empirical inference more complex. Consequently, in addition to examining the full 1870–1990 time period, we will also examine periods shorter than the full period, repeating each test for four time periods. Two of the time periods are periods of emerging U.S. leadership (1870–1913 and 1870–1945), one is a period of systemic leadership (1946–90), and the fourth one (1870–1990) encompasses the other three. Of course, the examination of periods that may be too short for long-term relationships to be fully manifested could introduce as much distortion as looking only at a longer period without being concerned about heterogeneity across time. Our compromise then is to look at both the longer and shorter periods in hopes of expanding our ability to correctly read the statistical outcomes.

Statistical Tests

The statistical investigation consists of Granger's (1969, 1980) causality tests (as in chaps. 2 and 6). Here, we also add tests based on distributed lag models. This approach is based on the basic assumption of time-series analysis that as long as the error term is white noise, the effects of other variables not included in the statistical model can be adequately represented by the lags of the included variables. As we have already noted, Granger's approach and distributed lag models are not meant to generate the last word on research questions. Despite their technical complexity, these models may be viewed as preliminary to the development of a more fully specified model. Yet, our immediate goal in what is a complicated and ambitious undertaking is not to model fully the relationships that pertain among our variables, but rather to systematically investigate them with the intent of formulating more ambitious models in the future.

It is worthwhile recapitulating the basics of the Granger approach in the context of this chapter. Granger suggests a causality test based on joint-significance F-tests from the coefficients of series x and y in equations (9) and (10), where y_t and x_t are the values of the variables whose causal relationship is being investigated, t denotes time, y_{t-k} and x_{t-k} are values k years ago, x_0 and y_0 are intercept terms, L_x, L_y, L'_x, and L'_y are the number of lags used, u_t and u'_t are error terms, and Greek symbols are coefficients. In general, these regressions may or may not include control variables. We include R_N, R_w, and W_N dummy variables to denote U.S. recessions, world recessions, and U.S. wars, respectively. Three causality tests are performed. The first tests the causality between the U.S. leading sector growth rate and world trade openness. The second tests the causality between U.S.-held share of world's leading sector production and world trade openness. The third tests the causality between the U.S. share of the world's naval capability and world trade openness.

$$x_t = x_0 + \sum_{k=1}^{L_x} \alpha_k x_{t-k} + \sum_{k=1}^{L_y} \beta_k y_{t-k} + \gamma R_{Nt} + \delta R_{Wt} + \mu W_N + u_t \qquad (9)$$

$$y_t = y_0 + \sum_{k=1}^{L'_x} \alpha_k' x_{t-k} + \sum_{k=1}^{L'_y} \beta_k' y_{t-k} + \gamma' R_{Nt} + \delta' R_{Wt} + \mu' U_N + u_t' \qquad (10)$$

The Granger's test results are interpreted as follows. If the coefficients β_k in (9) are significantly different from zero, the inclusion of past values of y will yield better forecasts of future x than the use of x alone. Hence, one would conclude that y *causes* x. The roles of x and y are then reversed in (10) to test if x *causes* y. This is done by determining whether the coefficients α_k' are significantly different from zero. If both β_k and α_k' are significantly different from zero, *both variables cause each other.*

Granger's test does not show the signs of effects. However, hypotheses H12 and H14 also specify signs of effects. To that effect, one could treat equations (9) and (10) as distributed lag dynamic models and use them to investigate sign and speed of effects. Because Granger's equations include distributed lags, the *t*-statistics of the individual coefficients tend to be larger due to potential multicollinearity. The signs of the coefficients are nevertheless meaningful. In fact, several studies use such models to analyze the signs of effects as reflected by the model's coefficients.[3] However, distributed lag models typically include many coefficients, one for each lagged term. Those coefficients, in turn, may exhibit different signs and are therefore hard to interpret. Consequently, many studies that use distributed lag models inspect the sums of lag coefficients for both their signs and significance levels.[4]

The sums of lag coefficients deserve additional discussion. In a standard regression, the response of the dependent variable to a change in some independent variable is assumed to be complete at the end of the period used for the measurement. In distributed lag models, the comparable concept is the effect of a one-time change in the values of all the lags of a certain independent variable. Hence, the sums of lag coefficients in these models give the overall effect of a shock in an independent variable that lasts for a time period equal to lag length used for that independent variable. The longer the lag length involved, the slower is the propagation of the effect of the independent variable on the dependent variable. As detailed in Doan (1992), the sums of lag coefficients could be tested for their statistical significance using an appropriately constructed *t*-test.

As can happen with any regression or statistical model, Granger's test may miss variables. Attempting to deal with this claim, we add control variables. In the context of the analysis of this chapter, we believe that the most important control variables to include are the timing of U.S. wars and U.S. and world recessions. In our period, U.S. wars also include world wars, hence we also control for world wars. We mark wars by setting a dummy variable to one to indicate the presence of a war that involves the United States as a participant, and to zero otherwise. Recessions represent a faster dynamic than that of long cycles, which may be caused by different forces from those causing long cycles.[5] We mark recessions by setting two dummy variables, one for the United States and one for the world, to a value of one in years in which they occur. The recession data relies on the procedure advocated by Maddison (1992), which equates years of recession with years of negative growth in gross domestic product.

Finally, we generally assume that different statistical tests are complements to one another rather than substitutes. Along these lines, in the discussion of the empirical results we plan to integrate the information gained from the Granger tests with the information gained from testing the significance of the sums of these lag coefficients. This will allow us to paint a broader picture of the forces in the model (for technical details on Granger test design issues, see appendix A).

Data and Measures

Our empirical test requires measures or indicators of the leader's leading sector growth, leading sector production share, and naval capabilities share. The measurements of these concepts were discussed in detail in chapters 2 and 3. The current chapter makes use of these same empirical data. In addition, we need to describe the new data required for the specific analysis of this chapter, namely, world trade openness.

Our indicator of world trade openness employs a ratio of a measure of world trade to a measure of world economic activity. For our measure of trade, we rely on Maddison's (1991) total exports (i.e., from a country to the world). Our measure of economic activity is based on Maddison's (1991) gross domestic product (GDP) data. Both of these measures are available for sixteen of the economically most important states in the system: Australia, Austria, Belgium, Canada, Denmark, Finland, France, Germany, Italy, Japan, the Netherlands, Norway, Sweden, Switzerland, the United Kingdom, and the United States.

During our 1870–1990 period, the total exports and GDPs of these countries represent the lion's share of world exports and GDP, respectively. Recalling that exports are the imports of some other country, our world trade measure is given by the sum of the total exports of the preceding countries. Our measure of world economic activity is given by the sum of the GDPs of those countries. The measure of world trade openness is then generated by taking the ratio between these two numbers, at any given point in time.

Empirical Results

Table 7.1 reports the significance levels obtained from the Granger causality tests and the lag length for which each particular result is obtained. Low significance levels indicate that the null hypothesis of no causality in a certain direction is rejected. Beginning with Panel A of table 7.1, the causality from leading sector growth to world trade openness is statistically significant in two out of the four periods. The causality from leading sector production share to world trade openness is significant in all periods. Hence, the causality from U.S. economic leadership to world trade openness is more pronounced in the case of leading sector production shares than in the case of leading sector growth rate. These results support hypotheses H12 and H14. The causality from U.S. political power, as measured by its naval capabilities share, to world trade openness is also significant in all periods. This result supports hypothesis H12. In all, these results illustrate that world trade openness is preceded by both political and economic variables pertaining to the U.S. leadership position in the world system.

Panel B of table 7.1 illustrates the existence of statistically significant effects of world trade openness on U.S. economic and political power, which supports hypothesis H14. It is interesting to note that these effects are the least significant during the 1870–1913 period. This particular outcome is intuitive since during this period the U.S. economy was relatively closed to trade, and its innovations were still in a formative stage. We believe that the effects of world trade openness on U.S. political and economic power generally work through technological diffusion from the leader to follower economies that results in increasing foreign production in the new industries. In this respect, the 1870–1913 period would be too early to expect much in the way of diffusion-stimulated feedback. We further investigate these ideas in the analyses reported in table 7.2.

Table 7.1 shows that the lag lengths in Panel A (reporting causality results from U.S. leadership to world trade openness) are generally shorter than those in Panel B (reporting causality results from world trade openness to U.S. leadership). Specifically, the average lag length in Panel A is 3, versus 9.5 for Panel B. This observation implies that the effects of U.S. leadership impact world trade openness relatively quickly, while the effects of world trade openness impact U.S. leadership more slowly.[6]

The results in table 7.1 then support an interpretation according to which politicoeconomic leadership and world trade openness affect each other. The signs of these effects can be inferred from the sums of lag coefficients in the causality regressions. In Panel A of table 7.2, world trade openness is the dependent variable, whereas in Panel B of table 7.2 it is the independent variable. In each case, we list the sum of lag coefficients and note their statistical significance as in table 7.1.

TABLE 7.1. Causality between U.S. Leadership and World Trade Openness

Period	Leading Growth	Leading Share	Naval Share
A. U.S. Leadership → World Trade Openness Significance Levels			
1870–1990	0.36 (1)	0.01 (15)***	0.00 (3)***
1870–1913	0.12 (1)*	0.08 (2)***	0.00 (5)***
1870–1945	0.05 (2)**	0.02 (11)***	0.03 (2)***
1946–90	0.28 (2)	0.20 (8)*	0.08 (2)***
B. World Trade Openness → U.S. Leadership Significance Levels			
1870–1990	0.00 (10)***	0.06 (2)**	0.01 (15)***
1870–1913	0.11 (2)*	0.18 (9)*	0.50 (13)
1870–1945	0.00 (12)***	0.03 (9)***	0.00 (2)***
1946–90	0.00 (11)***	0.05 (15)***	0.00 (14)***

Note: Entries are Granger's significance levels, followed by the lag length used to obtain it, written in parentheses.

*significance at the 20% level; **significance at the 10% level; ***significance at the 5% level.

In Panel A of table 7.2, the sums of lag coefficients of U.S. leading sector growth are statistically significant at the level of 20 percent only during the 1870–1913 period. These causal effects were also weak in Panel A of table 7.1. Taken together, these results imply a weak effect of U.S. leading sector growth on world trade openness, which supports hypothesis H12. Note that the effect of leading sector growth on world trade openness is negative at all periods. The consistency of sign is interesting and could reflect an initial tendency of the world trade system to close due to domestic pressures when facing rising competition from a new leading sector. The effect of U.S. leading sector share on trade openness is positive in three out of the four periods, including the full period. Recalling the significant causal results in all periods in Panel A of table 7.1 for that variable, these results point to a positive effect of the leader's leading sector shares on openness, which supports hypothesis H13. The effect of U.S. naval share in table 7.2 is again positive in three periods, including the full period. Recalling the causalities in table 7.1, Panel A, we conclude that the effect of U.S. naval share on world trade openness is also mostly positive.

The relatively weak negative effects of U.S. leading sector shares and naval shares on world trade openness during the 1946–90 period can be accounted for by our theoretical perspective. This period is one of both U.S. rise and decline. During the latter half of the 1946–90 period, U.S. leading sector and naval shares are generally declining. At the same time, its

TABLE 7.2. Sums of Coefficients in Causality between U.S. Leadership and World Trade Openness

Period	Leading Growth	Leading Share	Naval Share
A. Effects of U.S. Leadership on World Trade Openness			
1870–1990	−0.002	0.011***	0.004***
1870–1913	−0.008*	0.013***	0.054***
1870–1945	−0.002	0.004	0.001
1946–90	−0.004	−0.03*	−0.010
B. Effects of World Trade Openness on U.S. Leadership			
1870–1990	−3.49***	−0.24***	−0.03
1870–1913	−6.43**	−0.14	30.78
1870–1945	8.95***	−0.37	−2.04***
1946–90	−10.40***	−5.70***	−3.49***

Note: Entries are the sums of lag coefficients, when the number of distributed lags equals those reported in Table 7.1.

*significance at the 20% level; **significance at the 10% level; ***significance at the 5% level.

political elites were still deeply entrenched in a free trade ideology, an element that continues the generally positive effect of the United States on world trade openness, despite its relative decline. As noted by Salvatore (1998) and Baldwin (1995), however, there are also tendencies for protectionism to rise in new and nastier forms starting in the mid-1970s, which agrees with hypothesis H12. Hence, overall, we may conclude that a rise in U.S. leadership exerts a positive effect on world trade openness, which supports hypothesis H12.

Finally, the results in Panel B of table 7.2 generally support hypothesis H14. The growth rate of the U.S. leading sector is affected negatively by world trade openness in three out of four periods. Hence, as openness rises, U.S. leading sector growth falls. The only period where the two move in the same direction is 1870 through 1945. We believe this subperiod finding reflects the strong impact of the 1930s depression during which a sharp decline in world trade openness was associated with a sharp decline in world economic activity, including the United States (and its leading sectors). The effect of a rise in world trade openness on U.S. leading sector share is negative in all periods and, in particular, is large in the 1946–90 period. Combined with the statistically significant causal effect of world trade openness on the leader's leading sector share in table 7.1, Panel B, these results imply that the leader pays a price for inducing trade openness in the world economy even as it approximates its apex position.

The effect of world trade openness on U.S. naval share is negative in three out of four periods. The effect is not significant but positive when the 1870–1913 period is examined. In Panel B of table 7.1, the causal effect in the 1870–1913 period was statistically insignificant, but was statistically significant in the full period. Hence, taken together, these results imply that the effect of world trade openness on U.S. naval shares is mostly negative, which supports hypothesis H14. Furthermore, the negative effects are greatest during the 1946–90 period, most likely reflecting the intense catch-up nature of the second U.S.-led growth wave.

Conclusion

We have linked technological leads and naval capabilities—the asserted foundations of systemic leadership—to world trade openness behavior. We focused on the case of the United States and measured U.S. politicoeconomic systemic leadership as understood from a leadership-long cycle perspective. U.S. economic leadership was measured by the growth rate of its leading sector and its share of world production of that sector. U.S. military-political leadership was measured by its share of world naval forces. World trade openness was measured as the ratio between world trade and world GNP, where the world was defined as the aggregation of the sixteen economically largest industrialized countries given in the Maddison compilation. As noted, these countries account for the overwhelming majority of world trade and production activity at any point in time in our empirical sample. The empirical test focused on both Granger causalities and signs and speed of effects in the Granger regression, and the analysis was repeated in four time periods, including the overall 1870–1990 time period.

Our empirical results reveal clear patterns that support our approach. Before we summarize them, we need to note that our empirical analysis is not without limitations. We did not, and could not, include all the variables called for by our theoretical perspective. The processes investigated here thus test only part of the fuller story on long waves of economic growth and systemic leadership, and they suggest the need for more empirical work.[7]

The findings reported in this chapter support our three hypotheses. The empirical outcome suggests that there are unambiguous linkages between systemic leadership and world trade openness (fig. 7.1). Moreover, the causality works both ways—positively from leadership to openness and negatively from openness to leadership. The leader's economic and military-political leadership induces a fast and direct increase in world trade openness. Over a longer time-horizon, on the other hand, an increase in world trade openness contributes to the relative economic and military-political decline of the leader.

It is important to note that our results do not preclude the possibility of creating future world trade openness through alternative mechanisms than the one presented here. Nor do these results prove that systemic politicoeconomic leadership is either necessary or sufficient to the development of a more open world trade. Our empirical findings do reinforce the assertion that systemic leadership has been important to fluctuations in openness in the past. Moreover, the alternatives to hegemonic leadership or the preponderance of one political-economic-military leader remain largely hypothetical. The current world economy has been shaped to some considerable extent by fluctuations in the foundations and degrees of systemic leadership (see fig. 7.2 for highlights). Of course, invoking history does not mean that the same processes will have the same effects into an infinite future. But it does suggest that we should be reluctant to ignore the

Systemic Leadership and World Trade Openness

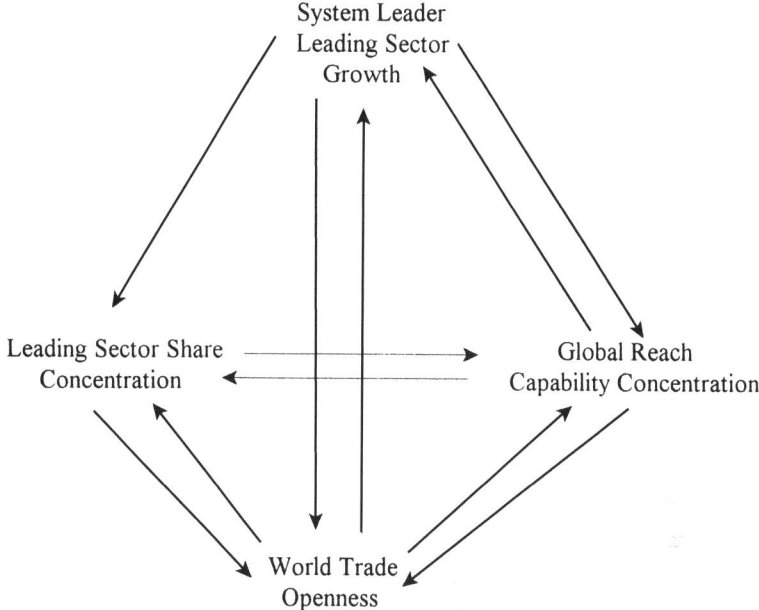

Fig. 7.1. Systemic leadership and world trade openness

importance of structural context. It has clearly mattered in the past. It could well continue to matter in the future, for it is not at all clear that the age of intermittent periods of high capability concentration and systemic leadership has passed.

One of the more recent candidates as an important agent promoting trading openness, somewhat ironically, is the tendency to regionalize trade barrier reduction efforts. The irony stems from the frequent assumption that regional trading blocs and protectionism go hand in hand, that when you encounter regional trading blocs, you should also expect to find increased protectionism. We think this assumption is at the very least highly dubious. Regionalism in trade need not always imply increased protectionism. By focusing on NAFTA within the longer-term context of U.S. trading patterns in chapter 8, we are able to evaluate some of the nascent domestic implications of the ongoing North American experiment. Our conclusion squares with those of others in the sense that the domestic impacts, especially in terms of the potential for trade diversion, have been less than

Growth, Trade, and Systemic Leadership

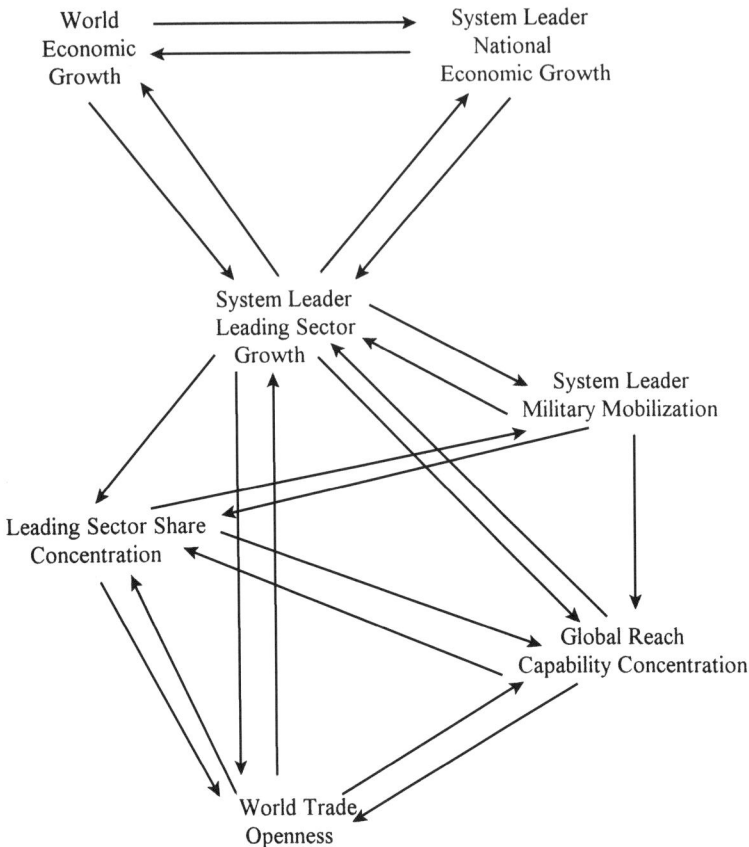

Fig. 7.2.   Growth, leadership, and openness

great. Next, we turn to the longer-term empirical relationships among tariff levels, trade regionalization, and trade openness. We find that in the U.S. historical case, these variables are less intercorrelated than is frequently imagined. In general, the emerging North American regional trading bloc has not led to a noticeable increase in protectionism or a decrease in trade openness. That need not be the case forever, but, in the interim, we need to reexamine some of our instinctive assumptions about international political economy processes. The unqualified equation of greater trade regionalization and less trade openness does not appear to be particularly valid.

8. Trade, Regionalization, and Tariffs: The Correlates of Openness in the American Long Run

The openness of the world economy is threatened—or so it would appear—by the formation of regional trade blocs. This tendency to trade more within a specific geographical region may be thought to be a relatively new phenomenon. In the late 1980s and 1990s, seemingly in emulation of the former, relatively unique, European Common Market, regional free trade areas proliferated around the world. In 1994, the North American Free Trade Agreement was signed by Canada, Mexico, and the United States. Yet it was only one of several new arrangements, joining others in South America (Mercosur) and the Pacific Rim (APEC), and anticipating the creation of other arrangements in the Caribbean, Central America, Africa, and the Middle East.[1]

The possibly alarming aspect of these regional trade pacts is the potential that they have for re-creating a world economy divided into exclusive trading zones, with each dominated by one of the major economies (i.e., Germany, the United States, and Japan). We have seen such arrangements before. Mercantilistic policy preferences led to the development of exclusive colonial zones as early as, if not long before, the putative division of the world between Spain and Portugal in the late fifteenth century. Breaking into Spain's Latin American preserve, or ensuring that the French did not inherit it, became one of the enduring frictions of European international relations for several centuries. Exclusive colonial trading privileges remained characteristic of the world economy in the early nineteenth century. Some overall movement toward freer trade was realized gradually, even though various states continued to harbor preferences for restrictions on trading openness, especially in times of political and economic crisis. Napoleon's Continental bloc scheme to preclude British economic domi-

187

nation in Europe, German plans for Mitteleuropa, and the Japanese idea of an East Asian co-prosperity sphere come readily to mind as examples.

Related to these older propensities is the idea that free trade has been championed by the leading economic power in the system (for the past few centuries, at least) as long as that power had little to fear in the way of production and trading competition. Once seriously challenged, though, Britain, the nineteenth-century leader, eventually retreated to a reliance on its advantages in serving its own imperial markets—another example of reversion to regional trading exclusiveness. The United States has been the leading economic power and the leading champion for free trade in the second half of the twentieth century. NAFTA, as well as the strong possibility of further expansion of FTAs throughout the Americas by the first decade of the twenty-first century, could be suggestive of a new retreat away from free trade principles on the part of a declining system leader.

Nevertheless, several questions need to be raised about these fears. Scholars have tended to focus on why and when trade blocs form, what form their general effects on regional and world trade take, and, more specifically, how blocs affect the overall welfare of members and nonmembers. Less likely to be addressed are the implications for domestic political economies. Who wins and loses at home once a state joins an FTA? Whatever the overall welfare shift, there is likely to be some unevenness in the domestic distribution of costs and benefits that may have some impact on whether these arrangements endure. At the same time, we also need to assess the assumption that trade regionalization tendencies can be equated with the closure of the world trading system. Underlying this correlation is another assumption: that all regional trading blocs at all times constitute relatively similar phenomena. However, number of scholars believe that regionalization can be either benign or malign.[2] There is no reason to assume that it is always a manifestation of a deteriorating international trade order. Ironically, perhaps, the new regionalization may even prove to be a substitute for a faltering multilateralism.[3]

This chapter examines the long-term movement toward regionalism in the important case of U.S. trade. The U.S. case has special significance because of the U.S. historical record as both system leader and free trade champion. In the past two hundred years, system leaders have been among the first to champion freer trade and among the last to retreat from free trade positions. If U.S. trade is becoming more encapsulated regionally, it may be taken as a leading indicator of a deteriorating trade regime first established in the aftermath of World War II. On the other hand, if

Trade, Regionalization, and Tariffs

NAFTA represents something other than increasing regional trade encapsulation, as we suspect, we have a useful warning that the proliferation of FTAs need not mean an automatic return to beggar-thy-regional-neighbor policies. This brings us to our primary hypothesis in this chapter.

> H15: Trade regionalization activities on the part of the system leader and the closure of world trade are not necessarily synonymous.

We begin by examining the possible domestic consequences of NAFTA. NAFTA is still very young, but we may still develop some sense of whether its impact is likely to be great or small. For various theoretical reasons, we do not anticipate that it will have a great impact in the near future, and this is basically what the empirical record suggests to date. We then turn to the related, longer-run question of whether U.S. trade regionalization necessarily implies a movement toward U.S. trade closure and protectionism. The catechism of international political economy portrays tariffs, trade proportions, and the regionalization of trade as an interdependent trinity. When tariffs and/or regionalization increase, trade openness must decrease (implying that the two causal relationships, tariffs → trade openness and regionalization → trade openness, are negative). When trade proportions (i.e., trade openness) increase, tariff levels and regionalization propensities must have declined. We are not so sure about the appropriate form of these relationships. Rather than assume their automaticity, we prefer to examine them more closely, over time, and with a highly selected country focus.

The point is not that every country is likely to be associated with a differently signed trinity. There are, after all, only so many possibilities given three variables. Rather, we suspect that, at the very least, some major examples—and the United States appears to be a good case in point—deviate from the usual assumptions made about these relationships. If we can develop empirical evidence pertaining to perceived exceptions, that may be all we accomplish. That is, what we are doing may simply amount to highlighting exceptions to the rule. Yet drawing attention to likely exceptions emphasizes the need to be wary of adopting assumptions about protectionist behavior—especially, when the rule itself has yet to be established empirically in any fashion. Moreover, we are dubious about any generalizations linking tariffs, trade openness, and trade regionalization that portray them moving in lockstep, either positively or negatively, with one another.

Our focus rests solely on the United States, some dimensions of its trading behavior over the last two centuries, and the North American trading region (Canada, Mexico, and the United States). We first explore the trade-diverting/trade-creating impacts of NAFTA and then examine the historical relationships characterizing U.S. tariffs, U.S. trade regionalization in North America, and U.S. trade proportions. Our specific expectations are that the overall net trade creation/diversion will not be great. We expect that both trade regionalization and the proportion of GNP constituted by trade are growing. We also expect a marked tendency for U.S. tariffs to decline at some point in accordance with expectations about the emergence of new politicoeconomic system leaders. In the last two centuries, in any event, the ascendancies of Britain and the United States have been closely associated (and credited) with ushering in new eras of freer trade. Whether that decline in protectionism leads to significantly higher trade proportions on the part of the system leader depends on the nature of the system leader's economy. In the U.S. case, where trade was not as major an economic factor as in the cases of earlier leaders, we doubt that there is or has been a close relationship. We also suspect that trade regional encapsulation tendencies in North America have increased across time, regardless of trade proportions and perhaps even tariffs.

The Impact of Trade Regionalization

Beginning in the late 1940s, U.S. support for multilateral trade agreements was reflected clearly by its initiation and stimulation of eight rounds of world trade and tariff reform within the context of the General Agreement on Tariffs and Trade (GATT). The relatively recent U.S. embrace of first NAFTA and then the Asia-Pacific Economic Cooperation (APEC) group has polarized scholars into two groups. Some believe that these regional groups facilitate a transition stage toward global free trade. Others worry that such arrangements distort trade patterns, complicate the regulation of trade, impose new trade barriers against nonmembers, lead to interregional trade wars, and, in all, slow down the movement toward freer trade on a worldwide basis.

In this section, we examine the theoretical economic effects of trade blocs on member countries. The literature on trade blocs is quite large, and it is not our intent to review it comprehensively. Rather, our present goal is to summarize the main insights offered by political economists, then apply them in our discussion of NAFTA. There are several types of trade blocs (preferential trade agreements or PTAs, free trade areas or FTAs, customs unions, economic unions). The following discussion applies, in principle, to all of these possible arrangements since they all involve lowered trade barriers among members while at least maintaining higher barriers toward nonmembers. The economics literature distinguishes between short-run and long-run effects of such arrangements. Short-run effects are based on a static economic analysis (that is, a cost-benefit analysis at one particular time). Long-run analysis permits gains and losses to accumulate over time and, therefore, is harder to conduct in a more formal fashion.

The short-run effects of trade blocs were first studied by Viner (1950) and then elaborated by Meade (1955) and Lipsey and Lancaster (1956).[4] The theory was formulated for a customs union—an area that prohibits trade barriers among members and harmonizes members' trade barriers toward the outside world. Nevertheless, Viner's insights also apply to other forms of trade blocs such as FTAs—arrangements that also prohibit trade barriers among members but stop short of harmonizing external trade policies.

Jacob Viner's static analysis emphasized the forces of trade creation and diversion. *Trade creation* occurs when the elimination (or reduction) of trade barriers among the trade bloc's members leads to more trade among them, thereby replacing domestic production. Viner and others have shown that trade creation increases the partners' welfare because it leads to greater specialization in production based on comparative advantage. Trade creation may create losses for some regional firms or industries, but the overall cumulative gains are believed to outweigh individual losses.

A trade bloc can also have a welfare-reducing effect. *Trade diversion* occurs when goods produced by less efficient producers inside the bloc replace the import of goods produced by more efficient producers from outside the bloc. This may happen if trade barriers are lowered among members but remain high toward nonmembers. Bloc consumers may then find it cheaper to buy goods produced inside the region. Yet the price of foreign goods is higher only because of trade barriers. This sort of trade diversion reduces welfare in that it entails a move away from the optimal production resource allocation of open markets. In principle, this effect is similar to other trade barriers. It distorts domestic consumption and production patterns and implies a move away from one's comparative advantage.

A trade bloc can exhibit both trade creation and diversion. Whether trade blocs are welfare reducing or not thus depends on the relative size of trade creation versus trade diversion. We should note that Viner's analysis is but one example of the economic theory of "the second best." The first-best policy in this respect is worldwide free trade. In the absence of the first best, a trade bloc can be a move in the correct direction, or a second-best policy. Nevertheless, the second-best policy may not increase members' welfare as long as there remain distortions that prevent market forces from arriving at optimal allocation of production resources.

The second-best theory has at least one important implication for the political economy of trade regionalism. The theory implies that only those trade blocs that generate a positive net benefit to members are likely to be either activated or reasonably stable. Otherwise, the losses associated with bloc formation are likely to motivate forces that will object to formation and continued membership. Of course, the political economy of bloc formation is more complicated than this simple model suggests. Such variables as winners' and losers' mobilization, organization, and access to power and other domestic factors are sure to make some difference as well. Periods of world depression and intense conflict are also notorious for encouraging exclusive trading blocs. Still, from a unitary state actor perspective, one can generalize that only trade blocs that entail a net gain will tend to be concluded and/or sustained.

Several scholars have investigated the theoretical conditions under which a trade bloc is more likely to create positive net gains.[5] One is that the higher the trade barriers between members prior to the bloc formation, the larger will be the size of trade creation once the barriers are removed. A second generalization is that the smaller the trade of the bloc with the outside world prior to group formation, the less likely trade diversion is. A related consideration pertains to the size of the bloc's external trade barriers. The lower are these barriers, the less trade diversion is likely. Moreover, the more countries choose to join the bloc (and the larger the size of their economies), the more likely trade creation is. This outcome is predicated on the assumption that the larger the bloc, the more probable it is that specialization and low-cost production of some goods will be located within the bloc. A fifth expectation is that trade creation will be greater for countries that are geographically proximate due to the reductions in transportation costs. Finally, competitive economies that also enjoyed a great degree of pre-bloc economic interaction are more likely to create trade than to divert it. In such situations, there are more possibilities for intratrade industry and production of differentiated goods. This implies that trade creation is more likely between two integrating competitive industrialized economies than between an integrating agricultural nation and a complementary industrial nation.

The second-best theory implies that country A, if given a choice between a preferential trade agreement with country B and free trade with country C, should go with C as long as the A-C trade creation effects are larger and the A-C trade diversion effects are smaller than in the A-B case. Yet country A might still choose to join in a bloc with country B if there is some promise of dynamic gains from their integration (i.e., gains that accumulate over time). This type of economic gain is normally not included in the trade creation/diversion static discussion.

Trade blocs can develop dynamic gains from several sources. First, trade blocs can increase the level of competition. Protected firms, in contrast, typically become less efficient over time. When trade barriers are removed, the previously protected sectors become exposed to new competition, which, in turn, should facilitate incentives to become more efficient. A second source of dynamic gain is that larger markets may encourage economies of scale. Facing expanding markets, firms may invest in new plants and equipment to serve their growing markets. Another possibility is that firms external to the bloc may establish production facilities inside the bloc in order to evade the external trade barriers. The ensuing increase in production facilities should further stimulate economic growth within the bloc.[6]

Bloc-joining considerations also include political motivations. As noted earlier, the literature on the politics of bloc formation is large, and we can only mention some of the ideas. One argument often invoked in the context of the European Union is that a substantial increase in economic interdependence can reduce the probability of warfare. Several of the EU founding fathers, such as Robert Schumann, the French foreign minister, and Jean Monnet, the French advocate of functionalist integration, held this view.[7] An alternative approach involves emphasizing the unification incentives stimulated by a common external threat. This type of argument is quite compatible with realist perspectives and is exemplified by Mearsheimer's (1990) work.[8] A third view is that trade blocs are formed in reaction to political pressure from various domestic and international groups. For instance, the Generalized System of Preference between developed and less developed countries (LDCs) that gives special trade preferences to LDCs was put in place in the 1970s under pressure from LDCs. A related argument is that trade blocs are a reaction to successful lobbying by exporters—an issue we turn to next.

The main gainers from free trade, consumers, are harder to mobilize than firms. This helps to explain why firms are able in many cases to lobby successfully for protection that is paid for in terms of higher prices by consumers. Exporters typically support free trade since it implies cheaper imported production inputs, frees up inputs for exporting sectors, and can lead to lower trade barriers abroad when a trading partner reciprocates with reductions in protectionist policies. As noted by Lawrence (1996), among others, these processes are not widely appreciated by the public. Unilateral trade liberalization as a consequence is difficult politically. Liberalization through multilateral agreements may not be as attractive as bilateral arrangements to exporters who see, as in GATT and the WTO, all members receiving most favored nation benefits automatically. Multilateral agreements may also reflect compromises that do not always match the specific needs or goals of a single country's economy. Bhagwati and Krueger (1995) argue that these types of objections are less likely to apply to trade blocs since the benefits are more visible, less diffused, and thus more apt to stimulate strong support from exporters.

The NAFTA Debate

The NAFTA case provides a useful empirical focus for some of the theoretical arguments and generalizations outlined in the previous section. The formation of NAFTA was controversial from the outset in large part because observers projected varying expectations concerning the likely adverse impact of its formation on the U.S. economy.[9] While NAFTA has not been around long enough to say much that is conclusive about its impact, the circumstances surrounding its formation are especially revealing for our interest in assessing trade regionalization phenomena in the U.S. case.

In January 1, 1994, the United States, Canada, and Mexico began the implementation of NAFTA. The agreement requires the three members to remove all tariffs on trade among the three states over a period of fifteen years. Some restrictions on farm products and the flow of foreign direct investment (FDI) are exempted. The agreement also imposes strict rules on the use of nontariff barriers, spells out regional antitrust and intellectual property right rules, and provides dispute settlement mechanisms. Each country can upgrade its own environmental standards as long as it can claim a scientific basis for changing standards. Attracting FDI is not regarded as an appropriate reason for lowering environmental standards.[10]

NAFTA is unique because it joins two developed countries with a less developed country. Other trade blocs tend to be more homogeneous in the economic sense and, therefore, more likely to generate higher gains. Indeed, much of the debate over NAFTA has been about the desirability of close and free links between the United States (and to a lesser extent, Canada) and Mexico. As we have pointed out, trade blocs are second best and, therefore, may reduce bloc members' welfare. But they are also capable of generating gains down the road. The resultant political game is often one in which short-run losers mobilize to thwart the bloc formation, while potential, long-run, winners promote the agreement. Since future gains usually are less visible than current losses, short-run losers tend to be quite vocal.

While many U.S. policymakers supported NAFTA in 1993, there was (and continues to be) considerable objection to the bloc arrangement, stemming mainly from three groups: (1) organized labor and owners of industries facing competition from cheaper LDC (i.e., Mexican) labor; (2) environmentalists; and (3) some consumer groups. NAFTA was only approved in the House of Representatives by a narrow margin (234 to 200) and remains contentious, as was demonstrated in the late 1997 debate over granting presidential fast-track authority to expand NAFTA to encompass additional states in South America.[11]

The objection to NAFTA, predicated on the U.S.-Mexico economic development differences, can be summarized in the following way.[12] It has been claimed that NAFTA would result in the loss of American jobs because Mexican labor is less expensive and its workplace standards are more lax, and therefore less costly.[13] The implication was that labor-intensive goods from Mexico would outsell U.S. labor-intensive goods. It was also claimed that whatever trade diversion is created could generate other economic losses and might also contribute to the deterioration of major trading partners of the United States, such as Japan and members of the EU.

Another assertion was that American firms would relocate to Mexico in order to avoid the higher costs of doing business in the United States. Polluting industries, in particular, might be encouraged to move south, thereby contributing to the degradation of the Mexican environment. All of these shifts would not only reduce U.S. leverage on Mexico to tighten its environmental regulations, it would also increase global pollution. Firms in the United States might also reduce their production standards and product quality in order to compete with less costly Mexican goods and firms producing in Mexico. To the more general extent that NAFTA bolstered Mexican elites and their positions within the Mexican polity, one might expect as well slower movement toward economic and political reforms unless those same reforms encouraged the countervailing formation of new elite-mass groups that benefited from the changes and were in a position to work toward expanding the reforms. Yet given universal tendencies toward some degree of societal inertia, one might expect a healthy lag between the successful impact of new group demands and the drag of established elite clout.

NAFTA supporters largely followed the logic normally associated with an emphasis on trade creation and free trade. According to one view, NAFTA would increase competition and lower prices. The potential dynamic gains have also been emphasized. Hufbauer and Schott (1992), for instance, estimated that NAFTA would lead to a decline of 150,000 unskilled U.S. jobs and an increase of 325,000 skilled jobs. Low wage zones in the United States might suffer, then, but other areas would benefit. Another argument was that NAFTA would allow U.S. industries to import labor-intensive goods from Mexico while keeping their main plant operations within the United States. Contrary to the criticism of jobs migrating south, NAFTA could provide an alternative for the relocation of American firms to low-wage countries. The attractions of low wages in Mexico should be offset by the equally low productivity or real output per Mexican worker.[14] In any event, the issue of trade diversion was thought to be exaggerated inasmuch as the United States already possesses very low trade barriers toward the outside world. Finally, supporters argue that any negative environmental impacts should be regulated within NAFTA-negotiated guidelines.

The Impacts of NAFTA

The relatively short time since its 1994 inception makes it a bit too early to fully assess the NAFTA outcome. Nevertheless, some interim observations are feasible. For our purposes, NAFTA effects can be grouped into two categories: economic and political.

In the summer of 1997, the Clinton administration issued a report on the economic impact of NAFTA (as was called for by the original legislation).[15] In general, the U.S. and Canadian impacts of the trade bloc agreement are modest, but it does seem to have made more of an impression on the Mexican economy. The small Canadian impact is due mainly to the earlier U.S.-Canadian free trade agreement (1989) and the fact that even before 1989 their bilateral tariffs were low. Moreover, the potential Canadian gains from free Mexican-Canadian trade are likely to be quite small.

U.S. exports to Mexico rose from $40 billion in 1993 to $57 billion in 1996. U.S. imports from Mexico rose from $39 billion to $73 billion over the same period. Just what proportion of these increases should be attributed to NAFTA trade creation is harder to estimate. The evaluation is further complicated by the sharp devaluation of the Mexican peso in 1994–95 and the recession it induced in Mexico. The peso devaluation alone must have worked toward boosting Mexico's exports and suppressing its imports. Recession might also be expected to have an import-suppressing effect.[16] More clearly, the effect on U.S. employment is not great. Ojeda et al. (1996) estimate that the net employment impact of NAFTA on U.S. employment amounted to a gain of 10,000 workers (within a pool of 120 million workers). U.S. foreign direct investment in Mexico since 1994 averaged less than $3 billion, which, again, is a rather small number.[17]

NAFTA's trade diversion effects are less than clear. Despite Hufbauer and Schott's (1993) prediction of little trade diversion, given low U.S. trade barriers, some trade diversion may be taking place. In the automobile industry, in particular, some of Asia's car exports to the U.S. market have been replaced by Mexican car exports. The combined decline in trade barriers attributable to NAFTA, the relocation of some American auto plants to Mexico, and the sharp decline in the value of the peso in 1994–95 resulted in almost doubling the number of cars and trucks exported from Mexico to the United States from 1994 to mid-1997.[18]

The positive effect of NAFTA on the Mexican economy, therefore, has been noticeable and is expected to grow further in the long term. As estimated by Klein and Salvatore (1995) and Salvatore (1998), the Mexican economy will gain from NAFTA in terms of export-led growth, reduced capital flight, and the encouragement of structural economic (and political) reforms vis-à-vis freer markets. Mexico's average yearly growth rate is forecast to be 5.2 percent from 1995 to 2005. Without NAFTA, it is estimated that it would have been about 3.8 percent per annum. NAFTA is also expected to boost FDI to Mexico by $3.2 billion per year over the same period, reduce inflation by 4.8 percent, and boost exports to the United States by 2.1 percent per year. However, the peso crisis dragged down performance (below the forecast) in 1995 and 1996. Only in late 1997 were there signs that the Mexican economy was recovering from its unanticipated recession. Even so, some authors have attributed the relatively quicker recovery, compared to the 1982 debt crisis, to NAFTA.[19]

The relatively small effect of NAFTA on the U.S. economy can be explained in two ways. Since U.S. trade barriers for all goods and states were already low, the trade bloc arrangement bestows little in the way of competitive advantage on Mexican involvement in the U.S. economy. A modest amount of overall trade diversion corresponds with this observation. Perhaps more important, the Mexican economy is around twenty-five times smaller than the U.S. economy. The largest share that Mexican firms had in any U.S. sector does not exceed 10 percent and in many cases is smaller than 2 percent (Leamer 1993). Mexico's economy could hardly be expected to satisfy U.S. import demands even in sectors that are considered to be within the domain of Mexican comparative advantage (for example, textiles).

Given the history of Mexican authoritarianism, it is not surprising that the political effects of NAFTA are frequently highlighted. Some authors (Poli 1995; Lopez-Villicana 1997) assert that NAFTA has locked in Mexico's commitment to liberal reforms. Tornell and Esquivel (1995) emphasize that the Mexican response to the peso/debt crisis of 1994–95 was much different than its response to the 1982 debt crisis. In the 1980s, Mexico reacted by raising its trade barriers sharply. In the mid-1990s, it again raised trade barriers toward the outside world but continued to cut tariffs on U.S. and Canadian trade. Thus, NAFTA has contributed to the credibility of Mexican commitment to liberal economic reforms. It is also possible to argue that NAFTA could be used as a political weapon against protectionist forces within Mexico that can be expected to become stronger in periods of economic crisis (Frankel, Stein, and Wei 1997).[20]

Symbolically, NAFTA obviously underlines closer U.S.-Mexican relations. Mutual foreign policy issues are more likely to be dealt with in an interdependent manner. From one U.S. perspective, a strategy for combating drug smuggling and illegal immigration is to facilitate the success of the Mexican economy. Should NAFTA-induced liberalization accelerate Mexican growth, as anticipated, the "Gringo-bashing" rhetoric of the past may decline.[21] The American embrace of Mexico was demonstrated in two recent cases. In 1994 and 1995, the United States rushed to put together a $50 billion rescue loan to support Mexico in the aftermath of the peso crisis. Two years later, the United States renewed Mexico's certification as an ally in fighting drugs even though large quantities of drugs are still smuggled from Mexico to the United States.

Finally, some observers have argued that NAFTA has had some impact on Mexico's domestic political system. Almazan (1997) argues that by transferring authority from state to markets, NAFTA has weakened the formerly highly centralized position of the Mexican government and, as a consequence, also strengthened rebels within the various indigenous communities. In a related fashion, Purcell (1997) suggests that Mexico's relatively low-key response to the Chiapas rebellion reflects Mexico's official concern with its image in the United States and the fear that a negative U.S. reaction to a stronger response might jeopardize NAFTA. Husted and Logsdon (1997) have also concluded that NAFTA encouraged more commitment to Mexican policies aimed at pollution reduction and environmental regulation enforcement.

In sum, NAFTA has had some impact, and it is likely to continue to do so. Nonetheless, its primary impact has been focused on the Mexican economy—the smallest member of the NAFTA trio. The net effect of that impact has been to open Mexican markets and not to close North American markets to outside participation. As long as opening works to the benefit of Mexican economic development, the general impact should, in principle, be beneficial for freer trade in the world economy. At the same time, the Mexican contribution to the world economy is rather small. Therefore, we assume the net impact of NAFTA on the world economy will not be any larger. However, if NAFTA per se does not constitute a major shift away from freer trade, either in North America or the world at large, we still do not know what the general relationships are, and have been, among trade regionalization tendencies, expanding trade, and protectionism. That is the topic to which we turn in the second half of this chapter.

Trade Regionalization, NAFTA, and Openness

An early, highly influential article by Krasner (1976) established the trinity of tariff levels, trade proportions, and regional trade encapsulation as markers for the behavioral and institutional dimensions of trade structure. Krasner's argument revolved around several points. One was that no single indicator would suffice to capture trade structure. Tariff levels, in particular, are awkward in that they are difficult to operationalize and tricky to interpret. In addition, nontariff barriers to trade are often ignored. Krasner proposed to supplement tariff levels, an institutional indicator, with two behavioral indicators. One focused on the proportion of trade to national income or gross domestic product as a measure of the importance of external economic activity in comparison to domestic economic activity. The other indicator looked at the tendency for large states to protect their welfare by creating regional blocs through the concentration of their trade with nearby smaller states. The idea here is that political coercion is employed to distort what the trade outcome might have been if only comparative advantage was at stake.

A trade structure becomes more open, then, as tariffs fall, trade proportions rise, and regional encapsulation propensities decline. Krasner's reference point is clearly aimed at systemic structure. Since we are primarily interested in the U.S. case at this point, we are not necessarily challenging the accuracy of his aggregate structural generalization. In general, we accept the notion that falling tariffs, rising trade proportions, and declining regional encapsulation have been historical hallmarks of an opening trade structure. What we are curious about, though, is whether these relationships hold at less aggregated levels of analysis. Should we expect all states to be characterized by the same relationships? For that matter, should we expect the leader of the system to adhere to the aggregate pattern? There is also the question of novelty. Trade regionalization in the past has been equated with protectionist tendencies. That does not guarantee that the contemporary movement toward regionalization is equally protectionist in nature. Things change in international political economy as in other spheres of activity. Our suspicion, as suggested in hypothesis H15, is that not all trade regionalization activity is equally protectionist in nature. Some of it simply reflects the fact that longer distances for goods to travel tend to lead to higher prices. Some also connects to short-term political strategies that are not directly linked to trading patterns per se (e.g., as in bailing out a neighbor in trouble).

Krasner's (1976) historical evidence was at best ambiguous. In Europe, the 1820–79 period was described as one of decreasing tariff levels. In the years immediately leading up to World War I, European tariff levels, in most cases, rose and then increased again after World War I, most dramatically after 1930. After 1945, European tariffs decreased at least through the mid- to late 1960s. In contrast, the United States was described as remaining highly protectionist throughout the nineteenth century, especially after the American Civil War, until World War I, and then again in the early Depression years. Only in the mid-1930s did the United States take the lead in promoting lower tariff levels.

European trade proportions were described as paralleling tariff movements for the most part. Trade proportions in Europe increased in the nineteenth century through 1880, decreased between 1880 and 1900, increased from 1900 to 1913, and decreased in the 1920s and 1930s, before increasing again after 1945. The U.S. pattern is described and depicted as roughly holding constant at a low ratio throughout most of this same time period.

Regional encapsulation information is less easy to obtain. However, Krasner's data suggested some tendencies toward generally declining regionalization between 1890 and 1928, increasing encapsulation after 1928, and slowly decreasing regionalization after 1954. The data most pertinent to the U.S. case consist of the percentage of Latin American exports to the United States and the percentage of U.S. imports from Latin America (where Latin America is defined as Argentina, Bolivia, Brazil, Chile, Colombia, Ecuador, Mexico, and Paraguay). These data show increasing regionalization between 1890 and the 1950s and then declining percentages in the 1960s through 1967 or 1968.

There are of course some conceptual and empirical problems here. Krasner's tariff generalizations were not data-based, and the regional encapsulation data were limited in the number of observations that were examined. The encapsulation data are asymmetrical in that they look at "Latin American" flows to the United States but not U.S. flows to Latin America. One could also note that in the U.S. case, the question of regional encapsulation calls for an examination of trade flows to and from Canada as well as with southern neighbors. It is also awkward to evaluate movement in a few years in the 1960s as to whether a new trend line has been established. Mansfield (1994) notes, too, that after all is said and done, we end up with rather crude, dichotomous characterizations of periods of relative openness and closure.

Yet, index quibbling aside, the picture described by Krasner in 1976 has the United States beginning to lower its tariffs in the 1930s, not altering its trade proportion all that much, and retaining its regional trade biases well into the late 1950s. Such a picture suggests a rather uneven movement toward greater trade openness, with tariff decreases preceding deregionalization by several decades, which in turn precedes the relative absence of change in trade proportion or significance. This history does not necessarily violate the interdependence of the trinity, but it does suggest that the relationships among these three variables may be more complicated than is sometimes thought. Yet we are also left with something of an implied puzzle. If U.S. trade became less regional in scope only in the late 1950s, how should we regard the more recent interest in NAFTA? Does NAFTA represent still another reversal in regional encapsulation fluctuations? Is the United States hedging its openness bet as the post–World War II system leader by developing a regional enclave in its backyard much as the British did in the late nineteenth century with its more geographically extensive empire?

However we answer these questions, there are reasons to be cautious about interpreting NAFTA. On the one hand, it is an unfinished product (Weintraub 1997) that has yet to take full shape. At the same time, none of the members appears to have been motivated by a desire to reduce trade with nations outside the bloc. To the contrary, most accounts stress various types of trade liberalizing motivations and not straightforward protectionist urges, especially on the part of Mexico (see Haggard 1997; Weintraub 1997; Milner 1998).[22] Moreover, not only are there restrictions on what NAFTA covers, all NAFTA members are also members of APEC, the trans-Pacific arrangement. It has been noted that if NAFTA should expand to encompass the Americas, the APEC membership is retained and strengthened, and some new transatlantic arrangement were to be concluded, most of the world's trade would be encompassed in three overlapping "blocs" that would hardly represent blocs at all. The bottom line, already anticipated in earlier sections of this chapter, seems to be that we need not equate NAFTA, as a matter of assumption, with a retreat from free trade principles.

Long-Run U.S. Trade and Protectionism Data

One way to address some of these questions about the meaning of NAFTA is to develop a set of longer time-series for the U.S. case. We may then eyeball their patterns of fluctuations over time and also correlate the extent to which they covary. Figure 8.1 presents a long-run view of U.S. tariff levels, trade proportion, and regional encapsulation. The measure of U.S. tariff levels is nominal tariff rate averages (chap. 5). Trade proportion is the ratio of U.S. imports and exports to U.S. gross domestic product. Regional encapsulation is captured crudely by the size of U.S. trade with Canada and Mexico as a percentage of total U.S. trade with the world.[23]

Although subject to some extreme year-to-year fluctuations due to wars and depressions, the general patterns are reasonably clear. Tariff levels are shown as increasing to about 1835, decreasing to the Civil War, remaining mostly constant to the period just before World War I, then rising once again in the 1920s until they peaked prior to World War II. After 1940, they plummeted and remained low through the next fifty or more years. Keep in mind, however, that this series does not measure nontariff barriers

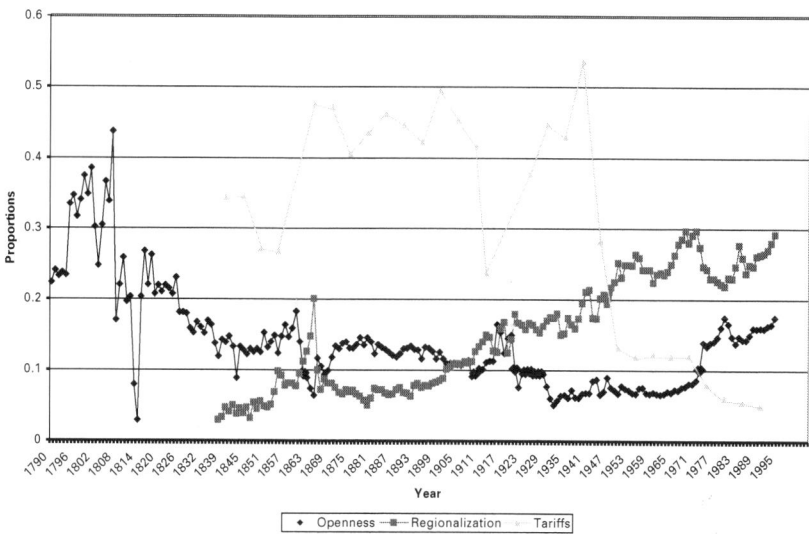

Fig. 8.1. Regionalization, tariffs, and openness in U.S. trade

(NTBs). If we had serial data on NTBs, the fifty-plus years of decreased protectionism might look a bit different, less oriented to free trade. At the same time, since the use of NTBs only intensified since the mid- to late 1970s (the last few years of our series), we may assume that their effect on our analysis is rather small.

Trade proportions were fairly high in the first few decades of U.S. history but also quickly began to decline. They continued to decline until the late 1960s and have more recently climbed back to levels not sustained since well before the American Civil War. Regional encapsulation, at least as we are measuring it (with an emphasis on North America), has been steadily trending upward for the last 170 years or so. Nevertheless, we do observe some short-term but recent decline in this propensity in the early 1970s that is not maintained after 1980 (which is presumably related to oil-pricing problems).[24] This departure from the trend line, though, does not appear to be the same shift captured in Krasner's Latin American series for the 1960s.

Data Analysis

We do not propose a definitive examination of the relationships among trade proportions, regional encapsulation, or tariff levels because, at this point, we do not have strong theoretical expectations about how they might be related, or what other variables might be critical. Our focus is also America-centric. A more definitive examination, minimally, would require a less selective country sample. Thus, our empirical examination is preliminary, exploratory, and aimed at evaluating hypothesis H15. There is some reason to anticipate, however, a less-than-perfect correlation among these variables, and we are curious just how much deviation from high correlations are observed. Yet our interest is not simply casual. The U.S. case, embodying the behavior of the post–World War II system leader, has more than average significance. While NAFTA may not be representative of other FTAs, it is certainly one of the more important regional trade arrangements—again, if only because it is centered on the system's lead economy of the twentieth century.

Our operationalizations of the three variables are straightforward and represent the same data discussed descriptively earlier in this chapter. Trade proportion is measured as the ratio of U.S. exports and imports to U.S. gross domestic product ("Trade/GDP" in tables 8.1 and 8.2). Regional encapsulation is the proportion of U.S. trade with Canada and Mexico in terms of total U.S. trade ("Regionalization"). Tariffs are measured as average tariff rates. The correlations among these three variables are based on the 1854–1990 period.[25]

Table 8.1 summarizes the correlational outcomes for two interpretations of the data. The first matrix is based on levels of the variables in question and without lagging (i.e., the contemporaneous relationship at t_0). The second matrix reports the unlagged correlations among the year-to-year change scores since the level data are characterized by discernible trends that might influence unduly the correlational outcomes. Given our sample size, correlations higher than +0.171 or lower than –0.171 are significant at the 0.05 level.[26]

The level outcomes certainly support the idea that these three variables have not moved in unison across time in the North American case. Trade proportion and regional encapsulation are negatively related, which is what we would expect if both variables measured trade openness/closure in similar ways. Note, however, that the correlation is only in the moderate range (–0.392). In marked contrast, however, the other two relationships are different from what might otherwise be expected. Trade proportion and tariff levels are not correlated in a statistically significant way (the association is –0.103). Tariff levels and regional encapsulation are highly and significantly correlated, but the relationship is negative (–0.785): lower U.S. average tariffs are associated with more U.S. regional encapsulation, or less U.S. trade with the world, a result which may seem a bit odd. Nevertheless, this last finding is not very mysterious. As we noted earlier, U.S. average tariff levels have been mostly decreasing in the post-1945 period, while U.S. regional trade has been increasing.

Yet the change scores (the second matrix in table 8.1) suggest something different. Changes in trade proportion and regionalization remain negatively related as in the levels case, albeit at a higher level of correlation (–0.547). Changes in average tariff levels and trade proportion are now negatively and significantly related at a moderate level (–0.311), which is a result to be expected based on short-run orientation of trade theory (see also hypothesis H11). Changes in average tariff levels and regionalization are now positively and significantly related (0.198). This means that, historically, a rise in average tariffs is positively associated with a rise in U.S. regionalization, all other things being equal. Theoretically, one would not expect changes in either one of these two variables to lead to positive changes in the other.

One possibility is that we are not working with the appropriate lag structure. If these variables are not perfectly correlated at t_0 and changes in

TABLE 8.1.   Correlation Matrix for U.S. Trade Regionalization, Trade/GDP, and Tariffs

	Regionalization	Trade/GDP	Tariffs
Level Scores			
Regionalization	—	–0.392*	–0.785*
Trade/GDP		—	–0.103
Tariffs			—
Change Scores			
Regionalization	—	–0.547*	0.198*
Trade/GDP		—	–0.311
Tariffs			—

Note: Entries are correlation scores between a variable whose name is written in a column with a variable whose name is written in a line.

*indicates statistical significance at 5% or better.

at least some of them do lead to changes in other values of the trio, we should look for lagged relationships, rather than t_0 relationships. Table 8.2 summarizes the outcome when one looks systematically at the six possible pairs of relationships subject to one- to five-year lags. The overall pattern that emerges suggests that these variables are even less interrelated than table 8.1's correlations might suggest.

The negative relationship between the U.S. trade proportion and regional encapsulation is most consistent for level scores (in all lags) and is concentrated at t_0 for the change scores. The U.S. trade proportion and regional encapsulation have moderately discouraged one another. But the lagged change score correlations and the size of the level correlations suggest caution in assuming that these processes necessarily have much of a causal relationship. The levels of trade proportion are not particularly related to tariff levels at any lag. Their moderate and negative relationship in the change scores is strongest in t_0 and generally supports the view that a rise in trade proportion drives a decline in tariffs (as reflected by the significant −0.218 and −0.190 scores).[27] Finally, regionalization and average tariff levels are negatively related at the highest levels reported in the table at all lags. But the change scores again suggest caution. They are much weaker, primarily insignificant, with the two significant scores having opposite signs (0.198 and −0.231). If there is a causal relationship

TABLE 8.2. Cross-correlations for U.S. Trade Regionalization, Trade/GDP, and Tariffs

$t-5$	$t-4$	$t-3$	$t-2$	$t-1$	t_0	$t-1$	$t-2$	$t-3$	$t-4$	$t-5$
Level Data										
Regionalization → trade/GDP						Trade/GDP → regionalization				
−.224	−.265	−.295	−.319	−.350	−.392	−.389	−.391	−.402	−.392	−.392
Tariffs → trade/GDP						Trade/GDP → tariffs				
−.035	−.049	−.067	−.083	−.096	−.103	−.074	−.032	−.020	−.080	−.144
Tariffs → regionalization						Regionalization → tariffs				
−.723	−.739	−.753	−.761	−.776	−.785	−.782	−.781	−.784	−.787	−.791
Change Score Data										
Regionalization → trade/GDP						Trade/GDP → regionalization				
.132	−.105	−.003	.020	.074	−.547	−.056	.171	−.157	.080	.196
Tariffs → trade/GDP						Trade/GDP → tariffs				
.187	.099	.019	−.045	−.149	−.311	−.218	−.119	−.190	−.111	.075
Tariffs → regionalization						Regionalization → tariffs				
−.231	−.048	−.012	−.026	.026	.198	.145	.009	.003	−.012	−.100

Note: Correlations higher than +0.171 or lower than −0.171 are significant at the 0.05 level.

between these variables, based on our results it is not clear what it might be. Thus, we see these preliminary results as supportive of hypothesis H15, which suggests only that trade regionalization and the system leader's trade closure are not identical processes.

Concluding Remarks

Overall, we can find long-run empirical relationships among U.S. regional encapsulation, trade proportions, and tariffs. However, the correlations are much less than unity and, in some instances, the relationships are either statistically insignificant (levels of tariffs and trade proportions) or signed differently than might have been expected (changes in regional encapsulation and tariffs). Only the correlation between average tariffs and regional encapsulation levels approximates the strong negative relationship that might be anticipated if the three variables were measuring processes that operated in parallel directions. Most of the other correlations we obtained here suggest weaker, more moderate relationships.

As we emphasized earlier, our analysis is not definitive and should be considered exploratory, in part because our number of country cases is one, and clearly a two-by-two correlation analysis falls short of a fully specified econometric model that links our variables. Yet the statistical outcome certainly supports the notion that trade regionalization, trade proportions, and protectionism do not necessarily go hand in hand. That is, trade regionalization does not necessarily mean an increase in protectionism. A considerable proportion of trade regionalization tendencies, no doubt, reflect the lower transportation costs associated with proximate economies and possibly political considerations of the bloc's members as suggested by several authors in the cases of the European Union and NAFTA.[28]

Other things being equal, we might expect neighboring economies to trade more with neighbors than with nonneighbors. This result is confirmed in numerous trade studies that have relied upon the bilateral trade gravity research design.[29] We might also expect, as reflected by our theoretical and empirical analysis, some tendency for trade diversion due to the formation of trade blocs. Yet this does not make trade bloc behavior necessarily malign, as some observers have contended. The important question is at what point trade regionalization takes on an exclusive flavor in which trade within the region and trade outside the region start assuming a zero-sum nature.

From what we find in our review of the NAFTA case, the trade diversion

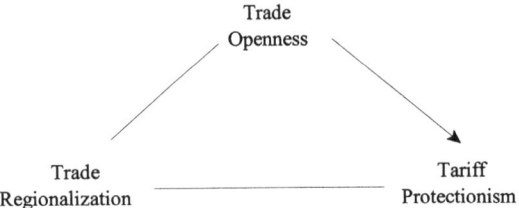

Fig. 8.2. Openness, regionalization, and tariffs

tendency of this trade bloc is not strong. That is, NAFTA per se has not constituted a major shift away from freer trade, either in North America or the world at large. This U.S. tendency is also evident in our longer-run data analysis. Of course, trade blocs can become malign. But a zero-sum movement toward trade regionalization would seem to require explicit political interventions. Intraregional activities would have to be given priority over extraregional activities by either prohibiting extraregional trade or by making it relatively too expensive to compete. Politically sanctioned regional trade encapsulation has certainly occurred before. But, in the U.S. case at least (and we suspect elsewhere as well), regional trade encapsulation can coexist with declining tariffs and expanding trade proportions. Increasing propensities toward regional trade, as summarized in hypothesis H15, cannot be interpreted automatically as a movement away from (or toward) freer trade order.

As a consequence, we view figure 8.2 as a reasonable way to organize provisionally the ways in which trade openness, trade regionalization, and tariff protectionism are related. We have reason to believe (from the findings discussed in chapter 6) that trade openness drives tariff protectionism more than the other way around. We can also link trade regionalization to trade openness and to tariff protectionism. Yet the linkages are probably not all that strong from a causal perspective. Sometimes they are related closely (as in the 1930s) and, at other times (the contemporary era), they do not appear to be closely linked. What this suggests is that some relationships are simply not time-invariant. Therefore, we need to be cautious in equating regionalization in trade flows with protectionism and closure of the world economy.

Contemporary trade regionalization activities might have constituted a threat to some of our basic arguments about the nature of systemic leadership and international political economy. That does not currently appear to be the case with the U.S. involvement in NAFTA. Thus, we need to add the linkages of figure 8.2 to our overall model. With that potential analytical problem out of the way, it is time to recapitulate our whole argument. Just what is it that our contentions, fifteen hypotheses, and findings add up to in terms of a bigger picture? The answer to this question is the focus of chapter 9, where we summarize what we have argued about and uncovered empirically in the last eight chapters.

9. Conclusion: Adding Things Up

Students of international relations sometimes debate which variables are most central to our understanding of how international politics and international political economy work. It is fairly obvious that we think system leadership should be listed as one of the most central keys to unraveling structure and behavior on the world stage. Yet we are also well aware that this position is not shared by many other scholars, especially in international political economy circles, even though one might argue that systemic leadership is particularly pervasive in IPE phenomena. Just why there is so much reluctance to embrace systemic leadership as a key factor is something of an analytical mystery.

It is not because leading IPE scholars have never considered the question. A number of influential figures have displayed some interest in the question. Even so, their interest has usually been either ambivalent or sporadic. Charles Kindleberger (1973) wrote a prominent study of the history of the interwar depression and concluded that a major factor was the absence of a hegemonic lender of last resort. Subsequently, he denied (1980) that one should make too much of the presence or absence of a hegemon. Yet he (1996) was also able, subsequently, to generate a book-length study focused explicitly on the last five hundred years or so of economic leaders. He came to the conclusion that there had been a tendency for one economy to achieve primacy in the world economy, and he expected that pattern to continue indefinitely into the future, with the United States eventually being replaced by some other economy.[1]

Stephen Krasner (1976) produced what has to be one of the most widely read article-length studies on the interaction of hegemony and protectionism. To be sure, his empirical outcome was less than completely supportive of his initial assumptions, but, more important, Krasner has never returned to that topic or the more general question of hegemonic influences (aside from Webb and Krasner 1989). Similarly, Robert Keohane (1980, 1984) demonstrated an early interest in the subject of systemic leadership and also appears to have abandoned the topic altogether. Joseph Nye (1990), a sometime coauthor with Keohane (Keohane and Nye 1977, 1989), picked up the topic briefly, but his interests, too, appear to have moved elsewhere. Even Robert Gilpin appears to have lost what was initially a very strong interest. Gilpin (1975) contrasted British and American leadership in the nineteenth and twentieth centuries, respectively. Gilpin (1981) next advanced a theory of hegemonic decline and war. Gilpin (1987) almost acknowledged explicitly that the world economy is geared to a rhythm of systemic leadership and long economic waves. Still, in Gilpin (2000), an assessment of the contemporary and immediate future of world economy governance, any references to systemic leadership and long waves of economic growth driven by radical technological innovation are virtually absent.[2]

IPE is well-known for its faddishness. For example, many of the early students of contemporary IPE had moved away from studying regional integration, which appeared to have lost its momentum in Europe by the end of the 1960s. The early 1970s was a time in which the Pax Americana was clearly in trouble. Vietnam, the abandonment of the gold standard, and the rise in Middle Eastern oil prices all suggested that the old post-1945 order was coming to an end. Hegemonic decline was thus an attractive topic, not unlike dependency, that was briefly adopted by some as an alternative, central question only to be discarded for greener pastures such as the study of international regimes, neoinstitutional practices, sovereignty, legalization, and a host of others. Presumably, many, if not all, of these topics have been or eventually will be discarded as well. This fluctuation in attention span seems to be characteristic of the study of international political economy—which, after all, is unsurprisingly attentive to fluctuations and turbulence in its subject matter. If the subject matter seems less than stable, should we anticipate that its central questions are any more constant?

If the 1970s and 1980s were a time of flourishing interest in hegemonic decline, there was also a brief period of reaction in which scholars argued that hegemony persisted and had never declined (Russett 1985; Strange 1987; Nye 1990; Nau 1990). Then, the disintegration of the Soviet Union and the apparent triumph of liberalism seemed to have resolved that question. A new world order was proclaimed by the chief executive of the surviving superpower. The world had suddenly turned unipolar, major power war was a thing of the past, and international relations would never be the same again—or so it was thought.

Since the 1990s, the payoffs from unipolarity and world order have seemed elusive. Major power warfare has certainly not been prominent, but two U.S.-led coalitions against minor-league challengers in Iraq and Afghanistan have captured a good deal of attention. At the same time, world economic governance does not appear to be faring any better than in the 1970s and 1980s. G-8 meetings continue without accomplishing much. The Southern debt crisis lingers on. Global inequalities have hardly lessened. World economic growth has been off and on, but mainly off. It certainly has not resembled the 1950s and 1960s.[3] WTO meetings are deluged by popular protests perhaps only camouflaging the lack of progress made within the formal negotiations. Protectionism seems to be on the rise, although in more subtle ways than in the old days of tariffs. Finance has led the way in the extent to which it has become a globalized activity and seemingly beyond the control of national governments. Environmental pollution, climate change, and disease problems continue to go largely unaddressed. Perhaps it is a good time to return to the question of systemic leadership. We believe that the notion of leadership has played and will continue to play a crucial role in shaping international political economy processes.

Of course, it is not only mainstream IPE that fails to sustain a continued interest in the question of systemic leadership. Mainstream economics has no room or tolerance for the idea that some actors are more critical than others to the functioning of markets.[4] As we have noted in earlier chapters, there is beginning to be a flicker of interest in the idea that some industries may be more important than others, as exemplified by the interest in general purpose technologies. But these studies so far stop short of embracing the kindred notion that critical industries tend to be concentrated spatially and temporally. As a consequence, one economy is most likely to take the lead for finite periods of time. As long as this basic idea is so alien to the majority of economists and their formal theories, it may be that little progress can be anticipated in IPE on this dimension. Since the majority of noneconomist IPE scholars take their cues about the dynamics of economic processes from the economics discipline, ideas that are alien to economists thus meet considerable resistance in mainstream circles within the field of IPE.

But there are even a number of long wave scholars—that is, analysts who accept the idea that fluctuations in long-term growth are geared to the rise and routinization of technologies and important industries—who balk at the idea of giving special emphasis to the system leaders who generate the industries and profit most handsomely for doing so. Systemic leadership is absent in Kondratieff (1979), Schumpeter (1939), Rostow (1978), and van Duijn (1983). The tendency for some economies to do better than others in matters of commercial and technological innovation is acknowledged in what might be called the Sussex school (for example, Freeman and Perez 1988) but otherwise largely ignored. Even the lateral pressure analyses of Goldstein (1988, 1991) and Pollins (1996), who recognize systematic connections between central economic processes and hegemony, characterize these connections as loose and intermittent.[5] For a number of reasons, then, systemic leadership is not currently one of the key variables to deciphering the long-term dynamics of international political economy. We think it should be. This book, focusing on growth and trade, has attempted to suggest some reasons why that should be the case and, just as important, has attempted to demonstrate empirically that systemic leadership is critical to the processes of economic growth, trade openness, and protectionism.

Recapitulating Our Model and Findings

In some respects, a formal conclusion to this study is not entirely appropriate; the activity reported in these pages represents work in progress. In other respects, however, we believe we have attained our immediate goals. As part of the IPE structural genome unraveling project mentioned in chapter 1, we have sought in this undertaking to establish the centrality of systemic leadership in major international politicoeconomic processes. Obviously, we cannot take on all IPE processes in one book. Some selectivity is therefore not only warranted but also inescapable. This study has emphasized aspects of economic growth, trade patterns, and trade policy—all of which are incontestably major processes of concern to IPE. Figure 9.1 recapitulates what has been learned and discussed in the past eight chapters. It also repeats chapter 1's figure 1.2 with little in the way of elaboration.

We contend that predominance in radical technological innovation and global reach capability are the principal resource foundations for systemic leadership. The innovations bestow lead economy status on one state. The surplus generated by innovation both funds and necessitates the development of a preponderance in global reach capability. It should hardly be controversial to point out that cotton textiles, iron production, steam engines, and railroads were sequentially prominent dimensions of British economic leadership in the late eighteenth and early to mid–nineteenth centuries. Steel, electricity, automobiles, semiconductors, and aerospace have been equally prominent industries in the emergence and maintenance of U.S. economic leadership in the twentieth century. We did not attempt to capture all facets of these phenomena, for to do so would be a rather ambitious undertaking. Instead, we focused on aggregated indicators of leading sector activity.

One index of the rise and decline of specific innovations or leading sectors that we have used is their rate of growth. When these industries are growing quickly, they are in their sunrise or ascent mode. When the rate of growth turns flat or negative, they are approaching sunset or decline status. A related index of significance used in this book is the share of leading sector production controlled by the system leader. As the leader's share rises, so, too, does the economic platform controlled by the system leader. One would expect the system leader's leading sector growth rates and leading sector share superiority to wax and wane in a corresponding fashion. The leader's share of naval capability, a major index of the ability to project force on a global scale, should also rise and decline in roughly synchronized fashion, albeit subject to some sort of lagged relationship to the economic foundations that both motivate and finance the expansion of naval power.

We contend that the trinity of leading sector growth rate, leading sector share, and naval power share should capture reasonably well the politicoeconomic and military foundation for systemic leadership—what we term the leadership platform. We need to stress that these indicators do not necessarily measure the success or even the exercise of leadership. What they measure are the capabilities that can be drawn upon if decision makers choose to exercise policy leadership for the world economy. Whether or not decision makers seek to exert policy leadership, it is unlikely that they will be very successful in doing so in the absence of an adequate resource platform. They will not have the resources. Nor will they have the begrudging acceptance, by at least some other parties in the world, that the most powerful actor in the politicoeconomic system, by default, is the most likely source of order. Everyone is unlikely to agree, but leaders need followers. Periods of high concentration in global politics are conducive to the development of followers. For that matter, policy success or even the specific exercise of leadership is not our immediate concern. What we are attempting to delineate are the empirical links—if they exist—among systemic leadership, via its resource platform, and growth and trade processes in order to assess our principal proposition.

> H1: World economic growth, trade, and systemic leadership covary causally and significantly.

Figure 9.1 indicates that the U.S. leading sector growth rate has anteceded the U.S. aggregate economic growth and the world economy's economic growth. U.S. aggregate economic growth also antecedes the world economy's economic growth. But world economic growth reverberates negatively in subsequent U.S. economic growth. Thus, we found ample empirical support for the three hypotheses confronted in chapter 2.

> H2: Leading sector growth in the lead economy drives the lead economy's aggregate economic growth.
> H3: Leading sector growth and aggregate economic growth in the lead economy drive world economic growth.
> H4: After some lag, world economic growth and leading sector growth in the lead economy are negatively related.

Figure 9.1 also links U.S. leading sector share and the U.S. global reach (naval) capability share. The U.S. leading sector growth and leading sector production share have also positively anteceded the U.S. naval capability share. There are also positive Granger causal relationships from military mobilization to leading sector growth and naval capability share, emphasizing how closely the components of the leadership platform are intertwined and reciprocal. These findings demonstrate empirical support for the hypotheses examined in chapter 3.

> H5: Leading sector growth in the lead economy supports the attainment of economic superiority in leading sector production.
> H6: Leading sector growth and superiority in leading sector production encourage the development of superiority in global reach capabilities.
> H7: The development of superiority in global reach capabilities reinforces an ascending system leader's military mobilization for warfare.

Conclusion

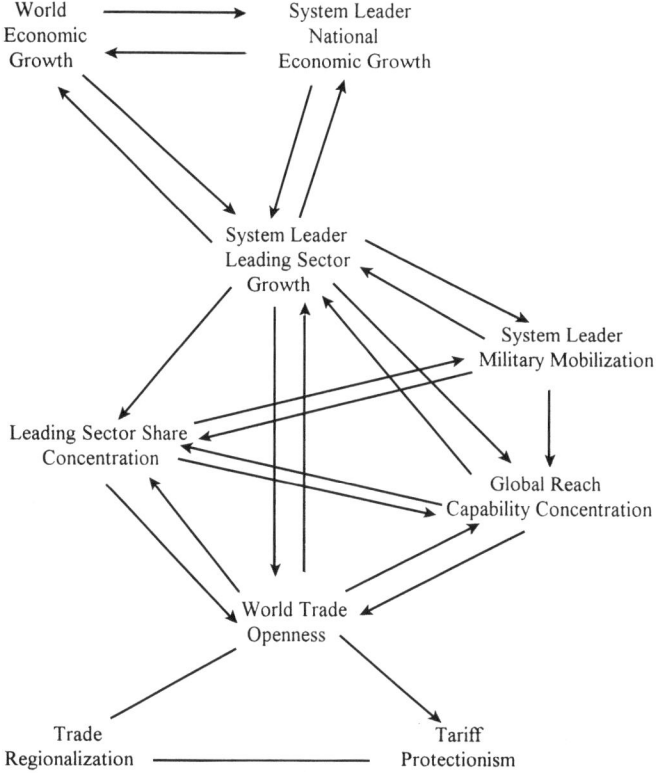

Fig. 9.1. The overall model

H8: Leading sector growth and economic superiority in leading sector production make the system leader's military mobilization for warfare more probable, which, in turn, encourages further leading sector growth and economic superiority.

But that is only the beginning of our understanding of the central role of systemic leadership in the IPE genome. We find strong linkages among the systemic leadership platform and fluctuations in trade and political behavior related to trade openness (i.e., protectionism). Figure 9.1 highlights the findings that world trade openness (world trade/world gross domestic product) generally antecedes tariff protectionism, rather than the other way around. This finding supports our claim that it is long waves of economic growth, systemic leadership, and various types of shocks related to these long waves, such as wars and depressions, that more fundamentally drive the major fluctuations in protectionism. Moreover, all of the many existing theories and models of protectionism reviewed in chapter 4 can be integrated by the common long wave denominator. The analyses conducted in chapters 4, 5, and 6 thus provide support for another set of hypotheses.

H9: Systemic leadership and long waves of economic growth and trade impose fundamental constraints on protectionist behavior.

H10: In the short term, protectionist behavior influences the volume of trade; in the long term, declining growth and trade influence the probability of protectionism.

H11: The long-term influence (trade → protectionism) is stronger than the short-term influence (protectionism → trade).

Figure 9.1 shows that all three legs of the leadership platform positively antecede world trade openness, while world trade openness negatively antecedes each part of the leadership platform. Trade openness is desired by the system leader, if for no other reason than that it can appreciate the virtues of openness when it has little in the way of genuine economic competition. A system leader can also engage in substantial trade regionalization activities without jeopardizing its commitment to freer trade on a planetary basis. But trade openness carries some hidden costs in the sense that openness also facilitates the catching-up of the leader's economic competitors—thereby eroding the relative edge of the leadership platform. Therefore, our last four hypotheses are also supported.

H12: After some lag, world trade openness will be positively influenced by systemic leadership, as reflected in the leader's leading sector production superiority and shares of global reach capability.

H13: The influence of leading sector growth in the lead economy on world trade openness is likely to be weak.

H14: After some lag, systemic leadership and the leader's leading sector growth, leading sector production superiority, and shares of global reach capability will be negatively influenced by world trade openness.

218

Conclusion

H15: Trade regionalization activities on the part of the system leader and the closure of world trade are not necessarily synonymous.

Added together, the linkages between and among the resources critical to the exercise of systemic leadership and the processes of economic growth and trade clearly covary. Systemic leadership in economic growth stimulates world economic growth and trade openness—but not without a price. The successful expansion of world economic growth and trade openness, along with the protection costs borne by the system leader, reverberate negatively in terms of the lead economy's own economic growth and systemic leadership position. This cyclical process of leading sector leapfrog is one of the most fundamental paths by which the world system expands its economic productivity over time. Despite its centrality to IPE, recognition of this process continues to be relatively marginal in that field. As long as we deny the existence of core processes, some difficulties in ascertaining the interplay of global structure and global dynamics should be anticipated.

Anticipating Some Objections

Should we expect our argument and findings to be embraced without reservation? While we might wish for such an outcome, we acknowledge that it is unlikely. Systemic leadership analyses, as we have repeatedly noted, are not central to IPE inquiry. If we are right, they should be. Instead, they remain hotly contested. Why that should be the case deserves more attention that it has received. One thoughtful exception (Sullivan 2001: 171–98) advances several criticisms of arguments about systemic leadership, trade fluctuations, and hegemonic stability.

1. The theoretical scope of long wave/long cycle analyses seems distant from the immediate concerns of the contemporary world.
2. The strength of the system leadership/hegemonic stability arguments is diluted by the disagreements about whether the system leader is declining or reviving. This problem is compounded by an observed tendency for analysts to diverge on their dependence on empirical measures. Analysts who rely more on empirical measures of system leader strength are more likely to see evidence of decline. Those who rely less on such measures are more likely to see little decline.

3. A basic question yet to be resolved is, When is a state the systemic leader or hegemon, and how can we tell? If there is no agreement on the thresholds or foci of concentration, it is difficult to evaluate claims about the alleged effects of the presence or absence of leadership.

4. Is hegemonic/system leader behavior deliberately hegemonic in motivation, or does it only appear to be while the behavior is due to other factors such as idiosyncratic ideas or domestic lobbying? On the other hand, does hegemonic/system leader motivation matter if it is primarily the economic performance of the system leader that leads to system transformation?

5. To the extent that long cycle analyses tend to envision impending returns to major warfare in an upcoming economic long wave, the existence of weapons of mass destruction implies a certain finality that is disheartening. Perhaps for this reason, long cycle analysts have "found reason to moderate their views about the finality of cycles" (179).

6. Debates about hegemony and system leadership nourish a "tankerful of ideological connotations" (188).

While not all of these criticisms speak directly to economic growth and trade issues, they all do address issues of interpretative face validity. As such, they are certainly germane here, for the strength of an argument and the empirical evidence associated with it are always in the eye of the beholder. If we can clarify some of these perceived problems, it is conceivable that we can speak to some objections before they are even raised. We have no illusions about completely heading off disagreement with the outcomes reported in chapters 2 through 8. But perhaps we can defuse or rechannel some of it.

The first criticism speaks to two decades or more of interest in questions related to global war on the part of leadership-long cycle analysts. Global wars are hardly trivial issues. They are also central components in the ascendance of system leaders. Over the past five hundred years, global wars have not been sufficient but they do appear to have been necessary to ushering in new system leaders. Global wars are the global system's functional equivalent of electoral contests. As such, they determine which of several contenders for succession to predominance emerges as the next system leader. As a consequence, the generation immediately following a global war should be the most promising for the exercise of systemic leadership. Rivals have been defeated, exhausted, and, in some cases, completely eliminated. The new system leader emerges from global war with its leadership platform enhanced. Global war benefits the system leader's relative economic edge over other economies and its lead in global reach capabilities.

Thus, an appreciation for the role of global war in facilitating the emergence of systemic leadership is crucial. New leaders do not just happen to emerge after big wars. Leadership and global war are closely and causally related in reciprocal fashion. Nye (1990) misses this point when he attributes the appearance of U.S. decline in the 1970s and 1980s to the "post–WWII effect." His argument is that the appearance of U.S. relative decline is simply a reflection of the inevitable diminishment of the huge lead the United States enjoyed at the end of World War II. Others were bound to improve their positions in the postwar era. To be sure, Nye is right to argue that some of the leading states weakened by global war participation were likely to recoup some of their losses. But the "post–WWII effect" is not an anomaly. It is the norm of long-term structural change. Global war enhances the triumphant system leader's relative economic and military position.[6] Even though the gap between the leadership platform and the resources of rivals is likely to be greatest in the immediate aftermath of war, this period is also likely to be characterized by substantial relative positional decline as other states catch up. The relative decline is probably inevitable. Whether it manifests itself in a corresponding deterioration of the exercise of systemic leadership is less inevitable.

This last point can be illustrated easily with a numerical example. Assume that a system leader's resource platform edge over states' resource platforms corresponds roughly to its ability to exercise systemic leadership. A small lead leaves little room for systemic leadership. Other states will pay less attention to the claims advanced by a weak leader. System leaders with very strong leads are like 800-pound gorillas. They are hard to ignore. All states in the system will not necessarily regard their preferences as authoritative and legitimate. But some will, especially if those preferences tend to match their own values. Others will depend on the 800-pound gorilla for economic assistance and military protection. Even so, global system leaders are not imperial hegemons able to demand that all states kowtow to their demands. Their leadership platforms, predicated on technological/commercial innovation and global reach capabilities, are limited. For instance, they have done better at sea where their capability edges are most prominent, but less well farther inland. Sea powers have defeated small land powers with coasts on occasion. Assistance from other land powers has been necessary to defeat larger land powers.

In any event, imagine that a system leader emerges from a global war with 75 percent of the system's leading sector production and global reach capability. Say it then loses 25 percent over the next twenty-five years. It still commands an impressive lead assuming that a rival does not control the remaining 50 percent. Thus, substantial relative decline need not mean the loss of a leadership position if a substantial lead is preserved and/or the disintegration of a major rival occurs. Alternatively, a declining lead can be renewed by innovation in new leading sectors. Both situations apply to the history of U.S. systemic leadership. It emerged from World War II in a very strong relative position. It experienced relative decline in its platform for systemic leadership through the 1970s and 1980s as other states narrowed the economic gap in a catch-up phase. The collapse of the Soviet Union at least temporarily ended the relative decline in its global reach capabilities. If one's major competitor drops out of the race, whatever resources remain are suddenly enhanced in a relative sense.

Global war, the initial size of a leader's edge, the possibilities for resource renewal, and fortuitous developments can all play some role in assessing the relative position of a system leader at any point in time. Still, global war is not the only topic of interest in long-term analyses. Considerable energies needed to be expended to persuade other analysts that some big wars were more significant for reasons other than simply their bigness. That debate continues. Yet it is appropriate that long cycle analyses spread their wings (so to speak) and take on other topics. That process is well under way. The current study, with its explicit focus on economic growth and trade openness, only exemplifies the search for what might be termed the "theoretical reach" of long cycle inquiry. In point of fact, we have only begun to explore the frontiers of long-term analysis. We do not yet know the full scope of its explanatory powers. However, we are confident in arguing that economic growth, protectionism, and trade openness are topics of immediate concern in the contemporary world.

Sullivan's second and third criticisms overlap. People disagree about the status of systemic leadership because they work with different pieces of the puzzle—or because they simply see the puzzle differently. If they think that leaders/hegemons are the most powerful states in the world, their identifications of who fits that bill depend on their sense of the sources of power in world politics. Some argue for the overall size of the economy.

Conclusion

Others think that only military power is critical. Still others bestow special significance on population size. We cannot expect to persuade everyone that our emphasis on leading sectors is critical to an understanding of long-term economic growth, but, at least, we have empirically demonstrated a Granger causality relationship between leading sectors and world economic growth.

Leading sectors are not the only drivers of world economic growth. For example, economic size and population size can matter. Taken by themselves, however, they are not especially illuminating. The respective leads of Russian economic size in the nineteenth century and Chinese population size in the twentieth century did not translate into anything resembling systemic leadership. It was the lead in technological innovation that was fundamental to systemic leadership in the nineteenth and twentieth centuries. The United States' larger economy and population meant that it was likely to supplant Britain eventually, if it also developed the lead in technological innovation, but the size of the economy and population were insufficient factors in the succession.[7]

Another reason for disagreement about decline has already been suggested. U.S. relative capabilities did experience decline in the post–World War II era. The question is not whether capabilities declined but, rather, whether the decline was sufficient to make a difference to the exercise of leadership. If one observer sees the continuing exercise of leadership despite erosion in capability position, it is only natural to downplay the significance of the positional erosion. It is equally natural to project positional erosion into the future, with the expectation, other things being equal, that at some future point the system leader will no longer be in a position to lead. Yet other things are not always equal. In the case of the U.S. systemic leadership, its lease on life appears to have been reinvigorated by the latest growth wave focused on information technology. With hindsight, one can trace the origins of this new growth wave back to earlier developments in transistors and computers during and shortly after World War II. But adequate hindsight is not always available when called upon to assess whether a system leader is currently ascending, declining, or running in place.

One of the advantages of focusing on the platform for systemic leadership is that we are not forced to say that in year X, the resource lead was sufficiently great that leadership began to be exercised, or that in year Y, the resource lead had evaporated and leadership was no longer possible. That is not the way systemic leadership works. U.S. systemic leadership behavior became most noticeable only during and after World War II. Some of the resource platform (technological innovation and superiority in leading sector production) for leadership was in place prior to World War II. If World War I had lasted longer or if the U.S. participation in that war had lasted longer, it is possible that U.S. global reach capability superiority would have emerged much earlier than it did. Yet even if all the resource platform ingredients for U.S. systemic leadership had been in place in 1919, it is not clear that U.S. leadership behavior would have been exercised in the interwar years along the lines manifested after World War II. There are other factors that are also critical, including the realignment of domestic elites and politics and a strong internal impetus to assert external leadership, which we have only hinted at in the hypotheses tested in this study.

Another advantage of our measurement approach is that we can capture dynamic shifts in the scale of leadership resource platforms. The usual alternative in empirical analyses is to take a long period such as 1815–1914, 1815–70, or 1945–73 and code each year as an equivalent period of system leadership/hegemony. As Mansfield (1994) has demonstrated, which years are used can make a significant difference in the statistical outcome. Our point is that there is no need to resort to the crude assumptions that a system leadership started and ended in any given year or that its leadership position (or behavior) was constant throughout its alleged tenure. Designating starting and ending dates is always an awkward exercise. Assuming constant positions and behavior is extremely difficult to justify because we have no reason to think that the real world works that way. Instead, we have devised and utilized several continuous measures of the level of economic and political leadership that are predicated on a framework emphasizing economic innovation and global reach capability.

Sullivan's fourth criticism raises a number of very interesting questions that remain somewhat tangential to our current concerns. Are system leaders self-aware when they exercise leadership? Or do we analysts simply assign leadership labels to the usual pursuit of self-interest, quite possibly driven by domestic politics rather than the perceived needs of the external arena? Is the system automatically transformed by the emergence of new lead economies? This last question is easiest to answer. The world economy is transformed by the emergence of new lead economies more or less automatically. The global political economy, however, may take more time to adjust. That is one of the reasons global wars are fought. To what extent decision makers are cognizant of leadership responsibilities remains a fascinating question. Their rhetoric would suggest some awareness. But this agreement falls short of telling us whether or to what extent they believe their own rhetoric. Still, probing this question much further would require a vastly different research design than the one we have developed for this study. We have focused on variables that are relatively easy to measure in order to best make and test our current argument about the covariance of systemic leadership, economic growth, and trade. Assessing why and how decision makers come to the conclusion that freer trade is preferred over protectionism is a different but no less worthwhile question that we must leave to other research venues and, we hope, other researchers.

The last two criticisms are in many respects the most tangential of them all for our present purposes. It is true that long cycle rhythms have built-in predispositions to go to major warfare every so many years. It is also hard to imagine the persistence of long cycle rhythms after a World War III. Yet the combining of these two facts does not imply conscious or subconscious ulterior motives on the part of long cycle analysts in exploring alternative futures. As far as we can tell, these long cycles have not been around since time immemorial. The leadership-long cycle argument (Modelski and Thompson 1996) is that they began to emerge one thousand years ago thanks to developments in Sung China and have evolved ever since. Global wars really only emerged in 1494 and did not begin to resemble the world wars of the twentieth century before 1585. According to Rasler and Thompson (1994; Thompson 2000), the global wars of the twentieth century were explicitly Eurocentric in nature. Once the European regional circumstances were transformed by 1945, future global wars were far less likely to be Eurocentric. They may also be far less likely. That depends not only on the fabled deterrence linked to the destructiveness of contemporary weapons arsenals but also on whether the regional circumstances that led to global war in Europe are replicated in a different theater—perhaps East Asia or, more generally, Eurasia. But that is another story and not one that is immediately relevant to our current preoccupation with economic growth and trade issues.

As for ideological considerations by the tankerful, we agree. But this observation no doubt holds equally well for both opponents and proponents of systemic leadership interpretations. For ourselves, we can only say that we are unaware of any personal or ideological attachment to the presence or absence of systemic leadership.[8] We have observed its presence and absence as regularities of world political economy. We have developed arguments about how it works and changes over time and space. We have tested these arguments and found them supported by empirical data. It is now up to others, if they are so inclined, to demonstrate equally empirically how we have gone wrong. Failing that, we hope others will build on our model and extend it in new directions.

More generally, in an assessment of contemporary IPE published in the journal *International Organization,* Katzenstein, Keohane, and Krasner (1998: 683) have lamented that "despite increasing sophistication, substantive findings remain meager. . . . counterintuitive, well-documented causal arguments are rare." Their judgment is sound, and we can appreciate the grounds for their disappointment. Yet increasing sophistication is no barrier to substantive findings of value. Our present findings are based on statistical techniques that can make a claim to a high degree of sophistication. Yet they are also fairly conservative tests. We were not assured of finding the large number of relationships that we did find. We were certainly not guaranteed of finding support for each one of our fifteen hypotheses.

We think the discovery of well-established linkages among systemic leadership, technological innovation, world economic growth, and trade openness can claim substantive significance in addition to statistical significance. Openness is an enduring question about the international trading system regardless of paradigmatic preferences. We have developed serial measures of world and national protectionism, conducted a variety of different types of tests pertaining to timing and causality, and can account for long-term fluctuations in both protectionism and openness/closure of the trading system. We have linked together a tripodal set of resources that we think provides a foundation for systemic leadership. These resources—which reflect the edges that system leaders possess over other actors in the world economy—can be linked to military mobilization, world economic growth, and trade openness. We find straightforward linkages between variable A and variable B. Yet we also find feedback loops between B and A that are sometimes differently signed than the A → B relationship. Systemic leadership contributes to the expansion and opening of the world economy, but, ultimately, the system leader pays for its success by creating situations in which other states can pass it by. However one assesses the ultimate costs, the dynamics at play guarantee system leaders a finite period of preeminence and leadership. These same dynamics also impart a cyclical rhythm to growth and trade.

Conclusion

None of these empirical linkages was simply stumbled onto in an ad hoc fashion. Our concatenated theory anticipated them. The relationships are expressed as causal relationships, just as our analytical procedures push the search for causality outside of laboratories as far as one can with quantitative data. No one yet has determined a way to fully establish causality with the type of data with which we are working, but we can establish patterns of antecedance—which variables are linked significantly to which other variables and which ones come first in the relationship. These are two critical characteristics of causal relationships. Whether they truly need to be counterintuitive is less clear to us. We can appreciate the appeal of the occasional counterintuitive argument that actually works. Too many counterintuitive findings, however, are worrisome from a causal point of view. Not all of our findings are obvious, but none seems particularly counterintuitive unless one insists that nothing beneficial can come from politicoeconomic power concentration. That should be reassuring vis-à-vis our claim that our arguments and findings represent causal linkages.

Thus, we provide both an explanation and evidence for cyclical behavior in IPE. In most cases, we do not attempt to compare explicitly or to integrate our explanation with others of a similar ilk. Chapters 4 and 5 are the principal exceptions. So we cannot claim to have fully resolved the debates (Mansfield 1994: 9) over which systemic models work best in deciphering IPE. We like to think, though, that we have definitely raised the bar for delineating a systemic model and generating evidence for its historical applicability. Much of the debate over systemic models has proceeded verbally and without much attempt at precision or evidence. We contend that theory, precision, and evidence should be minimal prerequisites for entering the debate. Those minimal prerequisites are satisfied in this study. We hope that alternative models can be articulated and put to equally exacting tasks so that we can compare the outcomes. If alternative models cannot be articulated and tested, there should be less reason for debate.

Our initial goals were (a) to establish the covariance of leadership, growth, and trade and (b) to explore the causal network of relationships that link these central IPE processes. Both goals have been attained via the development and testing of the fifteen hypotheses. Systemic leadership matters, and it seems to matter very much. What we cannot yet say is how much it matters in comparison to other variables that also may matter. We are not interested in developing a univariate theory of everything in IPE. But we have been interested in how far the reach of systemic leadership extends throughout the IPE universe. That quest will continue in future analyses, for it is one plausible strategy (among several) for mapping the genomic complexity of IPE.

Before moving on to a contemplation of future topics suitable for integration into our expanding model of the IPE universe, an epistemological aside is warranted. We think our modeling demonstrates especially vividly the limits to partitioning real-world phenomena into "political" and "economic" compartments. "Political economy" should work toward defeating that tendency, but it only rarely does. More often, it reinforces the artificial compartmentalization. We contend that the compartmentalization is artificial because the relationships and the ways in which they are linked, as we have seen in preceding chapters, simply do not lend themselves very well to disciplinary typecasting. For example, trade openness is an "economic" process pertaining to the relative size of trade that is influenced by technological innovation, economic growth, protectionism, and systemic leadership. Protectionism and systemic leadership are ostensibly political processes, but they, in turn, are influenced by technological innovation and economic growth. All of these processes are affected by global war, which economists would describe as another "political" intervention into the market even though one of its purposes is to resolve turbulence brought about by radically new patterns of innovation and economic growth. The more one tries to pigeonhole these processes along traditional lines, the more dizzying the attempt becomes.

As a consequence, we do not find the prevailing paradigms—liberalism, realism, and Marxism—all that helpful. Liberals seek to maintain some distance between politics and economics. They are also too quick to privilege economics as possessing its own autonomous marketplace dynamics. The pervasive influence of systemic leadership in matters of economic growth and trade suggests that these paradigmatic propensities are not well-founded.

Realists seek to downplay the central role of economic processes and, in doing so, bestow more autonomy than is warranted on the political sphere's logic of pursuit of national interest. Anarchy is also a rather dubious assumption if systemic leadership is as central to IPE dynamics as we think it is. The global system continues to lack a centralized government but it does not lack for centralized governance—albeit the amount of governance is less than constant over time. Assumptions about movements toward and away from anarchy might be more helpful to theory building than the present tendency to assume constant anarchy.

Conclusion

Marxists have more room for systemic leadership than do their liberal and realist brethren. Yet strong Marxist assumptions about core exploitation of the periphery and the hegemonic leader of the core detract from the centrality of the more important dynamic of technological innovation and its uneven diffusion. It is uneven technological diffusion, not capitalism per se, in conjunction with uneven development that accounts best for the world economy's inequalities. Much more might be done to attenuate inequality than is attempted by system leaders, but there is much more to Southern poverty than Northern exploitation. We do not see system leaders as particularly benevolent. Nor are their decision makers' intentions always benign. But that evaluation does not leave malign intentions as the only residual default option. Other forces explaining the persistent inequality are potentially more important, particularly those that affect the ability of the poor to absorb the radical innovations diffusing from the leader.

Future Directions

Our findings represent a good start, but there is much more to do and many more connections to test. One direction that could and should be pursued is the examination of domestic interconnections to the leadership platform. Leading sectors are the asserted engines of growth, but they do not spring forth unaided. We know they respond to processes external to the domestic economy in which they are generated. It may also turn out that they are driven, in turn, by other domestic processes. For instance, the long wave literature has debated the identity (or identities) of the primary drivers of long-term growth. Some analysts put their bets on radical technological innovation or leading sectors. Others give greater credit to investment in innovation, the development of infrastructure within which innovations can operate, fluctuations in profits, alternating incentives to allocate resources to primary resource extraction and cultivation versus manufacturing of finished goods, price and interest rate fluctuations, the impacts of war, and demographic changes. It does not require much imagination to see these processes as interconnected.[9] The principal questions should be how they are connected, which processes are primary drivers and which secondary, and what drives what.

Then, too, there are a number of political processes that appear to be tied to these fluctuations. Political realignments, in which national political systems undergo fundamental change as new governing coalitions emerge in response to technological change and new problems to solve or manage, appear to be related to long-term economic changes. Major shifts in public opinion favoring or opposing domestic and international activities by governments also appear to be connected to paradigmatic shifts in technology.[10] Regime types can also be related to development timing and the demands of industries attempting to cope with ongoing economic change.[11] Internationally, it can be argued, institutions are designed to deal with clusters of technologically induced problems that change over time and require major institutional adjustments. As a consequence, we have clusters of different types of international governmental and nongovernmental organizations that first emerged in the second half of the nineteenth century, the first quarter of the twentieth century, or the second half of the twentieth century. Some have disappeared as they became obsolete or ineffective, while others have survived because they have altered their organizational missions.[12] Moreover, there is the likelihood that social movements and religious identification are also tied in to these fundamental IPE shifts in the way we do things.[13]

But there are also a number of additional IPE processes that need to be drawn into the long-term, structural change web. Our own interests are attracted to North-South relationships. For instance, a number of analysts have related processes associated with the expansion and contraction of colonialism to systemic leadership, economic prosperity, and major power conflict. Colonial expansion is thought to be related to weak systemic leadership and increasing major power conflict. Whether prosperity or depression encourages Northern expansion into the South is disputed. Our suspicion is that these arguments can be generalized to fluctuations in systemic leadership and world economic growth leading to fluctuations in major power conflict and North-South relations.[14] We already have systemic leadership and world economic growth in our map. We need to introduce North-South conflict and major power conflict.

Another dimension of fluctuating North-South relations has to do with debt crises. Intermittently, Southern states experience major problems in paying the interest associated with loans advanced by Northern banks and states. While these crises seem merely intermittent, it has been argued that they are closely related to Northern economic growth processes.[15] Northern economic expansion leads to greater efforts to acquire Southern resources. Southern decision makers take advantage of this increased interest to attract Northern investment and loans in order to expand their export capability and overall economic development. Northern economic

Conclusion

contraction reduces Northern demand for Southern goods. It becomes more difficult to pay the interest on Northern loans to the South. Intermittent debt crises and defaults are the outcome. While intermittent, they are not randomly so. Rather, they are tied closely to the waxing and waning of world economic prosperity that, we have shown, is linked to systemic leadership. We need to introduce North-South debt crises to our model.

Another question of considerable interest to us is the eventual likelihood of economic convergence: As economic development proceeds, will economies become more alike and equally affluent? Some argue that IPE processes are predicated on well-entrenched inequalities that are unlikely to be overcome. Moreover, with each new wave of technological advance, some parts of the globe fall increasingly behind while others scramble to maintain their position on the technological and development gradients. If that is the case, economic convergence may be possible for only some limited parts of the world while economic divergence is more likely elsewhere. Are long-term economic growth and its paladin, systemic leadership, agents for greater or lesser world economic divergence and inequality? We suspect the answer varies according to which segments of the world's population we are addressing. Thus, the prospects for convergence and inequality also need to be related to the map laid out in figure 9.1.[16]

When all is said and done, however, what figure 9.1 hints at are major clues to how the world's political economy works. Completely unraveling how the world works is not the task of any one analyst or even a large team of analysts. It is a task in which all students of IPE should be involved. We hope that the findings put forward in this study will encourage others to explore the paths outlined, hinted at, and implied. In point of fact, other analysts already are pursuing these paths. What we need most is a better understanding of how the multiple paths of IPE connections fit together. We think that the systemic leadership platform that crops up repeatedly in our earlier chapters will prove to be useful for solving multiple international political economy pathways and puzzles.

Appendix A

This appendix describes technical details pertaining to the Granger causality statistical method that is used in chapters 2, 6, and 7. Several technical issues involve the design of a Granger causality test. A first issue deals with unit roots. A considerable number of studies doubts their practical importance, in particular when the error term in time-series regressions is without serial correlation (McCallum 1993, Doan 1992, Hamilton 1994). Nevertheless, we wish to reduce the risk associated with their presence (Hamilton 1994). Partially for this purpose, we use growth rates when appropriate. In addition, we rely on results from unit root tests and also plot our series with respect to time. If the plots reveal a nontrending picture fluctuating around zero, then our series are most likely stationary. We also check for the presence of unit roots and verify that there are no unit roots in our data. Since it is established that unit root tests have low power and results are sensitive to lag structure and test type, three tests (Dickey and Fuller, Phillips and Perron, and the conventional Durbin-Watson from regression of a series on a constant) are employed. The first two tests are described in Dickey and Fuller (1981) and Phillips and Perron (1988), respectively. Based on these tests, we find that our data generally have no unit roots. For this and another reason detailed below, we will report results from Granger causality regressions only if the error terms in those regressions are without serial correlation.

Granger investigations may also ignore relevant variables. To deal with the possibility of missing variables, we adopt Leamer's specification methodology (Leamer 1978). Starting with a bilateral model, we check robustness by adding related control variables, which are described in the particular chapters. Clearly, we cannot include all variables of possible interest in the investigation given the infeasibility of doing so and the problem of exhausting degrees of freedom. We therefore follow Hoole and Huang's (1989: 147) advice and assume that excluded variables will not affect the Granger regression when the error terms are white noise. We report results only if the error term is white noise from a significance level of 5 percent and better.

A third issue deals with the test for serial correlation in a Granger test. The Granger regression includes lags of the dependent variable on the right hand side. In this case, the standard Durbin-Watson test tends to be biased toward finding no serial correlation. The Durbin-h test statistic is sometimes used instead, but it only checks for serial correlation from the first order autoregressive type.[1] Other types of serial correlation could also be present. Accordingly, we use two methods to test for serial correlation, which are valid in the presence of dependent variable lags. One method uses the Q statistic from Ljung and Box (1979). The other method employs spectral analysis by computing the cumulative periodogram of the Granger regression's residuals and comparing it to a cumulative periodogram of white noise.[2] We report Granger causality results only if the error terms in the Granger regressions are white noise in both tests from a significance level of 5 percent and better.[3]

Another issue that is debated in the literature concerns the test's lag length. Kang (1989) notes that many Granger studies simply use 4, 6, 8, or 12 lags, but other studies try systematically various lag lengths, reporting the best results. Following the latter group, our approach is again conservative in that we systematically try several lag lengths, as is done in a relatively large number of studies.[4] Since the dynamics of our variables may be relatively slow for changes in one variable to register in the other variable, we try up to 15 annual lags in each of the tests.[5] Hence, for each time period we will obtain up to 15 Granger results, one from each lag structure used. We then report the lowest joint significance level obtained in any of these tests. This result represents the best fit of the model to the data in the Granger sense.[6]

A fifth issue concerns the significance threshold to use in evaluating results. Some studies use 5 and 10 percent significance levels. However, there is a debate in the literature about the utility of conventional levels in this case. By construction, Granger models exhibit collinearity that, while not biasing the results, reduces their significance. Moore (1995), for instance, reports results with 20 percent significance levels. Taking a middle ground position, we generally report results with 5, 10, and 20 percent significance levels.[7]

Dealing with time-series data requires some attention to the issue of detrending. In chapter 6, our Granger specification includes a time trend term since some of our time series in this case (tariffs) seem to be trending during some time periods. According to Kang (1985), a failure to detrend when needed may enhance causal relationships while detrending when not needed weakens causal relationships. Pursuing our conservative approach, in this instance we prefer to err by generating weakened causal results than to misidentify causal patterns that do not exist.

These issues, for the most part, continue to be debated.[8] Acknowledging them alerts us to the possible limitations of Granger's approach. However, as clearly pointed out by Freeman (1983) and Hamilton (1994), all these issues notwithstanding, Granger causality tests retain considerable empirical utility in assessing patterns of causality between variables. In particular, Granger's test is useful when used in light of theoretical expectations, as in our case.

Appendix B

This appendix discusses technical details related to several steps of our empirical analysis in chapter 3, which uses a vector auto regression model. To facilitate the discussion, we refer to the steps by using their number in the main text. The unit root tests we conduct in the first step of our analysis are known for their low power and several researchers doubt their overall importance in econometrics. For example, McCallum (1993), Doan (1992: 6–20) and Sims (1988) doubt the importance of unit roots, and Doan (1992: sec. 8-3) recommends to always use levels. Our approach, however, is conservative. In light of the low power of this test, we use three methods: (1) visual plots of series, (2) the Dickey and Fuller (1979) test, and (3) the Phillips and Peron (1988) test. If all our variables are nonstationary, their first differences may be used (if they are stationary). If the first difference is nonstationary, more differencing is needed. A cointegrated VAR may be used if the variables are co-integrated. If only one variable is nonstationary, the estimated regression from levels will be consistent. If some, but not all, variables are stationary the VAR may also be estimated in levels (Hamilton 1994).

In the unit root tests we tried systematically 1 to 10 lags for each of the series. Our sample size is 192. Therefore, the hypothesis of a unit root is rejected in all cases (except in the case of leading sector share which is rejected only when more than five lags are used, as noted in chapter 3, note 8) since the values of our test statistics are smaller than −3.15 (the critical value for our sample). The visual plots of all our time-series variables also show that they do not grow forever, which further supports the view that these series are stationary.

In the second step of the analysis we choose the lag length for the VAR. Sims's (1980) test determines the number of lags that best fit the data using a VAR by comparing a model of lag length N_1 is compared to a VAR model of lag length N_2. The statistical test then decides which model should be rejected in favor of the other. As we already noted, if the final chosen lag length is not appropriate, it will most likely be reflected by serial correlation in the error terms. To that effect, we inspect the estimated VAR for the presence of serial correlation.

VAR equations include lags of dependent variable. In this situation, the standard Durbin-Watson test tends to be biased toward finding no serial correlation. One alternative is to use the Durbin-h test. Yet this test is not always computable mathematically, depending on the sample size and the variance of the raw data, because it includes a square root from an expression that may be negative for some data sets. This happens to be our case. The pertinent mathematical details may be found in Greene (1997). Several researchers (e.g., Inder 1984) find that the Durbin-h test has low power and recommend against using it. In addition, it assumes that the serial correlation is an auto-regression order one type, but serial correlation of a different type could be present.

We use two methods to test for the presence of serial correlation in the VAR from our lag length, which are valid when a lagged dependent variable is included, the Q test (see Green 1997), and the cumulative periodogram test from spectral analysis. The cumulative periodogram test is based on the Fourier transform of the residuals. It is computed from the residuals of each equation in the model and compared to a cumulative periodogram of white noise from a Kolmogorov-Smirnov (K-S) test. If the two periodograms are statistically similar, the VAR's residuals do not contain any serial correlation, as discussed in Doan (1992).

The block exogeneity test conducted in our fifth step is a multivariate extension of Granger's (1969) test, suggested by Sims (1980). The restricted VAR includes some variables. The unrestricted VAR adds more variables as independent variables. The test statistics used (E) is distributed as χ^2 and is given by:

$$E = (T - C)[\, \log(\, |(\Sigma_r)| \,) - \log(\, |(\Sigma_u)| \,)\,],$$

where, Σ_r and Σ_u are the covariances of the two compared models, T is the sample size, and C is a correction factor. The null hypothesis is that the lags in a block of variables do not enter the equations in another block. Two limitations of the block exogeneity test should be noted however. First, the test does not involve all of the model's equations. Hence, some indirect effects may be missed. In this sense, the block exogeneity test suffers from the familiar limitation of the Granger causality test. Second, when a block of variables is found to not enter certain equations, this does not eliminate the possibility that individual variables from that block may still enter the equations.

The order of variables can make a difference in the results from the variance decomposition (step 6) and impulse response analysis (step 7) since it determines the Choleski factorization of the system and its orthogonalized form. Some ordering of the variables, however, must be chosen by the modeler because a VAR model is under-identified for the structural VAR. That is, it is not possible to trace (or identify) the impulse responses without imposing some restrictions on the original (unknown) structural equations. If the correlations among the variables are relatively low (say, 0.2), using different orders of variables may not matter. Of course, if these correlations are as low as 0.2, one may wonder why these variables are put in the same model in the first place. In our case, the correlations vary from around 0.2 to 0.8, depending on the identity of variables and their lag. Hence, the ordering of variables in our model may matter.

As we explain in the main text, we decided to use the variable ordering L, S, W, G. Nevertheless, we acknowledge that the issue of variable ordering in a VAR is not easy to resolve empirically. To check the sensitivity of our results to different ordering we also examined the ordering W, G, S, L. The spirit of the results from this ordering is mostly similar to the results reported here but the model fits the data somewhat less. Since both our ordering and the performance of the model using the ordering L, S, W, G are more in line with our theoretical interpretation than the ordering W, G, L, S, we use the former.

The Monte-Carlo simulations we use in the seventh step of our analysis includes several procedures. First, the covariance of the VAR coefficients is estimated from the data. Second, N impulse responses are computed where, in each computation, the coefficients of the VAR are drawn from a multivariate normal distribution with the above computed covariance and a mean equal to the estimated coefficients. Third, the N impulse responses are used to compute the standard deviation at each point of time along the trajectory. Fourth, confidence intervals around the trajectory from the original estimated coefficients are computed from a prespecified significance level.

Notes

Chapter 1

1. The idea of economic leadership is prominent in the work of a number of IPE analysts. See, for instance, Wallerstein (1974, 1980, 1983, 1989, 1996); Gilpin (1975, 1981, 1987); Kindleberger (1973, 1981, 1996); Krasner (1976); Keohane (1979, 1984); Bousquet (1980); Modelski (1981, 1982, 1987); Braudel (1984); Russett (1985); Thompson (1988, 2000); Chase-Dunn (1989); Lake (1993); Arrighi (1984); Modelski and Thompson (1996); Arrighi and Silver (1999); Knutsen (1999); and Boswell and Chase-Dunn (2000).

2. Arguments built around long waves of economic growth may be found in both mainstream and nonmainstream analyses. Compare, for example, Schumpeter (1939); Imbert (1959); Rostow (1978, 1998); Kondratieff (1979); Mensch (1979); Gordon (1980); Mandel (1980); Modelski (1981, 1982); Duijn (1983); Freeman (1983); Kleinknecht (1987); Vasko (1987); Chase-Dunn (1988, 1998); Freeman and Perez (1988); Goldstein (1988, 1991); Hall and Preston (1988); Ayres (1990); Rejinders (1990); Thompson (1990, 2000); Berry (1991); Tylecote (1991); Boswell and Sweat (1991); Murphy (1994); Bornschier (1996); Modelski and Thompson (1996); Murakami (1996); Neumann (1997); Pollins (1996); Soloumou (1998); Pollins and Murrin (1999); and Boswell and Chase-Dunn (2000).

3. Note that it is possible to use one concept without the other. Maddison (1991) stresses leaders and followers but only in the context of aggregate product growth. Kindleberger (1996) describes successive economic primacies without resorting to leading sector conceptualization. Kurth (1979a, 1979b) talks about the political implications of successive "product cycles"—an idea that is closely aligned with leading sectors—but does not do so in the context of a lead economy.

4. For instance, Mansfield (1994) notes that hegemons have been credited with stabilizing currencies, providing countercyclical liquidity and markets for distressed goods, acting as a lender of last resort, and maintaining an open trading system.

5. For an exposition of this literature, see Aghion and Howitt (1998b).

6. The significance of the insights gained from endogenous growth models, however, is not without critics (Pack 1994). Note, also, that a flow variable is measured per period, while a stock variable accumulates flow variables over time.

7. For example, see Rebelo (1991). The marginal product of capital is the addition to output from employing one more unit of capital.

8. Similar ideas emphasizing the buildup of labor skill (human capital) as the driving force of aggregate economic growth, and using a different mathematical setup, are found in Lucas (1988).

9. For related examples, see Grossman and Helpman (1991) and Aghion and Howitt (1992).

10. Olson argued that the decline of successful nations is due to the inevitable accumulation of institutional rigidities. The interpretation of Brezis, Krugman, and Tsiddon (1993) is narrower, emphasizing the different reactions of countries to technological innovation.

11. Related ideas may be found in Abramovitz (1986); Baumol, Batey, Blackman, and Wolff (1989); Nelson and Wright (1992); and Maddison (1991).

12. See Maddison (1982); Rosenberg and Frischtak (1983); and Solomou (1988).

13. See Jenks (1944); Cootner (1963, 1965); Fogel (1964); Mitchell (1964); Chandler and Solsbury (1965); Cochran (1965); and Hawke (1970).

14. See, for instance, Rostow (1978: 670–75). Jorgenson (in Jiminez 2001: 392) offers estimates for the percentage of U.S. growth attributable to information technology.

15. Some analysts insist that theories must be stated in formal, axiomatic-deductive fashion to qualify as theories. We disagree. While some types of behavior are conducive to deductive logics, it is not clear that all or even most of the ones that we deal with in IPE are susceptible to what Kaplan (1964: 298) calls hierarchical theorizing (i.e., "one whose component laws are presented as deductions from a small set of basic principles"). Instead, we are engaging in what Kaplan (1964: 298) termed "concatenated" theory (i.e., "one whose component laws enter into a network of relations so as to constitute an identifiable configuration or pattern . . . typically . . . [converging] on some central point, each specifying one of the factors which plays a part in the phenomenon which the theory is to explain"). While we do not see ourselves working with "laws" per se, this type of theory seems both more common in the social science outside of economics and more likely to facilitate the development of a general understanding of the phenomena in which we are most interested.

Chapter 2

1. Compare, for example, Rostow (1978, 1998); Modelski (1981); Freeman and Perez (1988); Thompson (1988, 1990, 1992); Chase-Dunn (1989); Tylecote

(1991); Rasler and Thompson (1994); Boswell and Misra (1995); Wallerstein (1995); Modelski and Thompson (1996); and Hopkins and Wallerstein (1996).

2. Among others, see Rostow (1978); Freeman, Clark, and Soete (1982); and Modelski and Thompson (1996).

3. Modelski and Thompson (1996) contend that this leadership innovation process has been ongoing more or less continuously for the past millennium, and that even earlier instances can be found going back five or six millennia from the present.

4. The period 1913–90 during which U.S. leadership was either gaining momentum or in full force was also used. The results were in the spirit of those reported here and are omitted to save space.

5. For example, see Granger (1980); Nelson and Kang (1984); McCallum (1993); Hamilton (1994); Doan (1992).

6. R_W is not included in the causality test involving only U.S. variables.

7. See Freeman, Williams, and Lin (1989: 586) and Moore (1995: 151).

8. As noted, we report results only when error terms are white noise. Hence, we may assume that other control variables will not affect our results (Hoole and Huang 1989). We had used other controls in earlier analyses, and they did not affect the substance of the results. In general, we attempt to limit the number of controls since we do not seek to fully model growth. War is another variable that could be introduced but not without interpretation problems as its effect on growth tends to be short term (Rasler and Thompson 1989). There is also the issue of whether to extend the war-induced impacts on growth into the postwar period and for how long. These are not casual questions and are better dealt with in more comprehensive examinations.

9. See Reuveny and Thompson (2001); Mintz and Huang (1990); Ward and Davis (1992).

10. Of course, we need to be careful in a visual analysis. To that extent we will also do statistical analysis and sensitivity investigations.

11. See Reuveny and Kang (1996), Thompson and Reuveny (1998), and others for a similar approach.

12. Since we know that U.S. leading sector activity peaked in the 1950s, we also investigated if its impact was waning toward the end of the 1946–90 period. This was done by using a sample that starts in 1870 and incrementing the end year by 10 years from 1949. We find that for the periods 1870–1949 and 1870–1959, the causality is reciprocal. For 1870–1969 and 1870–1979, GDP growth causes leading sector growth. Hence, once sectoral growth peaked, GDP growth dominated in the relationship.

13. Our comments refer only to trade. The U.S. economy was not closed to inputs of labor and investment capital in this period.

14. As Vivek Arora (IMF Survey, January 14, 2002: 10) puts it, the assump-

tion that the U.S. economy is the "engine of the world economy" lacks a "hard, quantified basis." Arora and Vamvadkis, two IMF economists, have recently examined this question of the United States as a driver of the world economy (over the past three decades) and stress that, so far, they are impressed by direct trade as an important transmission conduit. They also argue that developing countries with weaker economies are more likely to be affected by U.S. growth through trade channels than are stronger, industrialized economies.

Chapter 3

1. For a recent exposition of these ideas see, for instance, Modelski and Thompson (1996).

2. Ironically, Pollins and Murrin (1997; see also Bennett 1997) extend their focus on conflict to encompass nonwar, dispute events. Hence, we have representatives of the "weak connection" school expanding the scope of what is impacted by politicoeconomic and military change.

3. Throughout, we use the terms *leading sector growth rate* and *leading sector innovation* interchangeably.

4. In fact, a regression of the military mobilization index on a dummy variable denoting the presence or absence of U.S. warfare yields a coefficient of determination of 0.73 and a *t*-statistic that is highly significant (at the 0.001 level).

5. Weaker statistical results (in the sense of not being able to identify Granger causality) from using contemporaneous values as independent variables revealed that economic innovation was associated (or correlated) with economic and naval leadership.

6. See Freeman, Williams, and Lin (1989) for a review of those critics.

7. See, for instance, Freeman, Williams, and Lin (1989); Kinsella (1994); and Moore (1995).

8. Leading sector growth rates, global reach capabilities, and military mobilization are stationary. When more than five lags are used, leading sector share is also stationary. From a plot of leading sector shares, it does not expand forever. This observation supports the claim that this series is also stationary.

9. In this case, the restricted VAR consists of the equations for military mobilization and global reach capabilities. The unrestricted VAR consists of the same equations with the economic variables entering as independent variables.

10. The results also suggest that leading sector growth rates and leading sector shares are affected by their own dynamics. This is typically the case with macroeconomic variables such as ours.

11. Some VAR studies do not include a confidence interval analysis. This analysis is important, however, since impulse responses may not be statistically significant. If a response is assumed to be inside a confidence interval of 90 percent, in 900 simulations (out of 1,000) their replication should occur inside this interval.

12. In this exercise, shocks operate in isolation. Shocks may act simultaneously resulting in a more complicated response due to cross-effects. Such analyses are not easy to conduct and are typically not reported in VAR studies.

Chapter 4

1. For example, see Grilli (1988).

2. Dornbusch and Frankel (1987) also consider the effect of the exchange rate. An appreciation of the domestic currency raises domestic demand for imports and, therefore, protectionist pressures from import-competing domestic industries.

3. For examples, see McKeown (1986); Gallarotti (1985); Das and Das (1994); Krol (1996); and Hall, Kao, and Nelson (1998).

4. See Modelski and Thompson (1996) for a recent book-length exposition of these ideas.

5. See Thompson and Vescera (1992) and Thompson and Reuveny (1998).

6. See Ferguson (1984); R. Baldwin (1985); Strange (1985); Gourevitch (1986); Lavergne (1983); Frieden (1988); Milner (1988); and Busch and Milner (1994).

7. Milner's argument combines three different levels of analysis: firm, nation, and system.

8. See also Conybeare (1991) and O'Halloran (1994).

9. The Stolper-Samuelson theorem is a direct extension of the Heckscher and Ohlin model that includes two countries, two goods, and two production factors (labor and capital), and assumes that the production of one good employs relatively more labor than capital and the production of the other good employs relatively more capital than labor.

10. For various formulations and use of this theory see, for example, Magee and Young (1987); Stern (1987); Amelung (1989); Rodrik (1995); and Epstein and O'Halloran (1996).

11. Of course, it helps the bipolar conclusion if most, if not all, of the major trading states are attracted to one pole as opposed to being equally divided between antagonistic poles.

12. One concomitant of this reduced salience was, for instance, the apparent surrender of trade policy by Congress to the presidency.

13. See also Webb (1995).

14. Murphy (1994) has also stressed that international institutions, as responses to new technological problems, tend to have limited life spans of effectiveness. As new technologies emerge, the old institutions are not always capable of adapting to cope with the new problems.

15. See also Webb and Krasner (1989).

16. For an overview, see, in particular, Lake (1993).

17. For an early analytical treatment see Johnson (1954). Conybeare (1987) provides an example for a politicoeconomic analysis of trade wars.

18. For example, see Stern (1987); Bhagwati (1988a); and Salvatore (1998).

19. A different position is advanced by Blanton (1996) and Reuveny and Thompson (chap. 8, this book) who argue that, at least in the case of the United States, trading patterns are global regardless of the growth in its regional trade. Reuveny and Thompson also demonstrate that U.S. trade regionalization historically has not been closely related to tariff fluctuations.

20. Thompson and Vescera (1992) integrate five approaches from a long wave perspective.

21. For example, see Neumann (1997); Aghion and Howitt (1998); Helpman and Trajtenberg (1998). The interest of economists in long waves while currently not wide is, of course, not new and can be traced to Schumpeter (1934) and Kondratieff (1979).

22. See, for instance, Freeman and Perez (1988).

23. See Rasler and Thompson (1994); Modelski and Thompson (1996); and Thompson (2000).

24. See Kondratieff (1979). Testing this generalization depends on how one conceptualizes long waves. Kondratieff had a two-phased wave in mind: an upswing and a downswing. Others employ a Schumpeterian conceptualization of four phases in which recession and depression are two of the four phases. Hence, from the latter perspective, the timing of recessions is apt to be true almost by definition.

25. See Gowa (1994).

26. We should also note that our testing propensity is to compare protectionist levels in years of hegemonic ascent versus those of years of descent. Others may compare protectionist levels in years of recession versus those of years of positive growth. What we need to be working toward is looking at the combined effect of hegemonic trajectories and recession.

Chapter 5

1. McKeown (1984, 1986) and Gallarotti (1985) associate protectionism with national business cycles. Kindleberger (1975), Odell (1982), Goldstein (1986), and Rohrlich (1987) argue that ideologies shape trade policies. The role of surplus capacity is discussed by Strange (1979, 1985); Strange and Tooze (1981); and Cowhey and Long (1983). Frieden (1988) and Milner (1988) focus on the role of business elites. Ikenberry (1988), Haggard (1988), and James and Lake (1989) emphasize the role of institutions. Verdier (1994) emphasizes domestic politics. Gowa (1989) and Gowa and Mansfield (1993) discuss the impacts of bipolarity and multipolarity on free trade. For overviews of much of this literature, see Odell (1990), Lake (1993), and chapter 4.

2. We do not mean to suggest that these models exhaust the field of rival approaches. Other possibilities include, for instance, Gowa's (1989) argument about the relationship between polarity and free trade. Since there are a number of ways to measure polarity, pursuing that argument here is likely to divert considerable attention from our main question. Moreover, given the alternating pattern of protectionism fluctuations that most analysts describe, it also seems unlikely that the movement from multipolarity to bipolarity is likely to be equally helpful in capturing the periodicity of trade barriers in the nineteenth and twentieth centuries.

3. Thompson (1988) compares the hegemonic definitions of Wallerstein and Gilpin and argues that, as in the case of Krasner, there is a strong common denominator in the stress on technological preeminence.

4. Modelski and Thompson (1996), for instance, establish long waves as one of the fundamental motors of system leader ascent and decline, global wars, and the long cycle of global leadership. An alternative synthesis is offered by Goldstein (1988).

5. Frederick (1987: 202) notes that the volume of low-tariff grain imports increased substantially in Britain after the 1846 abolition of the Corn Laws. Low-tariff petroleum imports into the United States also increased dramatically after 1972 as well.

6. For a variety of empirical evidence and views on NTBs, see Walter (1972); Balassa (1978); Olechowski and Sampson (1980); UNCTAD (1983); Nogues, Olechowski, and Winters (1985); OECD (1985); World Bank (1987); Goldstein (1986); Bhagwati (1988b); Grilli and Sasson (1990); Verdier (1994); and Deardorff and Stern (1998).

7. See, for example, the discussion in Deardorff and Stern (1985); Corden (1987); Stern (1987); and Laird and Yeats (1990a).

8. Grilli (1990) aggregates several measures of NTBs utilized in large industrialized countries. He includes antidumping inquiries, countervailing procedures, and escape clauses of the United States along with safeguard, surveillance, antidumping inquiries, and countervailing procedures for the European Community. He then generates times-series plots of NTBs starting in 1968 and ending in 1986 that show "the explosion in demand for non-tariff protection during the mid- to late-1970s and from 1981 to 1984 in the United States and the EC" (146).

9. Salvatore (1993a, 1993b) argues that the trend in NTBs in the late 1980s and the beginning of the 1990s is one of increasing intensity.

10. Other countries that deserve attention include Russia, Belgium, the Netherlands, and Italy. At various points in time they controlled collectively some 10 to 25 percent of world trade. While tariff information on these states can be found in Ashley (1911), Isaacs (1948), Little, Scitovsky, and Scott (1970), Salvatore (1992), and Bairoch (1993), we were unable to locate enough serial information to make their inclusion feasible at this time.

11. This problem is associated with 9 of 36 French observations, 10 of 31 German observations, and 7 of 21 Japanese observations.

12. McKeown (1991), in contrast, does not weight his aggregation of import/GNP ratios. Instead, he calculates the average. But what does it mean to average the ratio of one country with little trade involvement with another with extensive trade involvement?

13. There is no particular consensus on how best to approach this question of transition. Long cycle and hegemonic analysts tend to isolate 1945 as the beginning point of the latest emergence of economic leadership. The period between World Wars I and II is often described as a time in which the British could no longer lead and the United States would not lead. In addition, Wallerstein (1983) and Keohane (1980) have made cases for not expecting leaders and their declines to be manifested simultaneously in all economic spheres or regimes. On the other hand, the leading sector underpinnings of the long wave approach is predicated on an 1890 transition in lead economies. Lake (1988: 61) uses 1912 as a relative labor productivity transition in his own treatment of this problem in attempting to explain American trade strategy in the late nineteenth and early twentieth centuries.

14. The systemic customs revenue series utilized by Thompson and Vescera (1992) represents an aggregation of different actors than those associated with the system protectionism indicator. To make the comparison as similar in structure as possible, we restrict (by recalculating it) the customs revenue/imports series discussed here to the same states (Britain, the United States, France, Germany, and Japan) used in the systemic tariff index. Weighted data for the United States and Britain (beginning in 1800), France (1850), Japan (1870), and Germany (1880) are combined to create a single index.

15. Other analysts share this view. See, for example, Bhagwati (1988a); Salvatore (1993a, 1993b); and Verdier (1994).

16. In contrast to technology gap trade models (e.g., Krugman 1979), alternative assumptions about the motors of trade include but are not exhausted by emphases on factor endowments (Ohlin 1933); demand patterns (Linder 1961); and size/distance factors (Linnemann 1966). These possible areas of elaboration are in addition to some of the needed theoretical construction recommended by Rosenberg and Frischtak (1994). They point out that long wave models rest on a number of causal assumptions about complex interactions among invention, investment, innovation, diffusion, recurrence, and economic impact that have yet to be sufficiently clarified theoretically or analyzed empirically. Nevertheless, the focus on innovation-driven economic growth seems to be making some headway even within mainstream economics (Grossman and Helpman 1991; Brezis, Krugman, and Tsiddon 1993).

Chapter 6

1. Examples include Kindleberger (1973); Krasner (1976); Conybeare (1983); Keohane (1984); Gilpin (1987); Lake (1988); Milner (1988); Webb and

Krasner (1989); Cohen (1990); Odell (1990); McKeown (1991); Mansfield (1994); and Gowa (1994).

2. For an overview of the development of this debate, see Lake (1993).

3. For a discussion of the contrast between popular myths about beggar-thy-neighbor policies in the 1930s and the contrary findings of economic historians, see Strange (1985: 239–40).

4. A number of examples of studies in economics that find a short-term decline in economic growth related to protectionism are listed in Mansfield and Busch (1995: 725 n. 3).

5. Different theoretical perspectives and empirical evidence on long-term patterns in economic growth and/or protectionism can be found in Goldstein (1988); Hall and Preston (1988); Freeman and Perez (1988); Thompson (1990); Maddison (1991); Berry (1991); Thompson and Vescera (1992); Tylecote (1993); Modelski and Thompson (1996); and Reuveny and Thompson (1997).

6. Bairoch (1993) emphasizes that the historical relationship between protectionism and national economic growth is by no means obvious and quite possibly positive in nature.

7. Challengers, those follower states that might possibly unseat the incumbent leader, especially need protection to realize their potential. Successful liberal challengers eventually will display patterns found in leader cases. Unsuccessful challengers are more likely to display cyclical protectionist tendencies.

8. The primary trade and GDP sources are Mitchell (1992, 1993, 1995) (for, respectively, Britain, France, and Germany; the United States; and Japan). The data on Japanese trade flows to and from the other four have been supplemented by information from Liesner (1988). Data after 1988 are taken from OECD (1992) and IMF (1991). The 1854 starting date for these series is based on our inability to find systematic British import data broken down by country source prior to the mid-1850s.

9. Too much data are missing to analyze Germany in the 1914–45 or 1854–1990 period.

10. Earlier applications and discussions of some type of a trade ratio indicator include Hirschman (1945); Gasiorowski and Polachek (1982); McKeown (1991); and Reuveny and Kang (1996).

11. Another limitation of average tariffs is their potential volatility due to changing import prices. Irwin (1996) uses both import prices and tariff regimes to explain average tariffs. While this boosts R^2 only from 0.94 to 0.96, the effect may be larger in some short periods. We, however, are not modeling tariffs in short periods. Nor are we attempting to develop a fully specified model of tariffs.

12. See Deardorff and Stern (1985); Bhagwati (1988); Grilli (1990); and Laird and Yeats (1990).

13. We do not assume that NTBs were nonexistent prior to 1968 but only that their short-term impact, especially given relatively low tariffs, was greater after 1968 than before.

14. See, for example, Mansfield (1994) and Gowa (1994).

15. Thirty-three unit root tests are conducted for each country and for the aggregate series, for each of four periods. All of the national and systemic trade ratios are stationary without unit root. However, the tariff series may include unit roots, depending on sample size, lag length, and the type of test used. Two versions of Dickey and Fuller's test and two versions of Phillips and Perron's test, with one version using the t-test statistics and the other focusing on sample size (1 – the autocorrelation coefficient), in addition to the standard Durbin Watson test of the series on a constant, were utilized. But as long as the error terms in the Granger regressions are white noise, the results are considered reliable (see McCallum 1993; Hamilton 1994).

16. Bairoch (1993: 20–21), for instance, notes some British tariff reductions in 1833 and 1842 but he associates, fairly conventionally, the emergence of a free trade stance with the 1846 abolition of the Corn Laws and some duties on manufactured goods.

17. The mid-series trade spike is something of an artifact of a trade index restricted to major economic powers. During World War I, France relied enormously on Allied imports to sustain its economy. Thus the spike captures a genuine trade expansion of sorts, but it is one restricted to wartime exigencies and does not describe what happened to French exports.

Chapter 7

1. The first set of dates is from Gilpin (1975, 1981, 1987), and the second from Wallerstein (1983).

2. The 1815–1914 measure, for instance, does well in the Mansfield examination possibly because it includes a period of British hegemonic decline (1873–1914), which is not found in the second measure that also happened to be a period of considerable trade expansion.

3. See, among others, Freeman, Williams, and Lin (1989) and Reuveny and Kang (1996, 1998).

4. Full details on distributed lag models can be found, for example, in Greene (1997).

5. However, we make no claim that recessions are completely independent of long cycles.

6. As could be expected, note also that the effects of leading sector growth rate in both panels are generally faster than those of the shares variables.

7. At the same time, this particular limitation is shared by all empirical investigations of our type, and in a way by all econometric investigations.

Chapter 8

1. Grilli (1997), however, reminds us that the more recent spate of regional arrangements actually represents a second, post–World War II wave. The first wave occurred between 1957 and 1975, generating the EC in western Europe, LAFTA and CACM in Latin America and the Caribbean, ACM in the Middle East, and UDEAC, SACU, CEAO, and ECOWAS in sub-Saharan Africa. Most of these arrangements were intra-Southern affairs and were less than successful (see Deutsch 1977; Langhammer and Hiemenz 1990; and Salvatore 1998). The second wave has tended to be more North-South in orientation.

2. Analysts disagree on the likely outcome of trade regionalization. Analysts who emphasize negative consequences include Gilpin (1987), Bhagwati (1991, 1993), Krugman (1991a), and Garten (1992). Oye (1992) and McDonald (1998) are among those who argue for positive consequences. In between are scholars such as Viner (1950), Lawrence (1996), Grilli (1997), and Haggard (1997).

3. Analysts also disagree about whether the new or reinvigorated regional arrangements constitute movement toward trade exclusivity. Pomfret (1988) argues that regionalism is not increasing. Grieco (1997: 172) suggests that there is considerable variation among different groups on this question. Mansfield and Branson (1997) demonstrate that one must control for other influences such as major power alliances in assessing the effects of trade blocs on the flow of trade. Faini (1997) argues that interbloc trade actually increased in the 1980s. El-Agraa (1997: 370) agrees and notes that both intra- and interbloc trade was able to increase thanks to overall growth in gross domestic product.

4. For a survey and more detailed development of these ideas, see Lipsey (1968), Pomfret (1986), and Bhagwati and Panagariya (1996).

5. This discussion summarizes ideas from Krugman (1991b); Frankel, Stein, and Wei (1993); Deardorff and Stern (1991); Lawrence (1996); and Salvatore (1998).

6. For instance, U.S. firms made massive investments in Europe following the 1957 formation of the European Common Market and then again after 1986 when the union membership grew to fifteen nations.

7. See Keohane and Hoffmann (1990).

8. As of 2002, Mearsheimer's prediction concerning European political instability following the end of the Cold War has not materialized outside of the Balkans. Nevertheless, it is clear that an emphasis on external threat does not help to explain cases, such as NAFTA, in which there is no overt perception of threat.

9. On the NAFTA debate and its expected impact on the U.S. economy, see, for example, Brown, Deardorff, and Stern (1992); U.S. International Trade Commission (1993); Fatemi and Salvatore (1994); Garber (1993); and Hufbauer and

Schott (1993). For critical views of the NAFTA impact on the Mexican economy, see, for example, the articles contained in Appendini and Bislev (1999).

10. For details on the agreement, see Bannister (1997). Some protection from FDI will continue for Mexico's energy and railway sectors, the U.S. airline and communication sectors, and Canada's cultural sectors.

11. Ross Perot, the onetime presidential candidate, has been a leading opponent of NAFTA. See, for instance, Perot and Choate (1993).

12. It is interesting to note that the U.S.-Canadian 1989 FTA did not meet strong opposition. On the NAFTA debate, see, for example, Garber (1993). *The Economist* (November 13, 1993) provides a survey and summary of the opposing views.

13. For example, manufacturing wages in Mexico are roughly 10 percent of U.S. wages (Reyes 1999: 175 n. 24).

14. In 1995, for example, Mexico's GDP per capita was about one-tenth that of the United States. According to the World Bank, Mexico's labor productivity is roughly one-fourth of the U.S. level (see Husted and Melvin 1997).

15. For a summary of the U.S. administration's report, see the *Washington Post* (July 11, 1997) as well as reports issued by the Office of the U.S. Trade Representative and Related Entities at <www.sice.oas.org/forum/p_sector/govt/nafta_repe> (accessed April 20, 1999). On the 1989 U.S.-Canada free trade agreement and the Canadian gains from NAFTA see Lawrence (1996) and Salvatore (1998).

16. The *Economist* (July 5, 1997), the *New York Times* (December 19, 1996), the *Washington Post* (July 11, 1997), Husted and Melvin (1997), Sweeney (1997), and Bannister (1997) provide discussions of NAFTA's trade effects. In a 1997 study (cited in *Washington Post,* July 11, 1997 and <www.sice.oas.org/forum/p_sector/nafta_repe/chap1_1.stm>, accessed April 22, 1999) McGraw-Hill's DRI (a private consulting group) estimates that in 1996, NAFTA raised U.S. exports to Mexico by $12 billion and imports from Mexico by $5 billion.

17. On NAFTA's small effect on U.S. employment see also *Wall Street Journal* (November 17, 1993). Moreover, this small labor effect is reflected by the fact that by mid-1997, only 117,000 U.S. workers have signed on to receive government benefits offered to workers displaced by NAFTA. This number is quite small compared to the 2.8 million jobs created in the United States from 1994 to 1997 and the 1.5 million workers that lost jobs due to non-NAFTA related factory closures, corporate restructuring, and low demand. The FDI number is less than 0.5 percent of total U.S. firms' investments in new plants and equipment (*Economist,* July 5, 1997).

18. On the trade diversion interpretation of these Mexican car exports data, see the *Economist* (July 5, 1997). While less important due to its small size, Central American and Caribbean countries have also seen some of their trade diverted to Mexico following the agreement.

19. See <www.sice.oas.org/forum/p_sector/govt/nafta_repe/chap1_1.sum> (accessed April 28, 1999).

20. Panagariya (1995) and others have argued that commitment to trade liberalization through the WTO (and GATT) may work better than through the formation of a trade bloc.

21. This suggestion was advanced by former Clinton adviser Richard Feinberg: "We bought ourselves an ally with NAFTA" (as cited in *Economist*, July 5, 1997: 22). For a related argument, see Purcell (1997).

22. NAFTA nonprotectionist motivations do not appear to be all that unique in the latest wave of regional trading arrangements. See, among others, Lawrence (1996); Haggard (1997); Higgott (1998); Milner (1998); and Tussie (1998).

23. Mitchell (1993) represents the primary source for data on trade and gross domestic product. The sources for the tariff data are discussed in chapter 5 of this study.

24. Regional encapsulations are computed from ratios of trade values. As the price of oil rose sharply in the 1970s and early 1980s, the value of U.S. oil imports rose. Since U.S. oil is coming mostly from outside of NAFTA, the rise in oil price implied a decline in U.S. regional trade encapsulations during that period.

25. The 1854–1990 period stems solely from the authors' interest in paralleling other and earlier analyses of ours that involve other major economic powers and are restricted to 1854 starting points due to non-U.S. missing data problems.

26. A correlation of, say, 0.2, is not problematic in any way. However, while this correlation is statistically significant at the level of 5 percent in this sample, it probably means that the two variables are not the only determinants of each other.

27. Contrary to what one might expect, in the long-run trade volume Granger causes tariffs but the reciprocal relationship does not hold (chap. 6). We take this to mean that the main driving force is prosperity/depression. In a depressed era, trade volumes decline and tariffs are likely to rise, but the causal emphasis needs to be placed on the negative economic growth → trade volume relationship rather than the more celebrated, tariff → trade volume relationship.

28. As noted, some observers argue that the move to form the EU is also aimed to reduce the likelihood of warfare in Europe. Similarly, it is argued that the move to form NAFTA is also aimed to accelerate Mexico's democratic and free market reforms and strengthen U.S.-Mexico political relations.

29. See Frankel, Stein, and Wei (1997) for a review of the extensive trade gravity literature.

Chapter 9

1. Nevertheless, the following passage highlights Kindleberger's (1996: 13) own ambivalence.

There are many concepts like economic primacy . . . that cannot be defined rigorously, but most people know what is meant by them. Economic primacy cannot be measured exactly and, as Lord Elgin said, in such circumstances our knowledge is not completely satisfactory. Despite this, I assert that the idea has meaning, and that in the past, from time to time, perhaps a great deal of the time, economic primacy has had reality.

2. David Lake (1988) is another prominent IPE scholar who, aside from a 1993 postmortem, has also moved away from an initial interest in structural change and leadership.

3. From a twin-peaked perspective, the first growth surge is unlikely to match the second, catch-up growth wave.

4. Perroux (1979) was a clear and unusual exception. Maddison (1991, 1995) is another economist who comes close by acknowledging British and U.S. leadership in economic growth.

5. One reason may be the strong interest exhibited by lateral pressure studies in using price fluctuations, as opposed to technological innovation, as the main barometer of long economic waves.

6. This process occurs in multiple ways. Most obviously, rivals' positions deteriorate through exhaustion and defeat. But the system leader's leading sector production is stimulated by the demands of war. So, too, is the development of its global reach capability (Thompson 1988). There is also the matter of heading a wartime coalition of victorious states. The coalition is not guaranteed to survive intact forever, but the postwar leadership role seems more natural to the extent that it builds on patterns of wartime cooperation.

7. Global war was another seemingly necessary factor.

8. At the same time, there are undeniable benefits to be enjoyed from residing within the system's lead economy.

9. See Thompson (1990) for a discussion of the way analysts have connected these variables in previous arguments.

10. On the subject of political realignments and long waves, see Berry (1991); and Berry, Elliott, Harpham, and Kim (1998).

11. Pollins and Schweller (1999) link public opinion and long waves in the U.S. setting.

12. See Murphy (1994) on this topic.

13. Murphy (2001) takes on this question.

14. On this subject, see Chase-Dunn and Rubinson (1979); Bergesen and Schoenberg (1980); McGowan (1985); Boswell (1989); Strang (1991); Pollins and Murrin (1999); and Reuveny and Thompson (2002).

15. The most comprehensive analysis of debt crises in the long term is Suter (1992), but see, as well, Marichal (1989) and Reuveny and Thompson (forthcoming).

16. On the persistence of economic inequality from the perspective advanced in the present study, see Reuveny and Thompson (2003).

Appendix A

1. Whether the Durbin-h can be computed depends on the sample size and the variance of the raw data. See Greene (1997). The Durbin-h test is also criticized for having a low power. Some authors (e.g., Inder 1984) recommend not using it.

2. The cumulative periodogram test computes the Fourier transform of the residuals from the Granger regression. This cumulative periodogram is compared to a cumulative periodogram of white noise from a Kolmogorov-Smirnov (K-S) test. If the two cumulative periodograms do not differ statistically, then the Granger regression residuals are white noise and therefore do not contain any serial correlation. See Doan (1992).

3. On the role of ARIMA processes in Granger causality tests see, for example, Freeman (1983).

4. Mehra (1977), Huang and Kracaw (1984), Hoole and Huang (1989), Thompson and Reuveny (1998), and Reuveny and Kang (1996, 1998) try systematically different lag lengths. Sargent (1976) and Sims (1972) use fixed, but arbitrary, lag length.

5. The maximum number of lags that can be used is limited by the available degrees of freedom.

6. The number of lags that can be used is of course limited by the available degrees of freedom.

7. For more details, see Freeman, Williams, and Lin (1989).

8. See the discussions in Granger (1980); Freeman (1983); Nelson and Kang (1984); Freeman, Williams and Lin (1989); Hamilton (1994); and Reuveny and Kang (1996, 1998).

References

Abramovitz, M. 1986. "Catching Up, Forging Ahead, and Falling Behind." *Journal of Economic History* 46:386–406.

Adams, R. 1996. *Paths of Fire: An Anthropologist's Inquiry into Western Technology.* Princeton: Princeton University Press.

Aghion, P., and P. Howitt. 1992. "A Model of Growth through Creative Destruction." *Econometrica* 60:323–51.

———. 1998a. *Endogenous Growth Theory.* Cambridge: MIT Press.

———. 1998b. "On the Macroeconomic Effects of Major Technological Change." In E. Helpman, ed., *General Purpose Technologies and Economic Growth.* Cambridge: MIT Press.

Almazan, M. A. 1997. "NAFTA and the [Mexico] Mesoamerican States System." *American Academy of Political and Social Science* 550:42–50.

Amelung, T. 1989. "The Determinants of Protection in Developing Countries: An Extended Interest-Group Approach." *Kyklos* 42:515–32.

Angell, N. 1933. *The Great Illusion.* New York: Putnam.

Appendini, K., and S. Bislev, eds. 1999. *Economic Integration in NAFTA and the EU.* New York: St. Martin's.

Arrighi, G. 1994. *The Long Twentieth Century.* London: Verso.

Arrighi, G., and B. Silver. 1999. *Chaos and Governance in the Modern World: Comparing Hegemonic Transitions.* Minneapolis: University of Minnesota Press.

Arrow, K. J. 1962. "The Economic Implications of Learning by Doing." *Review of Economic Studies* 29:155–73.

Ashley, P. 1911. *Modern Tariff History: Germany, United States, France.* London: John Murray.

Ayres, R. 1990. "Technological Transitions and Long Waves." *Technological Forecasting and Social Change* 37:1–37.

Bairoch, P. 1993. *Economics and World History.* Chicago: University of Chicago Press.

Balassa, B. 1978. "The New Protectionism and the International Economy." *Journal of World Trade Law* 12:409–36.

Baldwin, D. A. 1979. "Power Analysis and World Politics: New Trends versus Old Tendencies." *World Politics* 31:161–94.

References

————. 1985. *Economic Statecraft.* Princeton: Princeton University Press.

Baldwin, R. E. 1984. "Recent Issues and Initiatives in U.S. Trade Policy." *NBER Conference Report,* ed. Cambridge, Mass.

————. 1985. *The Political Economy of U.S. Import Policy.* Cambridge: MIT Press.

————. 1995. "The New Protectionism: A Response to Shifts in National Economic Power." In J. Frieden and D. Lake, eds., *International Political Economy: Perspectives on Global Power and Wealth,* 339–52. New York: St. Martin's.

Banks, A. 1967. *Cross-Polity Time Series Data.* Cambridge: MIT Press.

Bannister, R. R. 1997. *The NAFTA Success Story: More Than Just Trade.* Washington, D.C.: Progressive Policy Institute.

Barnett, E. 1976. "The Gatt Tariff: Incidental or Effective Protection?" *Canadian Journal of Economics* 9:389–407.

Baumol, W. J., S. A. Batey Blackman, and E. N. Wolff. 1989. *Productivity and American Leadership.* Cambridge: MIT Press.

Bennett, S. L. 1997. "The Dynamics of Coevolving Systems and Armed Conflict." Revised paper presented at the 1996 annual meeting of the International Studies Association. Toronto.

Bergesen, A., and R. Schoenberg. 1980. "Long Waves of Colonial Expansion and Contraction, 1415–1969." In A. Bergesen, ed., *Studies of the Modern World-System.* New York: Academic Press.

Bernstein, A. M. 1940. "War and the Pattern of Business Cycles." *American Economic Review* 30:524–35.

Berry, B. J. L. 1991. *Long-Wave Rhythms in Economic Development and Political Behavior.* Baltimore: Johns Hopkins University Press.

Berry, B. J. L., E. Elliott, E. J. Harpham, and H. Kim. 1998. *The Rhythms of American Politics.* Lanham, Md.: University Press of America.

Bhagwati, J. 1988a. *Protectionism.* Cambridge: MIT Press.

————. 1988b. "The United States and Trade Policy Reversing Gears." *Journal of International Affairs* 42:93–108.

————. 1991. *The World Treaty System at Risk.* Princeton: Princeton University Press.

————. 1993. "Regionalism and Multilateralism: An Overview." In J. de Melo and A. Panagariya, eds., *New Dimensions in Regional Integration,* 22–51. New York: Cambridge University Press.

Bhagwati, J., and A. O. Krueger. 1995. *The Dangerous Drift to Preferential Trade Agreements.* Washington, D.C.: American Enterprise Institute for Public Policy Research.

Bhagwati, J., and A. Panagariya, eds. 1996. *Free Trade Areas or Free Trade? The Economics of Preferential Trading.* Washington, D.C.: AEI Press.

Blanton, R. G. 1996. "Diminished Giant or Vanguard for Liberalization? The US and the Regionalization of Trade." *Political Research Quarterly* 49:783–805.

References

Bornschier, V. 1996. *Western Society in Transition.* New Brunswick, N.J.: Transaction Press.

Borrus, M., and J. Zysman. 1992. "Industrial Competitiveness and American National Security." In W. Sandholtz et al., eds., *The Highest Stakes: The Economic Foundations of the Next Security System,* 7–52. New York: Oxford University Press.

Boserup, E. 1981. *Population and Technological Change: A Study of Long Term Trends.* Chicago: University of Chicago Press.

Boswell, T. 1989. "Colonial Empires and the Capitalist World-Economy: A Time-Series Analysis of Colonization, 1640–1960." *American Sociological Review* 54:180–96.

Boswell, T., and C. Chase-Dunn. 2000. *The Spiral of Capitalism and Socialism: Toward Global Democracy.* Boulder: Lynne Rienner.

Boswell, T., and J. Misra. 1997. "Cycles and Trends in the Early Capitalist World-Economy: An Analysis of Leading Sector Commodity Trades, 1500–1600/50–1750." *Review* 18:459–86.

Boswell, T., and M. Sweat. 1991. "Hegemony, Long Waves and Major Wars." *International Studies Quarterly* 35:123–49.

Bousquet, N. 1980. "From Hegemony to Competition: Cycles of the Core?" In T. K. Hopkins and I. Wallerstein, eds., *Processes of the World-System.* Beverly Hills, Calif.: Sage.

Brander, J. A. 1995. "Strategic Trade Policy." In G. M. Grossman and K. Rogoff, eds., *Handbook of International Economics,* vol. 3: 1395–1455. Amsterdam: Elsevier.

Brander, J. A., and B. Spenser. 1985. "Export Subsidies and International Market Share Rivalry." *Journal of International Economics* (February): 83–100.

Braudel, F. 1984. *The Perspective of the World.* New York: Harper and Row.

Brawley, M. R. 1993. *Liberal Leadership: Great Powers and Their Challengers in Peace and War.* Ithaca: Cornell University Press.

———. 1999. *Afterglow or Adjustment? Domestic Institutions and Responses to Overstretch.* New York: Columbia University Press.

Brenner, R. 1985. *Betting on Ideas: Wars, Inventions, Inflation.* Chicago: University of Chicago Press.

Bresnahan, T., and M. Trajtenberg. 1995. "General Purpose Technologies: Engines of Growth." *Journal of Econometrics* 65:83–108.

Brezis, E., P. Krugman, and D. Tsiddon. 1993. "Leapfrogging in International Competition: A Theory of Cycles in National Technological Leadership." *American Economic Review* 83:1211–19.

Brown, D. K., A. V. Deardorff, and R. M. Stern. 1992. "North American Integration." *Economic Journal* 102:1507–18.

Busch, M. L., and H. V. Milner. 1994. "The Future of the International Trading System: International Firms, Regionalism, and Domestic Politics." In R.

References

Stubbs and G. R. D. Underhill, eds., *Political Economy and the Changing Global Order*, 259–76. New York: St. Martin's.

Cass, D. 1965. "Optimum Growth in Aggregate Model of Capital Accumulation." *Review of Economic Studies* 32:233–40.

Caves, R. 1976. "Economics Models of Political Choice: Canada's Tariff Structure." *Canadian Journal of Economics* 9:278–300.

Chandler, A. D., Jr., and S. Salsbury. 1965. "The Railroads: Innovations in Modern Business Administration." In B. Mazlish, ed., *The Railroad and the Space Program: An Exploration in Historical Analogy*. Cambridge: MIT Press.

Chase-Dunn, C. 1989. *Global Formation: Structures of the World-Economy*. Cambridge: Blackwell. 2d ed., Boulder: Rowman and Littlefield, 1998.

Chase-Dunn, C., and R. Rubinson. 1979. "Toward a Structural Perspective on the World-System." *Politics and Society* 7:453–76.

Chen, J. 1974. "United States Concessions in the Kennedy Round and Short-Run Adjustment Costs." *Journal of International Economics* 4:323–40.

Choucri, N., and R. C. North. 1972. "In Search of Peace Systems: Scandinavia and the Netherlands, 1870–1970." In B. Russett, ed., *Peace, War and Numbers*. Beverly Hills, Calif.: Sage.

Cochran, T. C. 1965. "The Social Impact of the Railroad." In B. Mazlish, ed., *The Railroad and the Space Program: An Exploration in Historical Analogy*. Cambridge: MIT Press.

Conybeare, J. A. C. 1983. "Tariff Protection in Developed and Developing Countries: A Cross-Sectional and Longitudinal Analysis. *International Organization* 37:441–63.

———. 1987. *Trade Wars: The Theory and Practice of International Commercial Rivalry*. New York: Columbia University Press.

———. 1990. "A Random Walk Down the Road to War: War Cycles, Prices and Causality." *Defense Economics* 1:329–37.

———. 1991. "Voting for Protection: An Electoral Model of Tariff Policy." *International Organization* 45:57–82.

Cooper, R. 1968. *The Economics of Interdependence: Economic Policy in the Atlantic Community*. New York: McGraw-Hill.

———. 1987. "Trade Policy as Foreign Policy, from 1765 to 1985." In R. R. Stern, ed., *U.S. Trade Policies in a Changing World Economy*, 291–322. Cambridge: MIT Press.

Cootner, P. H. 1963. "The Role of the Railroads in United States Economic Growth." *Journal of Economic History* 23:477–521.

———. 1965. "The Economic Impact of the Railroad Innovation." In B. Mazlish, ed., *The Railroad and the Space Program: An Exploration in Historical Analogy*. Cambridge: MIT Press.

Corden, W. 1987. *Protection and Liberalization: A Review of Analytical Issues*. Washington, D.C.: International Monetary Fund.

References

Cowhey, P. F., and E. Long. 1983. "Testing Theories of Regime Change: Hegemonic Decline and Surplus Capacity?" *International Organization* 37:162–90.

Das, S., and S. P. Das. 1994. "Quantitative Assessment of Tariff Endogeneity: Interwar vs. Postwar." *Economic Letters* 44:139–46.

Davis, H. T. 1941. *The Analysis of Economic Time Series*. Bloomington, Ind.: Principia Press.

Deardorff, A., and R. Stern. 1985. *Methods of Measurement of Nontariff Barriers*. Westport, Conn.: Greenwood.

———. 1991. "Multilateral Trade Negotiations and Preferential Trading Arrangements." In A. V. Deardorff and R. M. Stern, eds., *Analytical and Negotiating Issues in the Global Trading System*, 27–85. Ann Arbor: University of Michigan Press.

———. 1998. *Measurement of Nontariff Barriers*. Ann Arbor: University of Michigan Press.

Destler, I. M. 1992. *American Trade Politics*. 2d ed. Washington, D.C.: Institute for International Economics.

Deutsch, K. W. 1977. "National Integration: Some Concepts and Research Approaches." *Jerusalem Journal of International Relations* 2:1–29.

Dicken, P. 1998. *Global Shift: Transforming the World Economy*. 3d ed. New York: Guilford.

Dickenson, F. G. 1940. "An Aftercost of the World War to the United States." *American Economic Review* 30 (supplement, part 2): 326–39.

Dickey, D., and W. A. Fuller. 1979. "Distribution of the Estimators for Time Series Regressions with a Unit Root." *Journal of the American Statistical Association* 74:427–31.

———. 1981. "Likelihood Ratio Test for Autoregressive Time Series with a Unit Root." *Econometrica* 49:1057–72.

Doan, T. A. 1992. *Regression Analysis of Time Series*. Evanston, Ill.: Estima.

Dornbusch, R., and J. A. Frankel. 1987. "Macroeconomics and Protection." In R. M. Stern, ed., *US Trade Policies in a Changing World Economy*, 77–130. Cambridge: MIT Press.

Dosi, G. 1982. "Technological Paradigms and Technological Trajectories." *Research Policy* 11:147–62.

———. 1983. "Technological Paradigms and Technological Trajectories: The Determinants and Directions for Technical Change and the Transformation of the Economy." In C. Freeman, ed., *Long Waves in the World Economy*. London: Pinter.

Duijn, J. J. van. 1983. *The Long Wave in Economic Life*. London: Allen and Unwin.

Duncan, G. T., and R. M. Siverson. 1982. "Flexibility of Alliance Partner Choice in a Multipolar System: Models and Tests." *International Studies Quarterly* 26:511–38.

References

El-Agraa, A. M. 1997. "Fortresses' and Three Trading Blocs?" In A. M. El-Agraa, ed., *Economic Integration Worldwide,* 368–78. New York: St. Martin's.

Epstein, D. O., and S. O'Halloran. 1996. "The Partisan Paradox and the U.S. Tariff, 1877–1934." *International Organization* 50:301–24.

Faini, R. 1997. "Integration or Polarization? Regionalism in World Trade during the 1980s." In R. Faini and E. Grilli, eds., *Multilateralism and Regionalism after the Uruguay Round,* 144–60. New York: St. Martin's.

Fatemi, K., and D. Salvatore. 1994. *The North American Free Trade Agreement.* New York: Pergamon Press.

Feige, E., and D. Pearce. 1979. "The Causal Relationship between Money and Income: Some Caveats for Time Series Analysis." *Review of Economics and Statistics* 61:521–33.

Ferguson, T. 1984. "From Normalcy to New Deal: Industrial Structure, Party Competition, and American Public Policy in the Great Depression." *International Organization* 38:41–94.

Finger, M. 1992. "Trade Policies in the United States." In D. Salvatore, ed., *National Trade Policies.* Westport, Conn.: Greenwood.

Finger, M., and A. De Rosa. 1979. "Trade Overlap, Comparative Advantage, and Protection." In H. Giersch, ed., *Free Trade in the World Economy: Toward an Opening of Markets.* Tübingen, Germany: Mohr.

Fischer, W. 1987. "Swings toward Protection and Free Trade in History." In H. Giersch, ed., *Free Trade in the World Economy: Toward an Opening of Markets.* Tübingen, Germany: Mohr.

Fogel, R. W. 1964. *Railroads and American Economic Growth: Essays in Econometric History.* Baltimore, Md.: Johns Hopkins University.

Frankel, J. A., E. Stein, and S. J. Wei. 1993. "Trading Blocs and the Americas: The Natural, the Unnatural, and the Supernatural." *Journal of Development Economics* 47:61–96.

———. 1997. *Regional Trading Blocs in the World Economic System.* Washington, D.C.: Institute for International Economics.

Frederick, S. 1987. "The Instability of Free Trade." In G. Modelski, ed., *Exploring Long Cycles.* Boulder: Lynne Rienner.

Freeman, C., ed. 1983. *Long Waves in the World Economy.* London: Butterworth.

Freeman, C., J. Clark, and L. Soete. 1982. *Unemployment and Technical Innovation: A Study of Long Waves and Economic Development.* London: Pinter.

Freeman, C., and C. Perez. 1988. "Structural Crises of Adjustment, Business Cycle, and Investment Behavior." In G. Dosi, C. Freeman, R. Nelson, G. Silverberg, and L. Soete, eds., *Technical Change and Economic Theory.* London: Pinter.

Freeman, C., and L. Soete. 1997. *The Economics of Industrial Innovation.* 3d ed. Cambridge: MIT Press.

References

Freeman, J. R. 1983. "Granger Causality and the Time Series Analysis of Political Relationships." *American Journal of Political Science* 26:709–29.

Freeman, J. R., J. T. Williams, and T. Lin. 1989. "Vector Auto-regressions and the Study of Politics." *American Journal of Political Science* 33:842–77.

Frieden, J. 1988. "Sectoral Conflict and U.S. Foreign Economic Policy." *International Organization* 42:59–90.

Gallarotti, G. 1985. "Toward a Business-Cycle Model of Tariffs." *International Organization* 39:155–87.

Garber, P. M., ed. 1993. *The Mexico-U.S. Free Trade Agreement*. Cambridge: MIT Press.

Garten, J. E. 1992. *A Cold Peace: America, Germany and the Struggle for Supremacy*. New York: Times Books.

Gasiorowksi, M., and S. Polachek. 1982. "East-West Trade and Linkages in the Era of Detente." *Journal of Conflict Resolution* 26:709–29.

GATT. 1979. *Working Groups Document 4900*. Geneva: General Agreement on Tariffs and Trade.

———. 1981. *Working Groups Document 5090*. Geneva: General Agreement on Tariffs and Trade.

Geweke, J. 1984. "Inference and Causality in Economic Time Series Models." In Z. Griliches and M. D. Intriligator, eds., *Handbook of Econometrics*. Amsterdam: North Holland.

Gilligan, M. J. 1997. *Empowering Exporters: Reciprocity, Delegation, and Collective Action in American Trade Policy*. Ann Arbor: University of Michigan Press.

Gills, B. K., and A. G. Frank. 1993. "World System Cycles, Crises, and Hegemonic Shifts, 1700 BC to 1700 AD." In A. G. Frank and B. K. Gills, eds., *The World System: Five Hundred Years or Five Thousand?* London: Routledge.

Gilpin, R. 1975. *U.S. Power and the Multinational Corporation: The Political Economy of Foreign Direct Investment*. New York: Basic Books.

———. 1981. *War and Change in World Politics*. New York: Cambridge University Press.

———. 1987. *The Political Economy of International Relations*. Princeton: Princeton University Press.

———. 1996. "No One Loves a Political Realist." In B. Frankel, ed., *Realism: Restatements and Renewal*. London: Frank Cass.

———. 2000. *The Challenge of Global Capitalism: The World Economy in the Twenty-first Century*. Princeton: Princeton University Press.

Goldstein, J. 1986. "The Political Economy of Trade: Institutions of Protection." *American Political Science Review* 80:161–84.

Goldstein, J. S. 1988. *Long Cycles*. New Haven: Yale University Press.

———. 1991. "A War-Economy Theory of the Long Wave." In N. Thygesen, K. Velupillai, and S. Zambelli, eds., *Business Cycles: Theory, Evidence, and Analysis*. New York: New York University Press.

References

Gordon, D. 1980. "Stages of Accumulation and Long Economic Cycles." In T. K. Hopkins and I. Wallerstein, eds., *Processes of the World-System.* Beverly Hills, Calif.: Sage.

Gourevitch, P. 1986. *Politics in Hard Times: Comparative Responses to International Economic Crises.* Ithaca: Cornell University Press.

Gowa, J. 1989a. "Bipolarity, Multipolarity, and Free Trade." *American Political Science Review* 83:1245–56.

———. 1989b. "Rational Hegemons, Excludable Goods, and Small Groups: An Epitaph for Hegemonic Stability Theory?" *World Politics* 41:307–24.

———. 1994. *Allies, Adversaries, and International Trade.* Princeton: Princeton University Press.

Gowa, J., and E. D. Mansfield. 1993. "Power Politics and International Trade." *American Political Science Review* 87:408–20.

Granger, C. W. 1969. "Investigating Causal Relations by Econometric Models and Cross-Spectral Methods." *Econometrica* 37:424–38.

———. 1980. "Testing for Causality: A Personal Viewpoint." *Journal of Economic Dynamics and Control* 2:329–52.

Greenaway, D. 1992. "Trade Policies in the United Kingdom." In D. Salvatore, ed., *National Trade Policies.* Westport, Conn.: Greenwood.

Greene, W. H. 1997. *Econometric Analysis.* Upper Saddle River, N.J.: Prentice-Hall.

Grieco, J. M. 1997. "Systemic Sources of Variation in Regional Institutionalization in Western Europe, East Asia, and the Americas." In E. D. Mansfield and H. V. Milner, eds., *The Political Economy of Regionalism,* 164–87. New York: Columbia University Press.

Grilli, E. 1988. "Macro-economic Determinants of Trade Protectionism." *World Economy* 11:313–35.

———. 1990. "Protectionism and the Developing Countries." In E. Grilli and E. Sassoon, eds., *The New Protectionist Wave.* New York: New York University Press.

———. 1997. "Multilateralism and Regionalism: A Still Difficult Coexistence." In R. Faini and E. Grilli, eds., *Multilateralism and Regionalism after the Uruguay Round.* New York: St. Martin's.

Grossman, G., and E. Helpman. 1991. *Innovation and Growth in the Global Economy.* Cambridge: MIT Press.

———. 1994. "Endogenous Innovation in the Theory of Growth." *Journal of Economic Perspectives* 8:23–44.

Haggard, S. 1988. "The Institutional Foundations of Hegemony: Explaining the Reciprocal Trade Agreements Act of 1934." *International Organization* 42:91–119.

———. 1997. "Regionalism in Asia and the Americas." In E. D. Mansfield and

References

H. V. Milner, eds., *The Political Economy of Regionalism,* 20–49. New York: Columbia University Press.

Hall, H. K., C. Kao, and D. Nelson. 1998. "Women and Tariffs: Testing the Gender Gap Hypothesis in Downs-Mayer Political Economy Model." *Economic Inquiry* 36:320–32.

Hall, P., and P. Preston. 1988. *The Carrier Wave: New Information Technology and the Geography of Innovation, 1846–2003.* London: Unwin Hyman.

Hamilton, J. D. 1994. *Time Series Analysis.* Princeton: Princeton University Press.

Hansen, A. H. 1932. *Economic Stabilization in an Unbalanced World.* New York: Harcourt Brace.

———. 1964. *Business Cycles and National Income.* Expanded ed. New York: W. W. Norton.

Hawke, G. R. 1970. *Railways and Economic Growth in England and Wales, 1840–1870.* Oxford: Clarendon Press.

Helleiner, G. 1977. "The Political Economy of Canada's Tariff Structure: An Alternative Model." *Canadian Journal of Economics* 10:318–26.

Helpman, E., ed. 1998. *General Purpose Technologies and Economic Growth.* Cambridge: MIT Press.

Helpman H., and P. Krugman. 1989. *Trade Policy and Market Structure.* Cambridge: MIT Press.

Helpman E., and M. Trajtenberg. 1998. "A Time to Sow and a Time to Reap: Growth Based on General Purpose Technologies." In E. Helpman, ed., *General Purpose Technologies and Economic Growth.* Cambridge: MIT Press.

Higgott, R. 1998. "The International Political Economy of Regionalism: The Asia-Pacific and Europe Compared." In W. D. Coleman and G. R. D. Underhill, eds., *Regionalism and Global Economic Integration: Europe, Asia and the Americas,* 42–67. London: Routledge.

Hirschman, A. 1980. *National Power and the Structure of Foreign Trade.* Berkeley: University of California Press.

Holtfrerich, C.-L. 1989. " Introduction: The Evolution of World Trade, 1720 to the Present," in C.-L. Holtfrerich, ed., *Interactions in the World Economy: Perspectives from International Economic History.* New York: New York University Press.

Hoole, F., and C. Huang. 1989. "The Global Conflict Process." *Journal of Conflict Resolution* 33:142–63.

Hopkins, T. K., and I. Wallerstein, eds. 1996. *The Age of Transition: Trajectory of the World System, 1945–2025.* London: Zed Books.

Hsiao, C. 1979. "Causality Tests in Econometrics." *Journal of Economic Dynamic and Control* 1:321–46.

Huang, R., and W. Kracaw. 1984. "Stock Market Returns and Real Activity: A Note." *Journal of Finance* 39:267–73.

Hufbauer, G., and J. Schott. 1990. *Economic Sanctions Reconsidered: History and Current Policy.* Washington, D.C.: Institute for International Economics.

References

————. 1992. *North American Free Trade: Issues and Recommendations.* Washington, D.C.: Institute for International Economics.

————, eds. 1993. *NAFTA: An Assessment.* Washington, D.C.: Institute for International Economics.

Husted, B. W., and J. M. Logsdon. 1997. "The Impact of NAFTA on Mexico's Environmental Policy." *Growth and Change* 28:24–48.

Husted, S., and M. Melvin. 1997. *International Economics.* Reading, Mass.: Addison-Wesley.

Ikenberry, J. 1988. "Conclusion: An Institutional Approach to American Economic Policy." *International Organization* 42:219–43.

Imbert, G. 1959. *Des Mouvements de Longue Durée Kondratieff.* Aix-en-Provence, France: La Pensée Universitaire.

IMF (International Monetary Fund). 1991. *Direction of Trade Statistics Yearbook.* Washington, D.C: IMF.

IMF Survey. 2002. "Interview with Arora and Vamvakidis: United States Increasingly Serves as 'Engine' for World Growth." *IMF Survey* 31 (January 14): 10–13.

Imlah, A. 1958. *Economic Elements in the Pax Britannica.* Cambridge: Harvard University Press.

Inder, B. A. 1984. "Finite Sample Power of Tests for Autocorrelation in Models Containing Lagged Dependent Variables." *Economic Letters* 14:179–85.

Irwin, D. A. 1996. *Changes in U.S. Tariffs: Prices or Policies?* National Bureau of Economic Research Working Paper No. 5665. Cambridge, Mass.

Isaacs, A. 1948. *International Trade: Tariff and Commercial Policies.* Homewood, Ill.: Irwin.

James, S. C., and D. A. Lake. 1989. "The Second Face of Hegemony: Britain's Repeal of the Corn Laws and the American Walker Tariff of 1846." *International Organization* 43:1–29.

Jenks, L. H. 1944. "Railroads as an Economic Force in American Development." *Journal of Economic History* 4:1–20.

Jiminez, A. 2001. "Interview with Dale Jorgenson: Revolution in Information Technology Requires a Revolution in Economic Thinking." *IMF Survey* 30 (December 10): 391–93.

Johnson, H. G. 1954. "Optimum Tariffs and Retaliation." *Review of Economic Studies* 21:142–53.

Jones, L. E., and R. Manuelli. 1990. "A Convex Model of Equilibrium Growth." *Journal of Political Economy* 98:1008–38.

Jovanovic, B., and R. Rob. 1990. "Long Waves and Short Waves: Growth through Intensive and Extensive Search." *Econometrica* 58:1391–1409.

Kang, H. 1985. "The Effects of Detrending in Granger Causality Tests." *Journal of Business and Economic Statistics* 3:344–49.

References

————. 1989. "The Optimal Lag Selection and Transfer Function Analysis in Granger Causality Tests." *Journal of Economic Dynamics and Control* 13:151–69.

Katzenstein. P. J., R. O. Keohane, and S. Krasner. 1998. "*International Organization* and the Study of World Politics." *International Organization* 52:645–86.

Kennedy, P. 1987. *The Rise and Fall of the Great Powers: Economic Change and Military Conflict from 1500–2000.* New York: Random House.

————. 1993. *Preparing for the Twenty-first Century.* New York: Random House.

Keohane, R. O. 1980. "The Theory of Hegemonic Stability and Changes in International Economic Regimes, 1967–1977." In O. R. Holsti, R. M. Siverson, and A. L. George, eds., *Change in the International System.* Boulder: Westview.

————. 1984. *After Hegemony: Cooperation and Discord in the World Political Economy.* Princeton: Princeton University Press.

Keohane, R. O., and S. Hoffmann. 1990. "Conclusions: Community Politics and Institutional Change." In W. Wallace, ed., *The Dynamics of European Integration.* London: Pinter.

Keohane, R. O., and J. S. Nye. 1977. *Power and Interdependence: World Politics in Transition.* Boston: Little, Brown. 2d ed., Glenview, Ill.: Scott Foresman, 1989.

Keynes, J. M. 1971 [1919]. *The Economic Consequences of the Peace.* London: Macmillan.

Kindleberger, C. P. 1973. *The World in Depression, 1929–1939.* Berkeley: University of California Press.

————. 1975. "The Rise of Free Trade in Western Europe." *Journal of Economic History* 35:20–55.

————. 1981. "Dominance and Leadership in the International Economy: Exploitation, Public Goods, and Free Riders." *International Studies Quarterly* 25:242–54.

————. 1996. *World Economic Primacy, 1500–1990.* New York: Oxford University Press.

————. 1999. *Essays in History: Financial, Economic, Personal.* Ann Arbor: University of Michigan Press.

King, R. G., and S. Rebelo. 1990. "Public Policy and Economic Growth: Developing Neoclassical Implications." *Journal of Political Economy* 98:125–50.

Kinsella, D. 1994. "Conflict in Context: Arms Transfers and Third World Rivalries during the Cold War." *American Journal of Political Science.* 38:557–81.

Kitschelt, H. 1991. "Industrial Governance, Structures, Innovation Strategies and the Case of Japan: Sectoral or Cross-National Comparative Analysis?" *International Organization* 45:453–93.

Klein, L., and D. Salvatore. 1995. "Welfare Effects of the North American Free Trade Agreement." *Journal of Policy Modeling* 17:163–76.

Kleinknecht, A. 1987. *Innovation Patterns in Crisis and Prosperity: Schumpeter's Long Cycle Reconsidered.* London: Macmillan.

Knorr, K. 1975. "International Economic Leverage and Its Uses." In K. Knorr and

References

F. N. Traeger, eds., *Economic Issues and National Security.* Lawrence, Kans.: Allen Press.

Knutsen, T. L. 1999. *The Rise and Fall of World Orders.* Manchester, U.K.: Manchester University Press.

Kondratieff, N. D. 1979. "The Long Waves in Economic Life." *Review* 2:519–62.

Krasner, S. D. 1976. "State Power and the Structure of International Trade." *World Politics* 28:317–48.

———. 1982. "Structural Causes and Regime Consequences: Regimes as Intervening Variables." *International Organization* 36:185–205.

———, ed. 1983. *International Regimes.* Ithaca: Cornell University Press.

Krauss, E. S., and S. Reich. 1992. "Ideology, Interests, and the American Executive: Toward a Theory of Foreign Competition and Manufacturing Trade Policy." *International Organization* 46:857–97.

Krol, R. 1996. "Testing Tariff Endogeneity in Japan: A Comparison of Pre- and Post-War Periods." *Economic Letters* 50:399–406.

Krueger, A. O. 1996. *The Political Economy of American Trade Policy.* Chicago: University of Chicago Press.

Krugman, P. 1979. "Increasing Returns, Monopolistic Competition, and International Trade." *Journal of International Economics* 9:469–79.

———. 1991a. "Is Bilateralism Bad?" In E. Helpman and A. Razin, eds., *International Trade and Trade Policy,* 9–23. Cambridge: MIT Press.

———. 1991b. "The Move toward Free Trade Zones." In *Policy Implications of Trade and Currency Zones.* Kansas City: Federal Reserve Bank of Kansas City.

Krugman, P., and A. Smith. 1994. *Empirical Studies of Strategic Trade Policy.* Chicago: University of Chicago Press.

Kuderle, R. 1985. "Political Economy of U.S. Protectionism." In P. Johnson and W. R. Thompson, eds., *Rhythms in Politics and Economics.* New York: Praeger.

Kurth, J. R. 1979a. "The Political Consequences of the Product Cycle: Industrial History and Political Outcomes." *International Organization* 33:1–34.

———. 1979b. "Industrial Change and Political Change: A European Perspective." In David Collier, ed., *The New Authoritarianism in Latin America.* Princeton: Princeton University Press.

Laird, S., and A. Yeats. 1990a. *Quantitative Methods for Trade Barrier Analysis.* New York: New York University Press.

———. 1990b. "Trends in Nontariff Barriers of Developed Countries, 1966–1986." *Weltwirtschaftliches Archiv* 2:299–325.

Lake, D. A. 1988. *Power, Protection, and Free Trade: International Sources of U.S. Commercial Strategy, 1887–1939.* Ithaca: Cornell University Press.

———. 1993. "Leadership, Hegemony and the International Economy: Naked Emperor or Tattered Monarch with Potential?" *International Studies Quarterly* 37:459–89.

References

Landes, D. S. 1969. *The Unbound Prometheus.* Cambridge: Cambridge University Press.

———. 1998. *The Wealth and Power of Nations.* New York: W. W. Norton.

Langhammer, R. J., and U. Hiemenz. 1990. *Regional Integration among Developing Countries: Opportunities, Obstacles and Options.* Tübingen, Germany: J. C. B. Moher.

Laux, J. K. 1991. "Limits to Liberalism." *International Journal* 46:113–36.

Lavergne, R. 1983. *The Political Economy of the U.S. Tariff: An Empirical Analysis.* New York: Academic Press.

Lawrence, R. Z. 1996. *Regionalism, Multilateralism, and Deeper Integration.* Washington, D.C.: Brookings Institution.

Leamer, E. 1978. *Specification Searches: Ad Hoc Inference with Non-experimental Data.* New York: Wiley.

———. 1993. "Wage Effects of a U.S.-Mexican Free Trade Agreement." In P. Garber, ed., *The Mexican-U.S. Free Trade Agreement,* 57–125. Cambridge: MIT Press.

Lerdau, E. 1957. "On the Measurement of Tariffs: The U.S. over Forty Years." *Economia Internazionale* 10:232–44.

Lew, K. 1987. *New Protectionism in World Trade: Political and Economic Aspects of New Protectionism.* Bloomington: School of Public and Environmental Affairs, Indiana University.

Lewis, W. A. 1978. *Growth and Fluctuations, 1870–1913.* London: George Allen and Unwin.

Li, R. Y., and W. R. Thompson. 1978. "The Stochastic Process of Alliance Formation: A Time Series Systems Analysis." *American Political Science Review* 72:1288–1303.

Liesner, T. 1988. *One Hundred Years of Economic Statistics.* New York: Facts on File.

Linder, S. 1961. *An Essay on Trade and Transformation.* New York: Wiley.

Lindert, P. H., and C. P. Kindleberger. 1982. *International Economics.* 7th ed. Homewood, Ill.: Irwin.

Linnemann, H. 1966. *An Econometric Study of International Trade Flows.* Amsterdam: North Holland.

Lipsey, R. G. 1968. "The Theory of Customs Unions: A General Survey." In R. E. Caves and H. G. Johnson, eds., *Readings in International Economics.* Homewood, Ill.: Irwin.

Lipsey, R. G., C. Bekar, and K. Carlaw. 1998. "What Requires Explanation?" In E. Helpman, ed., *General Purpose Technologies and Economic Growth.* Cambridge: MIT Press.

Lipsey, R. G., and K. Lancaster. 1956. "The General Theory of the Second Best." In K. Lancaster, collective volume, *Trade, Markets and Welfare,* 193–220. Cheltenham, U.K.: Elgar.

Liska, G. 1990. *The Ways of Power.* Cambridge: Blackwell.

References

Little, I., T. Scitovsky, and M. Scott. 1970. *Industry and Trade in Some Developing Countries: A Comparative Study.* New York: Oxford University Press.

Ljung, G., and G. Box. 1979. "On a Measure of Lack of Fit in Time Series Models." *Biometrika* 66:265–70.

Lopez-Villicana, R. 1997. "Mexico and NAFTA: The Case of Ministers of Foreign Affairs." *Annals of the American Academy of Political and Social Science* 550:122–29.

Lucas, R. E., Jr. 1988. "On the Mechanics of Economic Development." *Journal of Monetary Economics* 22:3–42.

Maddison, A. M. 1982. *Phases of Capitalist Development.* Oxford: Oxford University Press.

———. 1992. *Dynamic Forces in Capitalist Development: A Long Run Comparative View.* New York: Oxford University Press.

———. 1995. *Monitoring the World Economy, 1820–1992.* Development Center Studies. Paris: OECD.

Magaziner, I., and R. Reich. 1982. *Minding America's Business.* New York: Random House.

Magee, S. P., W. A. Brock, and L. Young. 1989. *Black Hole Tariffs and Endogenous Policy Theory: Political Economy in General Equilibrium.* Cambridge: Cambridge University Press.

Magee, S. P., and L. Young. 1987. "Endogenous Protection in the United States, 1900–1984." In R. R. Stern, ed., *U.S. Trade Policies in a Changing World Economy,* 145–95. Cambridge: MIT Press.

Mandel, E. 1980. *Long Waves of Capitalist Development: The Marxist Interpretation.* Cambridge: Cambridge University Press.

Mankiw, G. N. 1995. "The Growth of Nations." *Brookings Papers on Economic Activity* 1:275–326.

Mankiw, G. N., D. Romer, and D. N. Weil. 1992. "A Contribution to the Empirics of Economic Growth." *Quarterly Journal of Economics* 112:407–37.

Mansfield, E. D. 1994. *Power, Trade and War.* Princeton: Princeton University Press.

Mansfield, E. D., and R. Bronson. 1997. "The Political Economy of Major-Power Trade Flows." In E. D. Mansfield and H. V. Milner, eds., *The Political Economy of Regionalism,* 188–208. New York: Columbia University Press.

Mansfield, E. D., and M. L. Busch. 1995. "The Political Economy of Nontariff Barriers: A Cross-National Analysis. *International Organization* 49:723–49.

Mansfield, E. D., and H. Milner. 1999. "The New Wave of Regionalism." *International Organization* 53:589–627.

Marichal, C. 1989. *A Century of Debt Crises in Latin America: From Independence to the Great Depression, 1820–1990.* Boulder: Westview.

Martin, L. 1992. *Coercive Cooperation: Explaining Multilateral Economic Sanctions.* Princeton: Princeton University Press.

References

Mastanduno, M. 1991. "Do Relative Gains Matter? America's Response to Japanese Industrial Policy." *International Security* 16:73–113.

Mastel, G., and S. Andrew. 1997. "China's Growing Trade Surplus: Why It Matters." *Washington Quarterly* 20:201–12.

McCallum, B. T. 1993. "Unit Roots in Macroeconomic Time Series: Some Critical Issues." *Economic Quarterly* 79:13–44.

McDonald, B. 1998. *The World Trading System: The Uruguay Round and Beyond.* New York: St. Martin's.

McGowan, P. 1985. "Pitfalls and Promise in the Quantitative Study of the World-System: A Reanalysis of Bergesen and Schoenberg's 'Long Waves' of Colonialism." *Review* 8:177–200.

McKeown, T. 1983. "Hegemonic Stability Theory and Nineteenth Century Tariff Levels in Europe." *International Organization* 37:73–91.

———. 1984. "Firms and Tariff Regime Change: Explaining the Demand for Protectionism." *World Politics* 36:215–33.

———. 1986. "The Limitations of Structural Theories of Commercial Policy." *International Organization* 40:43–64.

———. 1991. "A Liberal Trade Order? The Long-Run Pattern of Imports to the Advanced Capitalist States." *International Studies Quarterly* 35:151–71.

Meade, J. 1955. *The Theory of Customs Unions.* Amsterdam: North Holland.

Mearsheimer, J. J. 1990. "Back to the Future: Instability in Europe after the Cold War." *International Security* 15:5–56.

Mehra, Y. P. 1977. "Money Wages, Prices, and Causality." *Journal of Political Economy* 85:1227–44.

Mensch, G. 1979. *Stalemate in Technology: Innovations Overcome the Depression.* Cambridge, Mass.: Ballinger.

Messerlin, P. 1992. "Trade Policies in France." In D. Salvatore, ed., *National Trade Policies.* Westport, Conn.: Greenwood.

Metcalfe, J. S., and M. Gibbons. 1991. "The Diffusion of the New Technologies: A Condition for Renewed Economic Growth." In *Technology and Productivity: The Challenge for Economic Policy.* Paris: OECD.

Milner, H. V. 1988. *Resisting Protectionism: Global Industries and the Politics of International Trade.* Princeton: Princeton University Press.

———. 1998. "Regional Economic Cooperation, Global Markets and Domestic Politics: A Comparison of NAFTA and the Maastricht Treaty." In W. D. Coleman and G. R. D. Underhill, eds., *Regionalism and Global Economic Integration: Europe, Asia and the Americas,* 19–41. London: Routledge.

Mintz, A., and C. Huang. 1990. "Defence Expenditures, U.S. Economic Growth and the Peace Dividend." *American Political Science Review* 84:1283–96.

Misra, J., and T. Boswell. 1997. "Dutch Hegemony: Global Leadership during the Age of Mercantilism." *Acta Politica* 32:174–209.

References

Mitchell, B. 1964. "The Coming of the Railway and United Kingdom Economic Growth." *Journal of Economic History* 24:315–36.

———. 1992. *European Historical Statistics, 1750–1988.* 3d ed. New York: Stockton.

———. 1993. *International Historical Statistics: The Americas, 1750–1988.* New York: Stockton.

———. 1995. *International Historical Statistics: Africa, Asia and Oceana, 1750–1988.* New York: Stockton.

Modelski, G. 1981. "Long Cycles, Kondratieffs, and Alternating Innovations: Implications for U.S. Foreign Policy." In C. W. Kegley Jr. and P. J. McGowan, eds., *The Political Economy of Foreign Policy Behavior.* Beverly Hills, Calif.: Sage.

———. 1982. "Long Cycles and the Strategy of United States International Political Economy." In W. Avery and D. P. Rapkin, eds., *America in a Changing World Political Economy.* New York: Longman.

———. 1987. *The Long Wave in World Politics.* London: Macmillan.

———. 1989. "Long Cycles and Global War." In M. Midlarsky, ed., *Handbook of War Studies.* Boston: Unwin Hyman.

Modelski, G., and W. R. Thompson. 1988. *Sea Power in Global Politics, 1494–1993.* London: Macmillan.

———. 1996. *Leading Sectors and World Powers: The Coevolution of Global Politics and Economics.* Columbia: University of South Carolina Press.

———. 2000. "The Long and Short of Global Politics in the Twenty-First Century: An Evolutionary Approach." *International Studies Review* 1 (special issue): 109–40.

Moore, W. H. 1995. "Action-Reaction or Rational Expectations? Reciprocity and the Domestic-International Nexus during the Rhodesia Problem." *Journal of Conflict Resolution* 39:129–67.

Murakami, Y. 1996. *An Anticlassical Political-Economic Analysis: A Vision from the Next Century.* Stanford: Stanford University Press.

Murphy, C. 1994. *International Organization and Industrial Change: Global Governance since 1850.* New York: Oxford University Press.

Nau, H. R. 1990. *The Myth of America's Decline.* New York: Oxford University Press.

Nelson, C., and H. Kang. 1981. "Spurious Periodicity in Inappropriately Detrended Time Series." *Econometrica* 49:741–51.

———. 1984. "Pitfalls in the Use of Time as an Explanatory Variable in Regression." *Journal of Business Economic and Statistics* 2:73–82.

Nelson, R. R., and S. G. Winter. 1982. *An Evolutionary Theory of Economic Change.* Cambridge: Harvard University Press.

Nelson, R. R., and G. Wright. 1992. "The Rise and Fall of American Technological Leadership: The Postwar Era in Historical Perspective." *Journal of Economic Literature* 30:1931–64.

References

Neumann, M. 1997. *The Rise and Fall of the Wealth of Nations: Long Waves in Economics and International Politics.* Cheltenham, U.K.: Elgar.

Nogues, J., A. Olechowski, and L. A. Winters. 1985. *The Extent of Nontariff Barriers to Industrial Countries' Imports,* Report No. DRD115. Washington, D.C.: World Bank Development Research Department.

Nye, J. S. 1990. *Bound to Lead.* New York: Basic Books.

Odell, J. S. 1982. *U.S. International Monetary Policy: Markets, Power and Ideas as Sources of Change.* Princeton: Princeton University Press.

———. 1990. "Understanding International Trade Policies: An Emerging Synthesis." *World Politics* 43:139–67.

OECD (Organization for Economic Cooperation and Development). 1985. *Costs and Benefits of Protectionism.* Paris: OECD.

———. 1992. *Main Economic Indicators, December, 1992.* Paris: OECD.

O'Halloran, S. 1994. *Politics, Process, and American Trade Policy.* Ann Arbor: University of Michigan Press.

Ohlin, B. 1933. *Interregional and International Trade.* Cambridge: Harvard University Press.

Ojeda, R. H., C. Dowds, R. McCleery, S. Robinson, D. Runsten, C. Wolff, and G. Wolff. 1996. "North American Integration Three Years after NAFTA." *NAID Working Paper.* Los Angeles: UCLA North American Integration Development Center <http://naid.sppser.ucla.edu/nafta96/> (accessed April 23, 1999).

Olechowski, A., and G. Sampson. 1980. "Current Trade Restrictions in the EEC, the United States and Japan." *Journal of World Trade Law* 14:220–31.

Olson, M. 1982. *The Rise and Decline of Nations.* New Haven: Yale University Press.

Organski, A. F. K., and J. Kugler. 1980. *The War Ledger.* Chicago: University of Chicago Press.

Oye, K. A. 1992. *Economic Discrimination and Political Exchange: World Political Economy in the 1930s and 1980s.* Princeton: Princeton University Press.

Paarlberg, R. L. 1978. "Food, Oil, and Coercive Resource Power." *International Security* 3:3–19.

Pack, H. 1994. "Endogenous Growth Theory: Intellectual Appeal and Empirical Shortcomings." *Journal of Economic Perspectives* 8:55–72.

Page, S. A. B. 1981. "The Revival of Protectionism and Its Consequences for Europe." *Journal of Common Market Studies* 20:17–40.

Panagariya, A. 1995. *The Free Trade Area of the Americas: Good for Latin America?* College Park: University of Maryland Center of International Economics.

Pastor, R. A. 1980. *Congress and the Politics of U.S. Foreign Economic Policy.* Berkeley: University of California Press.

Perot, H. R., and P. Choate. 1993. *Save Your Job, Save Our Country: Why NAFTA Must Be Stopped—Now!* New York: Hyperion Press.

Perroux, F. 1979. "An Outline of a Theory of the Dominant Economy." In G.

References

Modelski, ed., *Transnational Corporations and World Order.* San Francisco: W. H. Freeman.

Phillips, P. C. B., and P. Perron. 1988. "Testing for a Unit Root in Time Series Regression." *Biometrika* 75:335–46.

Pierce, D. A. 1977. "Relationships—and Lack Thereof—between Economic Time Series, with Special Reference to Money and Interest Rates." *Journal of the American Statistical Association* 72 (applications section): 11–22.

Pierce, D. A., and L. Haugh. 1977. "Causality in Temporal Systems: Characterizations and a Survey." *Journal of Econometrics* 5:265–93.

Poli, E. 1995. "NAFTA and Mexico: An Example of Cooperation between Developed and Developing Countries." *Economia Internazionale* 48:569–97.

Pollins, B. M. 1996. "Global Political Order, Economic Change and Armed Conflict: Coevolving Systems and the Use of Force." *American Political Science Review* 90:103–17.

Pollins, B. M., and K. P. Murrin. 1999. "Where Hobbes Meets Hobson: Core Conflict and Colonialism, 1495–1995." *International Studies Quarterly* 43: 427–54.

Pollins, B. M., and R. L. Schweller. 1999. "Linking the Levels: The Long Wave and Shifts in U.S. Foreign Policy, 1790–1993." *American Journal of Political Science* 43:431–64.

Pomfret, R. 1986. "Preferential Trading Agreements." *Weltwirtschaftliches Archiv* 122:439–65.

———. 1988. *Unequal Trade: The Economics of Discriminatory International Trade Policies.* Oxford: Blackwell.

Prestowitz, C. V., Jr. 1995. "Beyond Laissez Faire." In J. A. Frieden and D. A. Lake, eds., *International Political Economy: Perspectives on Global Power and Wealth,* 506–18. New York: St. Martin's.

Purcell, S. K. 1997. "The Changing Nature of U.S.-Mexican Relations." *Journal of Interamerican Studies and World Affairs* 39:137–52.

Rasler, K., and W. R. Thompson. 1989. *War and State Making: The Shaping of the Global Powers.* Boston: Unwin Hyman.

———. 1991. "Technological Innovation, Capability Positional Shifts and Systemic War." *Journal of Conflict Resolution* 35:412–42.

———. 1994. *The Great Powers and Global Struggle, 1490–1990.* Lexington: University Press of Kentucky.

———. 2000. "Global War and the Political Economy of Structural Change." In M. Midlarsky, ed., *Handbook of War Studies II.* Ann Arbor: University of Michigan Press.

Rebelo, S. 1991. "Long Run Policy Analysis and Long Run Growth." *Journal of Political Economy* 99:500–521.

Rejinders, J. 1990. *Long Waves in Economic Development.* Brooksfield, Vt.: Elgar.

References

Reuveny, R., and H. Kang. 1996. "International Trade, Political Conflict/Cooperation, and Granger Causality." *American Journal of Political Science* 40:943–70.

———. 1998. "Bilateral Trade and Political Conflict/Cooperation: Do Goods Matter?" *Journal of Peace Research* 35:581–602.

Reuveny, R., and W. R. Thompson. 1997. "The Timing of Protectionism." *Review of International Political Economy* 4:179–213.

———. 1999. "Economic Innovation, Systemic Leadership, and Military Preparations for War: The United States Case." *Journal of Conflict Resolution* 43:570–95.

———. 2001. "Leading Sectors, Lead Economies and Their Impact on Economic Growth." *Review of International Political Economy* 8:689–719.

———. 2002. "World Economic Growth, Northern Antagonism, and North-South Conflict." *Journal of Conflict Resolution* 46:515–46.

———. 2003. "Exploring the North-South Gap." *Japanese Journal of Political Science* 4:77–102.

———. Forthcoming. "World Economic Growth, Systemic Leadership, and Southern Debt Crises." *Journal of Peace Research.*

Reyes, E. D. 1999. "Regionalism: The Case of North America." In K. Appendini and S. Bislev, eds., *Economic Integration in NAFTA and the EU,* 161–77. New York: St. Martin's.

Richardson, D. J. 1990. "The Political Economy of Strategic Trade Policy." *International Organization* 44:107–35.

Richardson, N. R. 1995. "International Trade as a Force for Peace." In C. W. Kegley Jr., ed., *Controversies in International Relations Theory: Realism and the Neoliberal Challenge,* 281–94. New York: St. Martin's.

Rodrik, D. 1995. "Political Economy of Trade Policy." In G. M. Grossman and K. Rogoff, eds., *Handbook of International Economics,* vol. 3, 1457–94. Amsterdam: Elsevier.

Rogowski, R. 1989. *Commerce and Coalitions: How Trade Affects Domestic Political Alignments.* Princeton: Princeton University Press.

Rohrlich, P. E. 1987. "Economic Culture and Foreign Policy: The Cognitive Analysis of Economic Policy Making." *International Organization* 41:61–92.

Romer, P. M. 1986. "Increasing Returns and Long Run Growth." *Journal of Political Economy* 94:1002–37.

———. 1990. "Endogenous Technological Change." *Journal of Political Economy* 98:71–102.

Rose, A. 1941. "Wars, Innovations and Long Cycles: A Brief Comment." *American Economic Review* 31:105–7.

Rosecrance, R., and J. Taw. 1990. "Japan and the Theory of International Leadership." *World Politics* 42:184–209.

Rosenberg, N., and C. R. Frischtak. 1983. "Long Waves and Economic Growth: A Critical Appraisal." *American Economic Review* 46:341–52.

References

———. 1994. "Technological Innovation and Long Waves." In N. Rosenberg, ed., *Exploring the Black Box: Technology, Economics, and History.* Cambridge: Cambridge University Press.

Rostow, W. W. 1978. *The World Economy.* Austin: University of Texas Press.

———. 1998. *The Great Population Spike and After: Reflections on the Twenty-first Century.* New York: Oxford University Press.

Russett, B. 1985. "The Mysterious Case of Vanishing Hegemony: or, Is Mark Twain Really Dead?" *International Organization* 39:207–31.

Salvatore, D. 1992. *International Handbook of National Trade Policies.* Westport, Conn.: Greenwood.

———. 1993a. "Protectionism and World Welfare: Introduction." In D. Salvatore, ed., *Protectionism and World Welfare.* New York: Cambridge University Press.

———. 1993b. *International Economics.* New York: Macmillan.

———, ed. 1997. *Trade Protectionism across Countries and Sectors.* Norwell, Mass.: Kluwer.

———. 1998. *International Economics.* Upper Saddle River, N.J.: Prentice-Hall.

Sargent, T. 1976. "A Classical Macroeconometric Model for the United States." *Journal of Political Economy* 84:207–37.

Sato, K. 1992. "Trade Policies in Japan." In D. Salvatore, ed., *National Trade Policies.* Westport, Conn.: Greenwood.

Schumpeter, J. 1934. *The Theory of Economic Development.* Cambridge: Harvard University Press.

———. 1939. *Business Cycles.* New York: McGraw-Hill.

Shell, K. 1966. "Toward a Theory of Inventive Activity and Capital Accumulation." *American Economic Review* 56:62–68.

Simon, J. L. 1981. *The Ultimate Resource.* Princeton: Princeton University Press.

Sims, C. 1972. "Money, Income, and Causality." *American Economic Review* 65:540–52.

———. 1980. "Macroeconomics and Reality." *Econometrica* 48:1–49.

———. 1988. "Bayesian Skepticism on Unit Root Econometrics." *Journal of Economic Dynamics and Control* 12:463–74.

Snidal, D. 1985. "The Limitations of Hegemonic Stability Theory." *International Organization* 39:579–614.

Snyder, G. H. 1984. "The Security Dilemma in Alliance Politics." *World Politics* 36:461–95.

Solomou, S. 1987. *Phases of Economic Growth, 1850–1973: Kondratieff Waves and Kuznets Swings.* Cambridge: Cambridge University Press.

———. 1998. *Economic Cycles: Long Cycles and Business Cycles since 1870.* Manchester: Manchester University Press.

Solow, R. M. 1956. "A Contribution to the Theory of Economic Growth." *Quarterly Journal of Economics* 70:65–94.

References

———. 1994. "Perspectives on Growth Theory." *Journal of Economic Perspectives* 8:45–54.

Spiegel, M. R. 1988. *Theory and Problems of Statistics.* New York: McGraw-Hill.

Stein, A. 1984. "The Hegemonic Dilemma: Great Britain, the United States and the International Economic Order." *International Organization* 38:355–78.

Stern, R. M., ed. 1987. *U.S. Trade Policies in a Changing World Economy.* Cambridge: MIT Press.

Stolper, W. F., and P. A. Samuelson. 1941. "Protection and Real Wages." *Review of Economic Studies* (November): 58–73.

Strang, D. 1991. "Global Patterns of Decolonization." *International Studies Quarterly* 35:429–54.

Strange, S. 1979. "The Management of Surplus Capacity; or, How Does Theory Stand Up to Protectionism?" *International Organization* 33:303–44.

———. 1985. "Protectionism and World Politics." *International Organization* 39:233–59.

———. 1987. "The Persistent Myth of Lost Hegemony." *International Organization* 41:555–74.

Strange, S., and R. Tooze, eds. 1981. *The International Politics of Surplus Capacity.* London: Allen and Unwin.

Sullivan, Michael P. 2001. *Theories of International Relations: Transition vs. Persistence.* New York: Palgrave.

Suter, C. 1992. *Debt Cycles in the World-Economy: Foreign Loans, Financial Crises and Debt Settlements, 1820–1990.* Boulder: Westview.

Sweeney, J. 1997. *NAFTA's Positive Impact on the US: A State-by-State Breakdown.* Washington, D.C.: Heritage Foundation.

Taussig, F. 1964 [1931]. *The Tariff History of the United States.* 8th rev. ed. New York: Capricorn Books.

Thompson, W. R. 1983. "Cycles, Capabilities, and War: An Ecumenical View." In W. R. Thompson, *Contending Approaches to World System Analysis.* Beverly Hills, Calif.: Sage.

———. 1988. *On Global War: Historical-Structural Approaches to World Politics.* Columbia: University of South Carolina Press.

———. 1990. "Long Waves, Technological Innovation and Relative Decline." *International Organization* 44:201–33.

———. 1992. "Systemic Leadership and Growth Waves in the Long Run." *International Studies Quarterly* 36:25–48.

———. 2000. *The Emergence of a Global Political Economy.* London: Routledge.

Thompson, W. R., and R. Reuveny. 1998. "Tariffs and Trade Fluctuations: Does Protectionism Matter as Much as We Think?" *International Organization* 52:421–40.

Thompson, W. R., and L. Vescera. 1992. "Growth Waves, Systemic Openness, and Protectionism." *International Organization* 46:493–532.

References

Tornell, A., and G. Esquivel. 1995. "The Political Economy of Mexico's Entry to NAFTA." *NBER Working Paper 5322.* Cambridge, Mass.: National Bureau of Economic Research.

Trotsky, L. 1973 [1923]. "The Curve of Capitalist Development." In L. Trotsky, ed., *Problems of Everyday Life.* New York: Monad Press.

Tussie, D. 1998. "In the Whirlwind of Globalization and Multilateralism: The Case of Emerging Regionalism in Latin America." In W. D. Coleman and G. R. D. Underhill, eds., *Regionalism and Global Economic Integration: Europe, Asia and the Americas,* 81–96. London: Routledge.

Tylecote, A. 1991. *The Long Wave in the World Economy: The Current Crisis in Historical Perspective.* London: Routledge.

Tyson, L. D. 1992. *Who Is Bashing Whom? Trade Conflict in High Technology Industries.* Washington, D.C.: Institute for International Economics.

UNCTAD (United Nations Conference on Trade and Development). 1988. *Consideration of the Questions of Definition and Methodology Employed in the UNCTAD Data Base on Trade Measures.* Geneva: UNCTAD.

U.S. Department of Commerce. 1975. *Historical Statistics of the United States, Colonial Times to 1970.* Washington, D.C.: U.S. Government.

———. 1983, 1992. *Statistical Abstract of the United States.* Washington, D.C.: U.S. Government.

U.S. Trade Commission. 1993. *Potential Impact on the U.S. Economy and Selected Industries of the North American Free Trade Agreement.* Washington, D.C.: U.S. Government Printing Office.

Vasko, T., ed. 1987. *The Long Wave Debate.* Berlin: Springer.

Verdier, D. 1994. *Democracy and International Trade: Britain, France, and the United States, 1860–1990.* Princeton: Princeton University Press.

Viner, J. 1950. *The Customs Union Issue.* New York: Carnegie Endowment for International Peace.

Vogel, S. 1992. "The Power behind 'Spin-Ons': The Military Implications of Japan's Commercial Technology." In W. Sandholtz et al., eds., *The Highest Stakes.* New York: Oxford University Press.

Wallerstein, I. 1974. *The Modern World-System.* Vol. 1. New York: Academic Press.

———. 1980. *The Modern World-System.* Vol. 2. New York: Academic Press.

———. 1983. "The Three Instances of Hegemony in the History of the Capitalist World Economy." *International Journal of Comparative Sociology* 24:100–108.

———. 1989. *The Modern World-System.* Vol. 3. New York: Academic Press.

———. 1995. "Peace, Stabilized Legitimacy: 1990–2025/2050." In G. Lundestad, ed., *The Fall of Great Powers.* New York: Oxford University Press.

———. 1996. "The Global Picture, 1945–90." In T. K. Hopkins and I. Wallerstein, eds., *The Age of Transition: Trajectory of the World-System, 1945–2025.* London: Zed Books.

References

Walter, I. 1972. "Nontariff Protection among Industrial Countries: Some Preliminary Empirical Evidence." *Economica Internazionale* 55:335–54.

Waltz, K. N. 1979. *Theory of International Politics.* Reading, Mass.: Addison-Wesley.

Ward, M. D., and D. R. Davis. 1992. "Sizing Up the Peace Dividend: Economic Growth and Military Spending in the United States, 1948–1986." *American Political Science Review* 86:748–55.

Webb, M. C. 1995. *The Political Economy of Policy Coordination: International Adjustment since 1945.* Ithaca: Cornell University Press.

Webb, M. C., and S. D. Krasner. 1989. "Hegemonic Stability Theory: An Empirical Assessment." *Review of International Studies* 15:183–98.

Weintraub, S. 1997. "The North American Free Trade Agreement." In A. M. El-Agraa, ed., *Economic Integration Worldwide,* 203–29. New York: St. Martin's.

Weiss, F. 1992. "Trade Policies in Germany." In D. Salvatore, ed., *National Trade Policies.* Westport, Conn.: Greenwood.

Williams, J. T. 1993. "Dynamic Change, Specification Uncertainty, and Bayesian Vector Autoregression Analysis." *Political Analysis* 4:97–125.

Williams, J. T., M. D. McGinnis, and J. C. Thomas. 1994. "Breaking the War-Economy Link." *International Interactions* 20:169–88.

World Bank. 1987. *World Development Report.* New York: Oxford University Press.

Yarbrough, B. V., and R. M. Yarbrough. 1992. *Cooperation and Governance in International Trade: The Strategic Organizational Approach.* Princeton: Princeton University Press.

Zellner, A., and F. Palm. 1974. "Time Series Analysis and Simultaneous Equation Econometric Models." *Journal of Econometrics* (May): 17–54.

Index

Index

Index

Index

Index

Index